Identity, Nationhood and Bangladesh Independent Cinema

This book analyses how independent filmmakers from Bangladesh have represented national identity in their films. The focus of this book is on independent and art-house filmmakers and how cinema plays a vital role in constructing national and cultural identity.

The authors examine post-2000 films that predominantly deal with issues of national identity and demonstrate how they tackle questions of national identity. Bangladesh is seemingly a homogenous country consisting 98% of Bengali and 90% of Muslim. This majority group has two dominant identities – Bengaliness (the ethno-linguistic identity) and Muslimness (the religious identity). Bengaliness is perceived as secular-modern whereas Muslimness is perceived as traditional and conservative. However, Bangladeshi independent and art-house filmmakers portray the nationhood of the country with an enthusiasm and liveliness that exceeds these two categories. In addition to these categories, the authors add two more dimensions to the approach to discuss identity: Popular Religion and Transformation. The study argues that these identity categories are represented in the films and that they both reproduce and challenge dominant discourses of nationalism.

Providing a new addition to the discourse of contemporary national identity, the book will be of interest to researchers studying international film and media studies, independent cinema studies, Asian cinema, and South Asian culture, politics and identity politics.

Fahmidul Haq is visiting professor at Bard College, New York, USA, and he has taught Mass Communication and Journalism at the University of Dhaka, Bangladesh for nearly two decades. He is also a former visiting research professor at University of Notre Dame, USA. His areas of interest include South Asian Cinema, Critical Media Studies and New Media Culture. His publications on South Asian film and media both in English and Bengali include *Cinema of Bangladesh: A Brief History* (2020). A human rights defender and public intellectual, Haq's online activism evolves around culture and politics of Bangladesh.

Brian Shoesmith was an honorary professor in Communications and Arts at Edith Cowan University, Perth, Australia. He was also Dean of Academic Development at the University of Liberal Arts Bangladesh (ULAB) for nearly a decade. He is the co-author of *Media Theories and Approaches: A Global Perspective* (2008) and co-editor of *Bangladesh's Changing Mediascape* (2013). He was a Founding Editor of *Continuum: Journal of Media and Cultural Studies* (Taylor and Francis). Dr. Shoesmith passed away on January 30th, 2020.

Routledge Contemporary South Asia Series

The Geopolitics of Energy in South Asia
Energy Security of Bangladesh
Chowdhury Ishrak Ahmed Siddiky

Transdisciplinary Ethnography in India
Women in the Field
Edited by Rosa Maria Perez and Lina Fruzzetti

Nationalism in India
Texts and Contexts
Edited by Debajyoti Biswas and John Charles Ryan

Gender Responsive Budgeting in South Asia
Experience of Bangladeshi Local Government
Pranab Kumar Panday and Shuvra Chowdhury

Gendered Modernity and Indian Cinema
The Women in Satyajit Ray's Films
Devapriya Sanyal

Reading Jhumpa Lahiri
Women, Domesticity and the Indian American Diaspora
Nilanjana Chatterjee

Indian Literatures in Diaspora
Sireesha Telugu

Identity, Nationhood and Bangladesh Independent Cinema
Fahmidul Haq and Brian Shoesmith

Media Discourse in Contemporary India
A Study of Select News Channels
Sudeshna Devi

For the full list of titles in the series please visit: https://www.routledge.com/Routledge-Contemporary-South-Asia-Series/book-series/RCSA

Identity, Nationhood and Bangladesh Independent Cinema

Fahmidul Haq and Brian Shoesmith

LONDON AND NEW YORK

First published 2023
by Routledge
4 Park Square, Milton Park, Abingdon, Oxon OX14 4RN

and by Routledge
605 Third Avenue, New York, NY 10158

Routledge is an imprint of the Taylor & Francis Group, an informa business

© 2023 Fahmidul Haq and Brian Shoesmith (this might be Fahmidul Haq and Vivien Shoesmith as Brian has passed away and Routledge signed the contract with his wife Vivien Shoesmith)

The right of Fahmidul Haq and Brian Shoesmith to be identified as authors of this work has been asserted in accordance with sections 77 and 78 of the Copyright, Designs and Patents Act 1988.

All rights reserved. No part of this book may be reprinted or reproduced or utilised in any form or by any electronic, mechanical or other means, now known or hereafter invented, including photocopying and recording, or in any information storage or retrieval system, without permission in writing from the publishers.

Trademark notice: Product or corporate names may be trademarks or registered trademarks and are used only for identification and explanation without intent to infringe.

British Library Cataloguing-in-Publication Data
A catalogue record for this book is available from the British Library

Library of Congress Cataloguing-in-Publication Data
A catalogue record has been requested for this book

ISBN: 978-1-032-22082-6 (hbk)
ISBN: 978-1-032-22084-0 (pbk)
ISBN: 978-1-003-27109-3 (ebk)

DOI: 10.4324/9781003271093

Typeset in Times New Roman
by MPS Limited, Dehradun

In memories of
Brian Shoesmith
The co-author who expired in the last stage of the book project

Contents

List of Figures viii
List of Tables ix
Acknowledgements x

Introduction 1

1 Nationhood, Identity and Independent Cinema 7

2 Identity Approaches of Bengali Muslims 30

3 The Making of Independent Cinema in Bangladesh 56

4 Textual Analysis: Foundational Films 87

5 Textual Analysis: Transitional Films 112

6 Textual Analysis: Contemporary Films 137

7 Representing Identity through Cinema 160

Conclusion 190

Index 197

Figures

4.1	Rabi Das (Jayanta Chattopadhyay), Banasreebala (Naila Azad Nupur) and Subal (Mamunur Rashid) in the green room of the *Jatra* stage	90
4.2	Majid (Raisul Islam Asad) in the shrine	97
4.3	Yakub (Riaz) and Rehana (Sohana Saba) in a moment of despair	104
5.1	Asma (Rimjhim) with a clay bird at her hand	114
5.2	Meher (Jaya Bachchan) in prayer	124
5.3	Amin Patwary (Kazi Shahir Huda Rumi) in front of a *halal* television	130
6.1	Ruhul (Fazlul Haque) comes back home from the city	140
6.2	Mithu (Noor Imran) enters Rima's (Sheena Chouhan) house and blackmails her	145
6.3	Roya (Shahana Goswami) in a dream sequence with garments workers	151
6.4	Kamal (Kamal Mani Chakma) with his bicycle	155

Tables

0.1	Selected films and their categories	4
3.1	Lists of selected early independent short films	61
3.2	Lists of selected films of the second phase (1993–1999) of the independent cinema movement	62
3.3	Format, length and funding details of selected feature films (2000–2010)	69
3.4	Selected global films	74
3.5	Selected documentaries	77

Acknowledgements

This book is an extended version of my doctoral research. Sometimes around 2011, I got together with Brian Shoesmith with an idea to convert my PhD thesis into a book project. What seemed like a straightforward and simple project, eventually, turned into a long one. The book project was delayed for two reasons. The preoccupation of both writers was one. Also, Brian's contract with the University of Liberal Arts Bangladesh (ULAB) came to an end and he had to return to Perth, Australia from Dhaka, Bangladesh in 2016. The collaboration continued but the process of writing chapters had slowed down. Meanwhile, the book project started getting revised and mounting bigger in volume. The number of selected films, from the initial four, had increased to ten. Theoretical approaches also went through some revisions as the context of analysis changed. There was a significant shift of our perception of the national identity in Bangladesh as well as some changes in the independent filmmaking practices in the country.

The project finally gained momentum when, in August 2019, I moved to the University of Notre Dame, USA as a visiting research faculty. The time at Notre Dame, especially Fall Semester of 2019, provided me with the opportunity to work fulltime on the book project. The first draft of the book was completed in June 2020 during the summer holidays.

The saddest part of the book project was the death of my co-writer. Brian died on January 30th, 2020 due to illness. I lost one of my dearest friends and a mentor in my mid-stage academic career. I missed him immensely when I was giving the final touch of the manuscript.

I sincerely acknowledge the support provided by the University of Notre Dame. James Collins and Pamela Robertson Wojcik, the Chairs of the Department of Film, Television and Theatre (FTT), Peter Holland, the Associate Dean of the College of Arts and Letters, University of Notre Dame and Michael Kackman, faculty of FTT deserve special mention for their support. I also thank New York-based International Institute of Education and Jan Dilenschneider for supporting the book project in different capacities. I thank Barbara Jasny for her copy-editing support before submitting the manuscript to the publisher.

Acknowledgements xi

I like to thank my PhD supervisor Shanthi Balraj at the University of Science Malaysia. I also thank the University of Dhaka for allowing my doctoral and post-doctoral leaves that had contributed to doing research and writing the book. I also acknowledge the ULAB for providing us a context to meet and work together.

I must mention film scholar Zakir Hossain Raju's engagement with the book project since the beginning and his comments and observations were beneficial. I must thank to Bard College, NY, a teaching-focused liberal arts college, where I am currently employed, for sparing some time to continue the last moment revisions of the book.

The directors of the selected films have been very cooperative in giving interviews and providing relevant information and data for the book. The photographs used in the book are provided by the directors. Thanks to all of them for their continuous cooperation throughout the prolonged book writing process. Lastly, I must thank Professor Ali Riaz and Dr. Mubashar Hasan for guiding me to revise some aspects of the manuscript on the way to reach Routledge for the final outcome.

Fahmidul Haq

Introduction

Bangladesh is apparently a homogeneous nation with over ninety percent (98%) of its citizens, both Muslim and Hindus, of Bengali ethnicity. A small minority of the population mostly situated in the Chittagong Hill Tracts (CHT) are indigenous tribal people of different ethnicity. Despite this seeming homogeneity, the complex history of Bangladesh ensures that identity is at the front and centre of the Bangladeshi narrative.

Historically, Bengalis have projected a sense of identity based on language and culture and are located largely in the eastern part of the Indian subcontinent. By contrast, it is also fair to say that their fellow Indians from other races have historically seen Bengalis as different, as arrogant, pedantic and insular. This sense of difference is complicated by a few factors. Here, we have been speaking of a unified people, the Bengalis, but they are divided by religion and nation, which are powerful factors in manufacturing differences. Nevertheless, Kolkata remains a dominant unifying force as the perceived centre of Bengali culture for both Indian Bengalis and Bangladeshi Bengalis. The shared language remains an important unifying factor. Both Indians and Bangladeshis revere the poets Rabindranath Tagore and Kazi Nazrul Islam, seeing them as epitomising the glories of the Bengali language and as the essence of 'Bengaliness'. However, the reverence for these poets blurs the edges of one major divide in determining Bengali identity: the sharp and fundamental divide between Islam and Hinduism. In discussing the identities explored in independent Bangladeshi film, we also have to look beyond the national, religious and cultural and take into account economic factors and class disparities (recent growth and development), region (city/mufassil divide), gender (e.g. the importance of the retail garments industry for young women), technology (television and social media) and syncreticism (Sufi and Baulism) versus political or Jihadist Islam in order to arrive at a clear understanding of how a contemporary identity is constructed in film in question. However, this is to note that while discussing the national identity of Bangladesh we will focus largely on 'Bengali Muslims' who have found a nation state of their own, Bangladesh in 1971 though we acknowledge, there are some other Bengali Muslims living mostly

DOI: 10.4324/9781003271093-1

in West Bengal, India and there are Bengali Hindus (8.5%) and indigenous people (1.8%) living in Bangladesh.

For having a tradition of the common culture of the Indian sub-continent, Bangladesh is also a cinephile country. It produces more than 50 films every year.[1] The audiences of Bangladesh indiscriminately enjoy Indian films, both Hindi and Bengali with a significant number of people watching Hollywood films. Indian films are generally not released in Bangladeshi theatres because of a previous ban. But there is no bar on Hollywood films and these films are usually released in selected multiplexes based in Dhaka. Indian films, as well as Hollywood films, are accessed by Bangladeshi audience through the internet and satellite TV channels. Due to the availability of films on the Internet, the audience also appreciates South Indian, Korean, Iranian and films from some other countries. However, they pay substantial attention to the local productions, all made in vernacular language. Theatre-based film production has been suffering since the middle of the 1980s after the advent of new technologies like VCR/VCP in the 1980s, satellite-based cable TV and genuine or pirated CD/DVD in the 1990s and the torrent and streaming sites in the Internet. Piracy became an issue, but the main problem was the failure of the industry to negotiate the newer reality and its failure to adopt the required changes in the process of film production. The inherent lack of talent was really felt when the audience left the theatres and started watching films on small screens. The euphoria of mediocrity ended at the end of the last century and the producers could not find anything except increasing the cheap elements like sex and violence in the filmic texts. However, the industry did quite well earlier in the 1960s and 1970s and had a big spectator base who were basically captive audience who would have to visit cinema halls for not having any other option of entertainment. Raju (2015) and Haq (2020) have discussed thoroughly how the mainstream film industry emerged in the mid-1950s, expanded in the late-1960s and in the 1970s, started declining in the 1980s and was nearly destroyed in the early 2000s. In post-2010 time with the help of the digital technology and a few new policy initiatives, some new producers created some buzz in the industry, but it was not enough to set it again in a strong foundation. *BBC Bangla* reports on December 1, 2017, once there were 1200 cine theatres in Bangladesh, the number has reduced to 300. Once Bangladesh Film Development Corporation (BFDC), the hub of mainstream productions, used to produce 100 films in a year, but the number has come down to 30.[2] According to the report of *The Business Standard* published on September 20, 2020, there were 185 theatres throughout Bangladesh in early 2020, but after the closing down of around 50 cinemas due to Covid-19 pandemic, there remained around only 135.[3]

Meanwhile, an out-of-studio independent filmmaking trend was seen in the mid-1980s which brought a serious kind of storyline and innovative film language. These films were primarily made in 16 mm format, short in length and were distributed informally at auditoriums, cultural clubs and even films were screened under the open sky. However, this trend grew later with no promise of entertainment or business rather with the commitment of art. The filmmakers described their creations as 'alternative films'. Though their claim was not always convincing, however, this sector was consistent in occasionally producing good quality of art-house cinema, bagging awards from overseas festivals and collecting funds from international agencies and even releasing films in the international market. Instead of the mainstream cinema, independent cinema is carrying the impression of 'national cinema' of Bangladesh, at least to the international audience. During the 2020–21 pandemic era, when Over The Top (OTT) platforms quickly grabbed the audiovisual market globally, new generation independent filmmakers started making films and web series both for local and Indian OTTs and thus the filmmakers have started expanding their spaces.

The independent and art-house filmmakers use cinema as a vehicle to tackle questions of national identity. For the most part, these films have reproduced dominant discourses of identity and nationalism. However, there are some attempts to portray alternative discourses. In this book, we will analyse how independent filmmakers from Bangladesh have represented national identity in their films.

We have selected films that span the history of independent cinema in Bangladesh and reflect the changing foci of the films and an increasing mastery of technique and film language. We have organised the films in three groups: foundational, transitional and contemporary. The foundational films focus on the 1971 Liberation War and rural life, exploring in depth the impact of the war on the lives of Bangladeshis. The foundational films also look at the Muslim identity of Bengalis from a linear point of view. The transitional films explore the 1971 war too, but with a sharper edge suggesting that as the country modernises the changing nature of Bangladesh society cannot be sufficiently explained by looking back to origins. As with the foundational group, transitional films have depicted the various versions of Muslim identities and the alternative narratives of the Liberation War. By contrast, the contemporary films explore the present, shifting the focus away from 1971 (although its presence is inescapable as a backdrop to contemporary Bangladeshi affairs) and focusing more on the transforming scenario in globalised Bangladesh. Thus, our categories were not developed according to strict temporal chronology but were devised by considering the nature and characteristics in portraying the identity of Bengali Muslims. We have selected 10 post-2000 films that predominantly deal with identity issues, and which are made by leading independent filmmakers. These 10 films were made in the time span of 15 years (from 2000 to 2015) and this time frame would be substantial for representing the discourse of independent filmmaking. These filmmakers are leading because some of them (Tanvir Mokammel, Morshedul Islam, Tareque Masud and Abu Sayeed) began and led the independent film movement in Bangladesh. Some other filmmakers (Mostofa Sarwar Farooki, Rubaiyat Hossain and Aung Rakhine) are some

4 *Introduction*

prominent names from the second-generation independent filmmakers who have earned some achievements in terms of getting critical acclaims and bagging awards nationally and internationally and who also set some examples of making better art-house films. Among selected films, there is one that is made in non-Bengali (Chakma) language, made by an indigenous filmmaker and depicts indigenous cultural identity. This will help us to understand the perspectives of identity from indigenous people. The selected films include:

Table 0.1 Selected films and their categories (something needs to be done with the graphics of the table – the first three films are Foundational, the next three are transitional and the last four are Contemporary. The present design of the table doesn't carry that information)

Year	Film	Director	Category
2000	*Kittonkhola*	Abu Sayeed	
2001	*A Tree Without Roots* (Lalsalu)	Tanvir Mokammel	Foundational
2006	*Dollhouse* (Khelghar)	Morshedul Islam	
2002	*The Clay Bird* (Matir Moina)	Tareque Masud	
2011	*Meherjaan*	Rubaiyat Hossain	Transitional
2012	*Television*	Mostofa Sarwar Farooki	
2010	*Runway*	Tareque Masud	
2013	*Ant Story* (Piprabidya)	Mostofa Sarwar Farooki	Contemporary
2015	*Under Construction*	Rubaiyat Hossain	
2015	*My Bicycle* (Mor Thengari)	Aung Rakhine	

Every film (except *My Bicycle*) predominantly deals with at least one of four approaches to greater Bengali Muslim identity we propose in this book – i. Bengaliness, ii. Muslimness, iii. Popular Religion and iv. Transformation. Bengaliness is an ethno-linguistic approach that emerged in the middle ages in Bengal through Bengali literature and culture. It reached its peak in the 1960s in the autonomy movement against the central West Pakistan government. This autonomy movement was inspired by the Bengali Language Movement in 1952 and contributed to the independence war of Bangladesh in 1971. Muslimness is a religious identity that first emerged in the 19th century Bengal as a result of Islamic reformist movements, such as the *Faraizi* Movement. In the 1910s–1940s, Muslimness stopped being synonymous with religious identity but instead became identified with the 'Pakistan Movement' in British India. Popular religious practices were once the basis of mainstream identity in the ancient and the middle age of Bengal. After the arrival of Muslim jingoism in the 19th century, popular religion went undercurrent in the Bengal society, which is now distinguished as a popular sub-culture. Buddhist Tantricism, Islamic Sufism and Hindu Vaishnavism – liberal streams of three major religions in the Indian sub-continent had led to popular religious practices in Bengal that came together under the umbrella of the Baul cult. Liberal humanist philosophy, some esoteric yogic practices and syncretic religious beliefs can be identified as the basic principles and practices of the popular religions. Bengal society, like others, has been going through a transformation from its early history, but here the fourth identity approach transformation is taking place in post-globalised and post-modern times which is shaped by two external factors – neoliberal economic and cultural globalisation and globalisation of Jihadist Islam in the post-9/11 era. These four identity approaches – Bengaliness, Muslimness, Popular Religion and Transformation – will be further discussed in Chapter 2 along with a historical background of the ethnicity of the people of Bangladesh.

We approach the issue of identity and film in a particular way, drawing upon a range of theoretical positions. We begin by discussing the various accounts of identity formation, focusing largely on Anderson (2006), Gellner (1983), Chatterjee (1993), Appadurai (2001), Bhabha (1990) and Hall (1999). We then will examine the current discourse regarding independent cinema, especially in Asia. By this means, we identify concepts that we think will help shed light on the state of independent film in Bangladesh. The discussion on the theoretical underpinnings related to this book and the identity discourses connecting to different Asian cinemas as well as the method of analysing the selected independent films from Bangladesh will be discussed in Chapter 1.

Chapter 3 is simply the historical discussion and characteristics of independent cinematic practices in Bangladesh. The chapter also includes the contemporary scenario of independent cinema. We consider it is important to look back to the historical account and characteristics of independent cinema before entering to analyse the content of the film texts and understanding the representation of national identity in those texts. This chapter previously appeared in an anthology (Shoesmith and Gelino 2013). However, this is a revised version here with new data.

The next three chapters (Chapters 4–6) are basically the textual analysis of three categories of the selected films – foundational films in Chapter 4, transitional films in Chapter 5 and contemporary film in Chapter 6. For analysing the film texts, a method of 'film narratology' has been applied which was derived from 'narrative discourse' formulated by structuralist cultural theorist Gerard Genette (1980). We will discuss on film narratology in Chapter 1.

Chapter 7 discusses how the national identity of Bangladesh is represented in independent films. The discussion finds some directors' bias to Bengaliness and artistic resistance to Muslimness, some directors' nuanced portrayal of three identity approaches – Bengaliess, Muslimness and popular religion. The chapter also shows the contemporary directors are more interested in portraying recent transitional and changing Bangladesh. We have also projected in the chapter that while representing national identity in the films, gender and class dimensions are also interlinked with the portrayal. The chapter also shows, independent cinema, the important cultural institution is sometimes entrapped in orientalising itself, especially for the global audience.

Notes

1 Bangladesh produced 35 films in 2019 and 50 films in 2018 and 58 in 2017 (See 'Annual Report 2019: The Worst Year of the Decade' [Saltamami 2019: Doshoker Sobcheye Baje Bochhor]. Accessed 30 May 2020 at https://bmdb.co/সালতামামি-২০১৯-দশকের-সবচ/).
2 See '50 Years of Modhumita Cinema Hall: The Heydays are Gone' (Dhakar Cinema Hall Modhumitar 50 Bochhor: Sei Romroma Obostha Ar Nai). Accessed on 10 July 2021 at https://www.bbc.com/bengali/news-42195711.
3 See 'Cinemas to Go Extinct if Steps Not Taken Soon'. Accessed 10 July 2021 at https://www.tbsnews.net/economy/industry/cinemas-go-extinct-if-steps-not-taken-soon-135169.

References

Anderson, B. (2006). *Imagined Community: Reflections on the Origin and Spread of Nationalism*. London: Verso.

Appadurai, A. (2001). Disjuncture and Difference in the Global Cultural Economy. In S. Seidman and J. C. Alexander (eds.), *The New Social Theory Reader: Contemporary Debates*. London: Routledge, pp. 253–265.

Bhabha, H. K. (1990). Introduction: Narrating the Nation. In H. K. Bhabha (ed.), *Nation and Narration* (pp. 1–7). London: Routledge.

Chatterjee, P. (1993). *The Nation and Its Fragments: Colonial and Postcolonial Histories*. New Jersey: Princeton University Press.

Gellner, E. (1983). *Nations and Nationalism*. London: Blackwell Publishing.

Genette, G. (1980). *Narrative Discourse*. Oxford:: Basil Blackwell.

Hall, S. (1999). Culture, Community, Nation. In D. Boswell and J. Evans (eds.), *Representing the Nation: A Reader* (pp. 33–44). London: Routledge and The Open University.

Haq, F. (2020). *Cinema of Bangladesh: A Brief History*. Dhaka: Nokta.

Raju, Z. H. (2015). *Bangladesh Cinema and National Identity: In Search of the Modern?* London: Routledge.

Shoesmith, B. & Gelino, J. W. eds. (2013). *Bangladesh's Changing Mediascape: From State Control to Market Forces*. Bristol: Intellect.

1 Nationhood, Identity and Independent Cinema

In this chapter, we discuss the theoretical underpinnings of our exploration of the different forms of identity representation found in the independent films of Bangladesh and the cultural institutions in which they are embedded. For that, we must discuss the idea of nation and national identity and the theoretical notion of representing national identity in different cultural forms. As we are dealing with film texts, which are frequently ephemeral and transitory, we will describe a method of textual analysis 'film narratology' which is derived from Gerard Genette's (1980) book *Narrative Discourse*. The chapter also reviews the existing literatures related to the topic of identity and representation, which provides us with some ideas about the prevailing situation in the global and Bangladeshi independent cinema culture. This may, in turn, indirectly help to construct a clearer picture of how representation of identity is achieved on the screen in the third world country. We begin with the theoretical notions of national identity.

Nationhood and Identity

Identity provides a link between individuals and the world in which they live (Woodward, 2000: 1). Having an identity allows individuals to share some awareness and involvement with other members of the society with whom they are linked. This *identification* grows in a person's mind within the context of different dimensions of class, gender, ethnicity or place. For national identity, the members of the nation unite through a 'moral conscience', as Ernest Renan suggests, a *large aggregate* of *men, healthy* in *mind* and *warm* of *heart, creates* the *kind* of *moral conscience* which *we call* a *nation* (Renan, 1990: 20). Benedict Anderson, on the other hand, sees the nation as an imagined political community – and imagined as both inherently limited and sovereign. It is *imagined* because the members of even the smallest nation will never know most of their fellow members, meet them or ever hear of them, yet in the minds of each lives the image of their communion (Anderson, 2006: 6).

DOI: 10.4324/9781003271093-2

8   *Nationhood, Identity and Independent Cinema*

In either case, both identity and the nation have non-material dimensions. They are what we and others think they are, which is why they are both such tricky theoretical elements to work with.

Identity is not fixed and unchanging, but the result of a series of conflicts and different identifications (Woodward, 2000: 17). Similarly, nations are not fixed and unchanging. The nation of Bangladesh today is not the same nation it was in 1971 when it was founded. History and perceptions have intervened. If one considers *place* or geographical territory as a determinant of national identity, nations typically go through a long process of the external and internal conflict, or at a minimum through a process of evolution, and the identity of the nation changes over time. The nation-state of Bangladesh now broadly has a Bengali Muslim identity that fit the majority of its population. However, it was a part of India before 1947, then became a part of Pakistan, and finally is now an independent state. At each of these stages, identity was conceived of and represented differently in culture. Before Partition people thought of themselves primarily as Bengali rather than Indian; during the Pakistan period, there was a failed attempt to create a Pakistani identity that combined elements of Bengali and what was essentially Panjabi culture. Today, the emphasis is emphatically on being Bangladeshi. Each of these stages leaves traces that can confuse the very idea of identity. For example, there has been a dichotomy associated with the notion of identity in Bangladesh, whether one is principally a Bengali in culture, custom and practice or a Muslim that is at the heart of current social tensions in the country, which we will address in detail below.

An important account of the origins of the nation as a concept is provided by the anthropologist and philosopher Ernest Gellner (1983). In Gellner's view, nations came into being with the advent of modernisation in general and industrialisation in particular. According to Gellner, modernisation refers to a complex and interrelated set of social changes that transformed agrarian societies and their simple patterns of hierarchy and religious integration into complex industrial and secular societies. In contemporary Bangladesh, we can certainly witness the process of modernisation at work, especially in the economy and the changing status of women as wage-earners but there is a monumental struggle going on at the social and cultural level between the secularists and the religious fundamentalists.

Gellner's account is a primary contributor to the theoretical discussion of nationalism. However, nationalism, according to Gellner, is a contingent, artificial and ideological invention (Gellner, 1983: 55). Nationalism uses pre-existing, historically inherited proliferation of cultures or cultural wealth and most often transforms them radically, a view that aligns with Benedict Anderson's ([1983]2006) dictum that sees a nation as an *imagined community*.

According to Anderson, the idea of identity has its limitations and strengths. It is imagined as *limited* because even the largest identity in the world will always see the existence of other identities, and no nation imagines itself as coterminous with mankind. A nation is imagined *sovereign* because a nation as a concept was born in an age in which the Enlightenment and Revolution actively destroyed the legitimacy of divinely ordained kings and their hierarchical dynastic realms. Also, a nation is imagined as a *community* in which a deep and horizontal sense of comradeship unites people when religion or language fails to unite them. To construct and perpetuate the existence of nation – the contingent, artificial, ideological invention and the imagined community – needs systematic representation of its imagined solidarity and uniformity. A film is a form of media that acts as a vehicle for systematic representation of nation-ness.

Scholars such as Partha Chatterjee have re-examined the justifications of the existence of nation-states in a time of globalisation and post-modernism. They have argued that Gellner and Anderson take a simplistic view of the condition contributing to the formation of a nation, which should instead be viewed as the product of complexity. Chatterjee attempts a critique of Anderson's idea of imagined communities in his book *The Nation and Its Fragments* (1993), which has a first chapter entitled 'Whose Imagined Community?' His challenge is that the meaning of the term 'imagined community' is not a universal one and he is sceptical about the idea of a nation being imagined from certain modular forms. If a nation is imagined at all, it must have a contextual aspect that is different from other nations. He identifies two sovereign domains of a nation. The first is the *material* domain, which encompasses the state plus formal elements, and which is an imitation of the West. Second is the *spiritual* domain, which consists of the 'national culture', i.e. the sovereign territory from which the colonial society emerged well before the beginning of its political battle with the coloniser. In the context of India, this would be before the establishment of Congress in 1885. It is in this sovereign spiritual domain that nationalism is said to have begun via the development of a native language, the writing of prose and novels, establishment of institutions such as secondary schools, reformation of the family and community and so on. In that process, national elites do not allow the intervention of the colonial State or European missionaries. Chatterjee based his proposition on colonial Bengal.

We consider Chaterjee's idea of spiritual domain in the formation of national identity important where national elites did not permit the contribution of the European missionaries or the colonial State to mould it and rather made a clear distinction from it. In our understanding, we also consider popular religions to have been a powerful force in the spiritual domain as they did not allow Bengaliness or Muslimness to intervene in the formation of a national identity in Bangladesh or at least resisted intervention, rather in the opposite way, it influenced those two aspects. Sufi Islam, as a liberal stream of Islam, helped to reduce religious dogma so that a tolerant Islamic society could form. The non-communal outlook of Bengaliness is partially borrowed from popular religions. Sufism and Baul's songs and poems helped Muslims (who are Bengalis at the same time) to internalise liberalism and Bengalis (who are Muslims at the same time) to create humanist literature and culture. The essence and role of popular religion in Bangladesh will be discussed in Chapter 2.

Arjun Appadurai argues that the central problem of today's global interactions is the tension between cultural homogenisation and cultural heterogenisation (Appadurai, 2001: 256). He points out that globalisation tends to homogenise cultures. In that process, there arises resistance against homogenisation by endorsing a promise to keep a heterogeneous world. In short, there are differing, competing ways of imagining the nation and this is clearly reflected in our choice of films.

In the 1990s, Bangladesh endorsed a free market economy as part of state policy and the rise of consumer culture was felt immediately in Bangladesh society. Bangladesh started becoming homogenised by the global culture which, to be more accurate, is American culture. An increase of Islamic fundamental values in the society may be considered as resistance to homogenisation. But homogenisation, according to Appadurai (2001), 'can be exploited by nation-states in relation to their own minorities' and thus 'one man's imagined community is another man's political prison'. This idea may be applicable to the ethnic minorities living in the Chittagong Hill Tracts (CHT) and other areas in Bangladesh. The CHT people have been fighting with the Bangladesh government to achieve special status over decades. One of our selected films (*My Bicycle*, 2015) portrays the life and culture of the Chakma ethnic group and describes the presence of military in the CHT area.

The question of identity, as Bhabha (1994) suggests, is never a self-fulfilling prophecy – it is always the production of an image of identity and the transformation of the person who assumes the contours of that image. This 'production of image' of the national identity may be transformed through education, as Ernest Gellner (1983) suggests, or by books and newspapers. Anderson (2006) holds a similar view by describing the significance of print in imagining a community; indeed he goes so far as to call the late 19th and early 20th century nation states 'print capitalism' as it is through this medium that a nation may be imagined. Here we add cinema as a vehicle to produce an image of identity. Stuart Hall (1999) summarises the whole process as a 'system of representation' as noted earlier. He argues, '[T]he nation-state was never simply a political entity. It was always also a symbolic formation – a "system of representation" – which produces an "idea" of the nation as an "imagined community"' (Hall, 1999: 38).

Bhabha (1990) adds to the conversation by comparing nations with narratives and argues that the image of the nation seems romantic and metaphorical though it emerges as a powerful historical idea through political thought and literary language (we add cinematic language) which can, he suggests, be a representational system. Bhabha states:

> [n]ations, like narratives, lose their origins in the myths of time and only fully realize their horizons in the mind's eye. Such an image of the

nation – or narration – might seem impossibly romantic and excessively metaphorical, but it is from those traditions of political thoughts and literary language that the nation emerges as a powerful historical idea in the west.

(Bhabha 1990: 1)

The contributions by Gellner (1983), Anderson ([1983]2006), Hall (1999) and Bhabha (1990) provide the theoretical vehicles that we will use to analyse the representation of the 'imagined' Bengali Muslim identity that graces the Bangladeshi screen. Additionally, we will also examine the filmic texts through the lens of the theoretical notions of identity provided by some Bangladeshi scholars.

Echoing Woodward, Afsan Chowdhury (2020) too indicates the changing nature of identity and argues it appears in history as a tool to achieve a collective goal rather than the final cultural construction destination. As history moves on, identities are also adjusted, prioritised and sometimes even perceived as different by the other. Chowdhury believes the notion of an essentialist/fundamentalist identity framework built around cultural constructs such as faith, language, ethnicity, territory, etc. In the identity of the majority population of Bangladesh, there is a strong presence of two major components – Bengaliness and Muslimness which grew on ethnicity/language and faith respectively. Chowdhury observes, according to such notions, only one identity is 'real' and the rest are 'false'. This depends on the political status of the interpreter at given moments of history. He highlights the multiplicity of national identity in the context of the ongoing identity formation process.

Akhand Akhtar Hossain (2016) also finds the multi-racial and multi-religious nature of Bangladesh society, but the political parties and the rulers try to impose the monopolistic views on various symbols of national identity. Hossain observes, there is a trend of 'torturous and prolonged' case of national identity formation and politics in Bangladesh. He thinks the extreme form of secularism is not acceptable to Bangladeshi Muslims. Nor does the overwhelmingly Muslim population of Bangladesh want an Islamic theocratic state, although they value all Islamic culture and traditions, including those which prescribe Islamic theocracy. He foresees, there is scope for Bangladesh to establish and sustainably institutionalise a post-Islamist political-governance framework that can be described neither as assertive secularism nor as extreme Islamism. This holistic ideological direction of Bangladesh politics could feasibly eventuate if the leading political parties such as Bangladesh Awami League (AL) and the Bangladesh Nationalist Party (BNP) both play a democratic game of politics under established, public interest institutions, rules and regulations.

Naseem Akhter Hussain (2010) explores how women in Bangladesh negotiate modernist and Islamist discourses and thereby engage in the politics of everyday living. She argues that women's agency moves beyond analysis of women as mere victims of ideological constructions. For that, she had to theorise the nature of Islam prevailing in contemporary Bangladesh. She finds, in Bangladesh, the Islamist forces are explicitly opposed to the Western concepts of women's rights which they perceive as part of a whole Western imposed social order and damaging to the fabric of Islamic society. Yet she discovers, there is an increasing trend of 'Islamic modernity' in the country. She observes that the Islamist forces accept some aspects of modernisation but not Westernization. Some Islamic groups are negotiating modernity and religion in order to adjust the forces of modernisation and globalisation, as they do not want to be driven out of the competitive market. However, they are selective about accepting avenues of Western modernity, as they, for example, use technology, press, media, education, English language, development organisations, market mechanisms and financial institutions. It is noteworthy that as a sign of modernity Islamists have ventured into the private sector to establish kindergartens, colleges and private universities where religious teaching is included in the curriculum. Besides traditional madrasas, the Islamists are expanding religious education among students of secular and even modern English-speaking schools in urban areas.

In this frame of Islamic modernity, women act as negotiators by wearing hijab in the public sphere, as well as performers of domestic roles in the private sphere. Hijab is a changing perception of modernity for women. While previously physical veiling was perceived as an absence of modernity and mostly practiced by rural middle class and illiterate women, in the present context, wearing hijab by educated, urban, middle class, young women exhibits their wealth and piety without losing modernity.

Chowdhury's idea of multiplicity and the ever-changing nature of Bangladesh's national identity and Hussain's notion of Islamic modernity will be used as guiding principles in analysing selected films. Also, Hossain's proposal for a democratic system of politics, which accommodates aspects of secularism, language, Muslim identity for forming and consolidating the country's multi-racial, multi-religious national identity over the long run and its survival as a sovereign state, would be consulted as a potential representation of identity on the screen.

In this study, we apply the idea of 'system of representation' to films because it too is formed and propagated by education, both formal and informal. It should also be noted that these meditations on the formation of the nation and national identity occurred at a historical moment that is identical with the making of the films we will analyse. That moment is the period when the nation and national identity appeared to be under assault from globalisation. By linking representations of identity, we add a new dimension to the study of the identity of Bangladesh, which hitherto has tended to be somewhat insular and closed.

Representation and Identity

The theoretical discussions above prove it eloquently that the discourse of nation is a narration through representational system. Now we need to discuss how the representations may take place. We also discuss here how cinema is a presentational system. According to Stuart Hall, representation means using language to say something about, or to represent, the world meaningfully to other people (Hall, 1997: 15). We live in a world of signs along with the world of reality, and we know the 'real' world through those signs – in other words, we live in a represented world through print (in all of its manifestation) and the image (photography, film, television and internet streaming). In our modes of communication, which range from interpersonal interactions to the mass-mediated world, we signify things and apply meaning to them through these systems of representation.

Hall broadly discusses three approaches to explain how representation of meaning through language works. He terms these the reflective, intentional and constructive approaches to cultural representation (Hall, 1997: 24–26). The *reflective* approach, according to Hall, carries the true meaning, as it already exists in the world; it functions like a mirror. Hall gives the example of the Greeks who, in the 4th century BC, used the notion of *mimesis* to explain how language, even drawing and painting mirrored and imitated nature. In the *intentional* approach, words (texts)do not imitate reality, but mean exactly what the author intends they should mean. It holds that it is the speaker (or author), who imposes his or her unique meaning in the world through language, which is the opposite of the reflective approach. In contrast, for the *constructive* approach things do not mean anything *per se*; meaning is constructed by using representational systems – concepts and signs. The approach recognises the public and social character of the language. Constructivists do not deny the existence of the material world, but it is not the material world that conveys meaning. Rather, it is the language system or whatever system we are using to represent our concepts that fulfil this function. Social constructionist views of language and representation owe a great deal to the work and influence of the Swiss linguist Ferdinand De Saussure. For Saussure, according to Jonathan Culler, the production of meaning depends on language: 'Language as a system of signs' (Culler, 1980 cited in Hall, 1997). Sounds, images, written words, paintings and photographs function as signs only when they serve to express or communicate ideas.

In cinema, directors use cinematic language to say something meaningful by using a system of signs that reflect, intend or construct. Francesco Casetti (1999) says cinema does not provide us with an image of the society, but with what society considers being an image, including a possible image of itself. For a filmmaker who does not 'reproduce' (or simply 'reflect') the reality, the way in which he 'deals with' (constructs) reality becomes important in studying cinema. We wish to emphasise this point as it informs our analysis of competing identities – secular versus religious, modernist versus traditionalist, Bengali versus Islamic – that the Bangladeshi independent films either implicitly or explicitly explore through their diverse systems of representation. In the selected films, it can be easily identified that the directors intend to project identity discourses. While doing so, some of them clearly state their preferred identity approach, some narrate the conflict between the identities and some provide nuanced perspectives of the identity politics in Bangladesh.

Within the context of Hall's notion of nation as a 'system of representation', we believe, cinema plays a vital role in the contemporary world for the symbolic formation of the nation. This is a topic that has generated a genre of writing, national cinema, that analyses in depth the relationship between cinema and its host society, the nation. Independent filmmakers of Bangladesh also deal with identity questions on a regular basis. In analysing 'the manner in which they deal with reality (here identity)', this book follows the constructivist approach of representation by relating the construction process in films to the greater societal and historical reality of Bangladesh.

Many new nation-states emerged in Asia and Africa in the middle of the 20th century as Western political colonialism ended. In this context, Bangladesh has followed a different trajectory. In effect, it underwent two stages of liberation from colonisation. It was liberated from British rule in 1947 when it became part of Pakistan. In many respects, Pakistan was a nation doomed to failure as it consists of two wings separated by 1000 miles of Indian territory as well as different regional cultures, customs and practices. The two wings only had Islam in common, and that proved ineffective in keeping the two parts together politically. Bangladesh as a nation was liberated from Western Pakistan in 1971, after a particularly nasty civil war, marked by unrestrained behaviour by the Pakistan troops towards the civilian population of the then East Bengal. Indeed, there are well-known parallels between Partition and the War of Liberation. Both events are pivotal to the narrative of the nation, both are traumatic events leaving a legacy of distrust and enmity, and their aftermath is still being played out (over Kashmir in the case of India and Pakistan and the International War Crimes Tribunal in the case of Bangladesh). Partition clearly left its mark on Bangladesh; the last aspect of Partition, resolving the status of the enclaves (small parcels of land technically belonging to India but surrounded by Bangladesh) has only occurred in 2016. However, in the grand narrative of what it is to be Bangladeshi, of where a identity was forged, the War of Liberation is the defining moment.

In the contemporary world, cinema has played a vital role in the symbolic formation of a nation, especially since the mid-20th century and the end of European colonialism. We would argue that this is particularly relevant to Bangladesh, which became a nation just as the world became image-saturated due to the expansion of global television. For example, events in Bangladesh in 1971 were widely circulated, especially on the British Broadcasting Corporation (BBC), as television began its trajectory as a global media, rather than a purely national one. Representing the nation has become an essential approach of cinema and other image-making media; the concept of national cinema in global film studies is the reflection of the approach. Above all, if in Jameson's (1986) account 'all third-world texts' necessarily project a political dimension in the form of 'national allegories', then cinematic representation of national identities are no different.

The filmmakers of Bangladesh, especially independent filmmakers, have engaged in dealing with identity questions from the very beginning. In their portrayals, they reproduce and sometimes redefine the prevailing discourses of identity. This book examines the nature of those portrayals.

Discourses on Independent Film: Global and Bangladeshi

Before entering our own discussion, we would like to look at what other scholars and writers thought about independent cinema and review prior discussions on cinema and identity, both from global and Bangladesh perspectives. According to film critic Roger Ebert, independent film is 'a film made outside the traditional [Hollywood] studio system, often with unconventional financing, and it's made because it expresses the director's personal vision rather than someone's notion of box-office success' (Ebert 1987 cited in Levy, 1999: 3). Emanuel Levy summarises the 'traditional' idea of an independent film as:

> Ideally, an indie [independent film] is a fresh, low-budget movie, which has a gritty style and off-beat subject matter that expresses the filmmaker's personal vision.
> (Levy 1999: 2)

From these definitions, we get two basic characteristics of independent cinema: production and content. An independent film is produced (made and distributed) without the intervention of any major film studio. The content of such a film reflects the filmmaker's personal vision and control. Independent filmmaking is thus an opportunity for some filmmakers to break the rules of traditional narrative and to experiment with new or different ways of telling stories. Sometimes independent films are closely related to underground films, alternative films, *avantgarde* or experimental films. They tend to be low budget and are not produced with the goal of profit-making. In the USA, although Hollywood is the strongest film industry in the world, there is also a stronghold of independent cinema. For Bangladesh, independent film is considered as an out-of-studio production which means that films are made outside of the control of the Bangladesh Film Development Corporation (BFDC)[2]. The director's artistic aspiration is to make his or her own film, the primary goal of which is not to make profit, but rather to portray social and political reality.

16 *Nationhood, Identity and Independent Cinema*

In the 1980s, new types of films began to be made outside of BFDC and contrary to the genres of the costume epic, fantasy and action films made by commercial approaches. People started disliking the cheap content and messy cinematic techniques of the commercial films made in BFDC and short films with serious content and fresh visual styles made the serious audience optimistic. The first short film from a film society activist, *Towards* (Agami), was made in 1984 by Morshedul Islam. *Towards* was a story of disillusionment in which freedom fighters were in a distressed situation in the independent country and the anti-Liberation force regained their strength. This was a very contemporary story for that time. The film received the best director award in Delhi International Film Festival. A few months after the release of *Towards*, Tanvir Mokammel released his film *Wanted* (*Hooliya* 1985). *Wanted* was the story of an outlaw political activist in the pre-Liberation War. The audience appreciated these two new kinds of art house films with political messages that they could relate to the situation in contemporary Bangladesh. *Towards* and *Wanted* were screened together in different parts of the country, through alternative distribution by film society activists. These two films were commercially successful. After this, an independent short film movement outside of the industry began and new directors became engaged with filmmaking. Mostofa Kamal's *Return* (Protyaborton 1986), Abu Sayeed's *The Cycle* (Abartan 1989), Tareque Masud's *The Inner Strength* (Adam Surat 1989) and Enayet Karim Babul's The Wheel (*Chakki* 1989) are some notable short films of the 1980s. Critics and audience appreciated that some of these films based on the Liberation War highlighted social problems, and also valued their comparatively modern filmmaking style.

Thus, the independent film movement began at a certain stage of film history in Bangladesh. Currently, it is facing a challenge as the film-watching habits of the audience have changed. Instead of going to the theatres, the audience enjoys both foreign and local films in DVD format, on cable channels, or by internet streaming at home. In the production aspect, independent filmmaking depends either on self-funding TV channels or foreign funds instead of tickets sold to audiences. Sometimes government grants are also available to use in generating funds. Hence in recent times, although independent cinema of Bangladesh has gained a degree of maturity in terms of content and form, it faces the challenge of maintaining its independent characteristics. This is especially true for the independent films produced by television channels. The filmmakers, who made short films in the 1980s, became the leaders of independent filmmaking in Bangladesh. They are also known as the renowned art-house filmmakers in Bangladesh, joined by more filmmakers in the contemporary decades. Actually, the national cinema of Bangladesh is represented in the global stage by these filmmakers whose creations will be analysed in this book.

Nationhood, Identity and Independent Cinema 17

Before entering the analysis of representation on identity in selected independent films, it is necessary to look at prior studies. In global film studies, much has been written about the independent film but very few authors examine the representation of identity in the independent films. Many of the books have been written on American independent films – the most vibrant independent filmmaking zone. The works by Emanuel Levy (1999), Greg Merritt (1999), Geoff King (2005) and Yannnis Tzioimakis (2006) are basically introductory, historical and interpretative accounts of indie cinema in the USA. They did not focus on how identity is represented in the American independent films, because they were either disinterested in the topic or assumed identity to be a given, not requiring elaboration. However, we will also attempt to review briefly some earlier works on the Asian national cinemas focusing on the representation of identity in independent films wherever possible. Indeed, the paucity of writings on independent cinema in Asia is noticeable.

Rey Chow and Sheldon Hsiao-Peng Lu are scholars of independent film in China, especially China's so-called Fifth Generation of Filmmakers exemplified by the directors Zhang Yimou and Chen Kaige. Rey Chow, in her book *Primitive Passions: Visuality, Sexuality, Ethnography, and Contemporary Chinese Cinema* (1995) finds that the early films of Zhang and Chen explore oppression, contamination, rural backwardness and the persistence of feudal values as the central themes of their version of the 'national allegory'. Although she praises the visual beauty captured in the films she identifies the tendency of portraying a backward, non-modern and oppressive Chinese society from the first half of the 20th century by those filmmakers, which she terms as 'primitive passion'. The subject matter and the visual beauty of the films have established the reputation of the filmmakers in the West, but she criticises them, essentially on issues of 'identity':

> [D]irectors such as Zhang are producing a new kind of orientalism ... this exhibitionism – what we may call Oriental's orientalism – does not make its critique moralistically or resentfully.
>
> (Chow, 1995: 171)

Sheldon Hsiao-Peng Lu (1997) in his edited collection *Transnational Chinese Cinemas: Identity, Nationhood, Gender*, examined Chinese language films produced in mainland China, Hong Kong and Taiwan. He observes that the political economy of these films is a colonial one as the films were funded by foreign capital (Hong Kong, Taiwan, Japan and Europe), produced by Chinese labour, distributed in a global network and consumed by an international audience. Consequently, he tags Fifth Generation films as 'transnational cinema', especially the films made by Zhang Yimou, and finds that the films are not 'purely' Chinese as they are 'periodically banned' by the Chinese authorities and not consumed in China. He states, 'like other national cinemas, Chinese cinema is the mobiliser of the nation's myths and the myth of the nation (Lu, 1997: 5).

While it is difficult to make direct comparisons between Chinese independent cinema and its Bangladeshi counterpart, it is important to recognise that Chow's concept of 'Oriental's orientalism' and Lu's idea of 'transnational Chinese cinema' are useful as theoretical tools to analyse the concept of identity mobilised and portrayed by independent filmmakers of Bangladesh, which will be discussed below.

The question of independent film has provoked considerable interest throughout Asia, largely, we would argue, because the 'national' screens of Japan, Hong Kong and China are dominated by the commercial cinema that is predominantly formulaic in their execution. Almost by definition independent filmmakers wish to escape this 'ideoscape' (Appadurai, 2001), which is predicated upon a set of assumptions about its audiences and what they willingly consume. In looking at independent film production in Hong Kong (Chu, 2003), Korea (Lee, 2000) and Japan (Davis, 1996) we accumulate a number of significant theoretical concepts that provide us with the tools to look at Bangladeshi independent films in greater depth.

Chu argues that Hong Kong has a 'quasi-national identity' that is reflected in its films, which have texts based on both the exclusion and inclusion of China's cultural identity (Chu, 2003). She points out that Hong Kong cinema projects this identity in two main areas: geopolitical cultural distinction and film narratives. Even after the unification of Hong Kong with China in 1997, the quasi-national identity portrayals remain unchanged. As China follows a 'one country, two systems' policy, the capitalist nature of Hong Kong as a state remains unchanged. Chu argues this situation is reproduced in the films and helps shape Hong Kong identity by their exclusion from mainland markets. This exclusion invites the local film industry to explore the territory's cultural identity in terms of political, economic and social integration with the mainland, which after the 1997 economic crisis in South East Asia entailed Hong Kong cinema seeking new sources of funding. Chu summarises:

> [T]he policy has encouraged the industry to seek overseas investment and markets which, as has been shown, will lead Hong Kong to take an increasingly global and pan-Asian outlook.
>
> (Chu, 2003: 132)

as opposed to an inclusive Chinese cultural perspective.

Hyangjin Lee studies six Korean films that are

> all constructed around the ideological tension between South and North, they invariably touch on the Confucian notion of family and connect it with their ideal nationhood. Their reliance on traditional

family values seems to suggest the enduring Confucian cultural root as a possible alternative to the current political ideologies to lay out an appropriate ground for establishing integrated nationhood.

(Lee, 2000: 106)

If the portrayal of Confucian cultural roots is common between two film traditions, they have, of course, displayed differences in portraying identity issues. In the North Korean films, anti-imperialism constitutes the core of their definition of nationhood. For South Korean films, anti-communism is the main cinematic crux (Lee, 2000). But since the late 1980s, as Lee (2000) observes, new independent filmmakers have emerged who give the appearance of politically conscious young filmmakers who challenge the ideological repression of the government on either side of the Korean divide (Lee, 2000). This interests us simply because mainstream Bangladeshi cinema strives to present an ideologically homogeneous culture in which difference is discouraged in favour of conformity. We will argue that many of the independent filmmakers seek to challenge the ideological conformity that characterises much of Bangladeshi cultural production, from traditional music to popular literature, albeit not always successfully.

Darrell William Davis, in *Picturing Japaneseness: Monumental Style, National Identity, Japanese Film* (1996), argues that films can be an active force, contributing to and even helping to create a nation's sense of its own identity. By concentrating on the Japanese cinema of the 1930s and 1940s, Davis shows how these movies distinguished Japanese culture from others. Davis describes how cultural and literary media play the role of portraying a Japanese identity and he puts film within that effort:

Between 1936 and 1941, there were strenuous efforts made to express, and define, what makes Japanese people and life so Japanese. ... Defining Japaneseness in the late 1930s, however become an institutionalised activity, as it today. Writers, artists, journalists company men, neighborhood associations, student activists, women's groups, boys' and girls' clubs were all organised for the express purpose of delineating the outlines of an authentic Japanese essence. Mass media, particularly the highly capitalised film, radio and mass circulation newspaper industries, were consolidated ad encouraged to generate representations of Japanese culture and behavior.

(Davis, 1996: 2)

Although Davis concentrates on earlier Japanese films, he states that this 'monumental style' of picturing Japaneseness is found in contemporary films as well. Davis alerts us to the fact that Bangladeshi cinema is very much geared toward the production of 'Bangladeshiness' with its emphasis on a few tried and tested cultural tropes; the language martyrs, the liberation war of 1971, the evils of the collaborators in that war, and the struggle to achieve nationhood. In addition, it has to distinguish itself from the other Bengali cinema based on Kolkata that for years was the cultural touchstone for Bangladeshis. There is an ambiguous relationship between the Kolkata industry of Bimal Roy, Satyajit Ray, Ritwik Ghatak and Mirnal Sen, which the Bangladeshi indie cinema at times claims as its own and at other times rejects. Kabir (1979), Hayat (1987) and Raju (2015) mention that one of the earlier feature films produced from Dhaka industry, *Asiya* (1960) was heavily influenced by Satyajit Ray's *Pather Panchali* (1956). Raju notes the words of Indian scholar Ravi Basudevan that the cultural-modernist Bengali Muslims and their film club discourse in the 1960s East Pakistan were then influenced by what he called the 'Satyajit Ray School' (Raju, 2015: 189–190). Satyajit Ray was one of the founders of Calcutta Film Society, which was established in 1948. As the Dhaka, based film clubs were the breeding ground of contemporary independent filmmakers in Bangladesh, the influence of Kolkata in Bangladeshi art and independent cinema is clearly evident. While writing on *The Clay Bird*, Claude-Marie Tremois called Tareque Masud 'a disciple of Ray' (Tremois 2003: 7). But by telling their own stories, Dhaka films are also different from Kolkata's, as these films portray rural Muslim society and the peoples' struggle in the Liberation War of Bangladesh and contemporary issues in urban society.

It is tempting to look to India as a point of comparison, but this would not be fruitful as Bollywood overwhelms Indian cinema and this flows on to Bangladesh, where the Indian spectaculars are freely available either through pirated DVDs, satellite television or streaming services on the Internet. However, studies have been conducted on the representation of identity in popular films that have some relevance to this enterprise; two book-length works can be found on the representation of identity in Indian popular films produced in Bombay. These are *The Cinematic ImagiNation: Indian Popular Film as Social History* by Jyotika Virdi (2003) and *National Identity in Indian Popular Cinema* by Sumita S. Chakravarti (1994). Virdi posits film as a kind of storytelling that provides a fascinating account of the social history and cultural politics of India, with the family deployed to symbolise the nation in Indian mainstream cinema. She observes that in popular Hindi films the nation is protected by the heroes of the films who:

> ... fights the nation's 'enemies' – threats to the nation at the moment of film's making. These enemies took the form of unprincipled profiteers in the 1950s, foreign aggressors in the 1960s, 'smugglers' in the 1970s, separatist 'terrorists' and politicians in the 1980s, and authoritarian patriarchs in the 1990s. While vanquishing enemies signifies the hero's passage to manhood, another battle, against the enemy within the family, marks his rite of passage.
>
> (Virdi, 2003: 87)

However, Virdi argues that the portrayal of the nation as a mythical community in popular Hindi films collapses under the weight of its own contradictions – incompatible differences that encompass gender, sexuality, family, class and religious communities.

By focusing on popular films in India, Chakravarti (1994) underpins a conjunctural picture of cinematic text, historical context and national interest. In doing so, she emphasises the cinema's characteristic forms, its range of meanings and pleasures, and, above all, its ideological construction of Indian national identity. She writes:

> The politics of film culture in postcolonial India that is treated in this book is also a politics of nostalgia, a genealogy of lost ideals in the nation's cultural and sociopolitical life.
>
> (Chakravarti, 1994: 9)

By analysing films directed by Vijay Anand, Raj Kapoor and Shyam Benegal (made in the 1950s–70s) she shows how 'imperso-*nation*', played out in masquerade and disguise, has characterised the representation of national identity in popular films. According to her, the concerns and conflicts over class, communal and regional differences are obsessively evoked, explored and neutralised through popular films. Thus, she delineates the function of popular cinema in the transgression of social codes and boundaries. She writes:

> The cultural elite, as official guardians of 'Indianness', labeled the commercial cinema as impersonating, debased, and parasitic form, thereby seeking to maintain and police cultural boundaries. The commercial cinema, meanwhile, has used the masquerade to transgress boundaries with impunity and to inscribe the national itself as the ideal-typical mode of impersonification.
>
> (Chakravarti, 1994: 5)

Finally, the Malaysian scholar Gaik Cheng Khoo (2006) has studied representations of identity in the films of Malaysia for several years, focusing mainly on the works of independent filmmakers. In *Reclaiming Adat: Contemporary Malaysian Film and Literature* (2006), Khoo reveals the tensions between gender, modernity and nation in Malaysian contemporary films and literature. The book makes a vital contribution to the analysis of the complexities ingrained in modern Malaysian culture, politics and identity. However, she has an interest in the representation of identity in the independent films of Malaysia. In her article *Art, Entertainment and Politics* (2005), she compares the ways in which mainstream Malay language cinema and independent cinema portray multiracial identity in the Malaysian context:

Malay cinema gives the impression of Malaysia as an ethnically homogenous nation. Often when actors of other ethnicities are cast, they are stereotypes: the crass Chinese businessman, the comic Indian character.... Indie films represent the polyglot that is Malaysia by being in Mandarin, Tamil, Cantonese, Hokkien, Malay, or English (always accompanied by English subtitles as a unifier).

Khoo (2005) praises independent films that portray racial disparity within an apparent homogenous Malaysian national identity propagated by the government:

Independent films like *6horts* (2002) and *The Big Durian* (2003) both by Amir Muhammad, cleverly broach topics tangential to ethnicity and culture such as Malay hegemony, the power of the Sultans, and systemic and structural racialisation sustained by corrupt crony politics and numerous laws that stifle freedom.

Again, these observations help us place the independent film of Bangladesh in a context. Bangladesh is a homogenous country in comparison with Malaysia but we have also selected the only film made in a non-Bengali language (*My Bicycle*), which provides us the opportunity to examine an ethnic culture and language under the hegemonic Bengali language and culture.

Now we need to look at how Bangladeshi scholars and analysts have looked at the portrayal of national identity in Bangladeshi cinema. Zakir Hossain Raju, in his book *Bangladesh Cinema and National Identity: In Search of the Modern?* (2015) highlights the tensions between Bengali-Muslim ethnicity and the purportedly secular nation-state of Bangladesh. He sees two conflicting identities emerging from these tensions, the secular-modern and the communal-Islamic. In Raju's view, the independent art filmmakers of Bangladesh stand for the secular-modern identity and these directors assume that the audience for their films will be members of the same identity group as themselves. These audiences, like the directors, received a Westernised secular education in schools that are part and parcel of the socio-politically consciousness of the art-loving urban and middle-class people. Raju's analysis leads him to identify two forms of modernity in Bangladesh that he terms the nation-state modernity and cultural-national modernity, which are portrayed and discussed in indie films.

In fact, he identifies two major schools of art cinema discourses in Bangladesh, which he terms middle cinema and independent cinema, respectively. According to Raju (2015), the middle cinema demonstrates the nationalising initiative of Bangladeshi art cinema that seeks to portray Bangladesh as a secular state. In short, this arm of the indie film sector represents the Westernisation of Bangladeshi art cinema, which Raju suggests is driven by economics. He identifies these films as part of the national treasury of 'high art' as they are palatable to western art-house audiences, where most the films are expected to recoup their costs, although this is unlikely in Bangladesh. Raju's basic argument is that the filmmakers, by consciously using the norms of Western/modern cinematic practices, are able to depict the conflict between the secular-modern and communal-Islamic forces in Bangladesh in the construction of the modern Bangladeshi identity.

Raju makes a further distinction in describing independent films in Bangladesh by positing additional analytic categories. One is the 'artisanal' short film, a trend which started in the mid 1980s and the other is the 'global' feature-length film, which started in the 1990s. These films were made by the same directors, such as Morshedul Islam, Tanvir Mokammel, Tareque Masud, and Abu Sayeed and represent the economics of independent filmmaking that are particularly acute in Bangladesh because investors and producers are unwilling to put money into potentially loss-making ventures. Both the 'artisanal' and 'global' films were financed from a multiplicity of sources; the 'artisanal film' by family or friends of the director or some individual producers, whereas the 'global' films tended to be funded by foreign sources. Both sources are notoriously fickle and unreliable. The mode of production and distribution of the films was clearly different from that of the mainstream popular films.

According to Raju, in the cinema environment of Bangladesh there is a dichotomy of 'trash versus taste', a conflict among both the critics and the audiences, in which the independent filmmakers claim themselves to be the advocates of taste. However, Raju perceives an irony at the core of this separation; while the independent films attempt to portray the life of ordinary people, standing for a cultural-modernist identity, these films were not appreciated by their intended audience because of their complicated narratives and abstract form. Raju adds that the independent feature films are more widely shown internationally than in Bangladesh, which is certainly true for films like *The Wheel* (1993) and *The Clay Bird* (2002). Raju goes further in criticising these global films. He argues, '[t]he global Bangladeshi cinema is presenting a "Bangladesh," that is, borrowing the words of Chow, "at once subalternise and exoticised by the West"' (Raju, 2015: 197).

However, setting this quibble to one side, we have used Raju's two main points as tools for further analysis: (i) that there are two conflicting identities in broader Bengali Muslim identity and that independent films deepens the conflict between the two and (ii) the idea of the Oriental's orientalism. This will be especially seen in the case of how these films represent identity.

Zakir Hossain Raju (2008) also discusses the portrayal of Bengali-Muslim identity in cinema and its role had in creating the nation-state of Bangladesh in a book chapter titled 'Madrasa and Muslim Identity on Screen: Nation, Islam and Bangladeshi Art Cinema on the Global Stage'. His analysis of the cinematic representation of Muslim identity, focuses on the madrasa, as a centre of Islamic learning and identity formation. He describes the bifurcated Bengali Muslim identity as comprising two conflicting categories: The Westernised secular ideology and pro-Islam rigidity and summarises his arguments thus:

> As the art cinema authors are busy in the act of orientalising Bangladesh for the global audience and Westernised Bengali-Muslims, in most cases, their representation of Islam and Islamic education deepens the Islam-Bengali dichotomy.
>
> (Raju, 2008: 140)

With the exception of *The Clay Bird*, Raju concludes:

> The Bangladeshi art cinema became overtly committed to cultural modernity of middle-class Bengali Muslims, a modernity that emphasises the secular notion of 'Bengali' cultural identity and opposes the 'Muslim-ness' of/within the Bengali Muslims.
>
> (Raju, 2008: 140)

Two other writers, Tanvir Mokammel and Manjare Haseen Murad, have also contributed to the debate around identity with several articles on independent cinema (which they call 'alternative cinema') in the local press. Both of them are independent filmmakers as well. It should be noted that in early phases, these films were known as alternative cinema and but the term 'independent cinema' has gained currency recently, hence our use of the term rather than alternative cinema.

In 1993, Tanvir Mokammel wrote an article entitled *Problematics of Alternative Cinema in Bangladesh: An Introspection*, in which the filmmaker-writer describes the background of independent cinema in an historical context – how it had begun, the situation in mainstream industry at the time, and how badly alternative ventures were treated by mainstream distributors. He develops an argument for the uniqueness of Bangladeshi independent film in comparison with other countries because of its thematic characteristics. At the same time, he acknowledges the limitations, especially in technical proficiency, of early independent films. He also describes the impediments placed on the films by the government, especially from the censorship board. In essence, the article is a plea for stakeholders, such as the government, TV channels and distributors to improve independent cinema through cash injections and provides better conditions for independent filmmaking.

Tanvir Mokammel (2006) adopts a more popular approach in *Twenty Years of Alternative Cinema: Experience and Achievement*, which is written in Bengali. In this article, he also describes the historical background of independent cinema of Bangladesh, which includes his early experiences, the limitations confronting him and others, the impediments from the government, and some unexpected success, particularly on the international stage.

What is important in this article is the writer's continuing desire to enhance independent cinema after twenty years of commitment to a largely ignoredgenre. He suggests independent films must be able to compete with mainstream movies, which requires the making of full-length along with short length films. He also acknowledges that independent cinema has to show more professionalism to achieve technical perfection, suggesting independent filmmakers work both inside and outside of the BFDC, which is the only studio of mainstream films in Bangladesh.

In order to achieve his goals Mokammel proposes that independent filmmakers put their own house in order by becoming better organisers, uniting to achieve public acceptance. He regards the current situation as dismal as directors have to depend on public support rather than government or capitalist sponsors. He proposes that film budgets should be kept low to avoid the need to compromise in order to obtain bigger budgets. He also adds the need to establish a film institute that acts as a centre to create an ideal cine culture. His extensive agenda of reform identifies documentary film as an important sub-genre of independent filmmaking and significantly he argues that indie filmmakers should not be wedded to a format of film but should be liberal and adopt newer digital ways of filmmaking.

In many respects Mokammel represents the purist's view of indie filmmaking that has prevailed in Bangladesh but with important exceptions; he is willing to experiment with formats and recognises that filmmakers also have to adjust to a market (the audiences) rather than relying on government largesse. These exception point towards a more sustainable future for indie filmmaking.

Leading documentary maker and independent cine activist Manjare Haseen Murad (2006) describes trends of alternative filmmaking in *Alternative Film of Bangladesh: Present and Future* and the future of the movement. After a brief background to independent cinema of Bangladesh, in which he identifies the contemporary state of independent film and the problems it faces, he goes on to discuss how the TV channels, which have swallowed the young filmmakers, are creating a crisis in the alternative film culture. On the question of format, the writer emphasises digital video format as an alternative to classical filmmaking. He also emphasises the necessity of disseminating the alternative film movement beyond the capital Dhaka to other major cities and small towns as he believes that is possible in a video format to create a broader potential market for the films than has been found in the metropolitan elite. He concludes by declaring his bias for a new cine culture, one which portrays the social and political realities of the country.

Film Narratology

The term *narratology* was introduced (according to Robert Stam et al. [1992]) by formalist Tzvetan Todorov for literary analysis; it has become the formal name for narrative analysis. In cinema, narration can be seen as a discursive activity that represents or recounts the events or situations of the story.

There have been innumerable accounts of how narrative works, especially in literature, from structuralists and post-structuralists to postmodernists, but for us the most useful is Gerard Genette's (1980) term *Narrative Discourse*. In our view it is invaluable in understanding narrative theory because of its systematic approach. As Culler points out, Genette is a more acute and perceptive analyst of fiction than his predecessors (Culler, 1980: 7). For the textual analysis of cinema, Robert Stam et al. (1992), argues that Genette's 'narrative discourse' has allowed film theory to describe the various narrative agents and levels in film in a precise manner. Film scholars like David Brodwell (1985), Murray Smith (2005), Seymour Chatman (2005) and Edward Braningan (1992) have endorsed this view and refer to Genette in their discussions of film narratology.

Bordwell (1985) states there are three threads to narratology. First and foremost, he says, we can treat narrative as a *representation*, constructing meanings through the depiction of the story's world and its portrayal of some sort of reality. Second, we can treat narrative as a *structure*, i.e. a particular way of combining parts to make a whole. Third, we can study narrative as the *process* of selecting, arranging, and rendering story material in order to achieve specific, time-bound effects on a perceiver. Bordwell also mentions that these three approaches have been addressed by different scholars, taking each thread individually or at times interweaving them into a layered account of film narrative. The second approach (narrative as a structure) is exemplified by Vladimir Propp's analysis of the magical fairy tale and by Tzvetan Todorov's (1969) studies of narrative 'grammar'. Claude Levi-Strauss' (1978) analysis of the structure of myth in order to reveal representational functions adds another dimension to this rich field of enquiry. By contrast, John Holloway (1979) considers representation and narration and their effect on structure. The central concern of Bordwell was elaborated in his book *Narration in the Fiction Film* (1985) adding a third approach to the analysis of film narrative, which he calls *narration*. Our reason for using Genette's 'narrative discourse' model, however, is straightforward. He addresses and covers all the three approaches of narrative analysis (*representation, structure* and *process*) within the one theoretical package.

Genette (1980) points out that the term 'narrative' has been used to cover three distinct notions: *recit, histoire* and *narration*. The *recit* (usually translated as narrative) is the signifier, statement, discourse or narrative text itself, i.e. the verbal or cinematic discourse that conveys the story-world to the spectator. The *recit* has both a material substance and a form. *Histoire* by contrast, is the signified or narrative content of the *recit*, i.e. the story world. *Narration* refers to the techniques, strategies and signals by which the presence of a narrator can be inferred, and the story is told. Genette subdivides *recit* into three categories: *tense*—the temporal relations between narrative and story; *mood*—the study of focalisation in terms of perspective and distance; and *voice*—the narrating instance or the marks of narration in the *recit*.

For the textual analysis of Bangladeshi independent film, we apply Genette's model of 'narrative discourse', which provides us with a systematic analytic tool for the analysis of the selected films. However, we have taken the liberty to reorganise the model in a simpler form, in which we use 'first *histoire* then *recit* and *narration*' method instead of the original 'recit-histoire-narration' order provided by Genette. We consider *histoire* as the story or signified in the text of the film, *recit* as the statement or signifier of the text of the film and *narration* as the technique or style in film language followed by the director in the narrative. The re-organisation of the model allows us to integrate the telling of the story of the film into an understanding of its meanings, constructed through narration. We stress this theoretical dimension to understanding film for one simple reason. This book is the first attempt to explain the theory of Bangladeshi film, more specifically independent film, rather than providing opaque renditions of an 'official' ideology.

Some of the data used in this book have been obtained through in-depth interviews with four leading independent filmmakers – Tareque Masud, Tanvir Mokammel, Morshedul Islam and Abu Sayeed. Also, we interviewed two film scholars, Zakir Hossain Raju and Sajedul Awwal. These interviews were conducted at different times in 2006 and 2007. However, another interview was taken in 2016 with filmmaker Mostofa Sarwar Farooki. Authorial observations integrate the interviews and the textual analysis of the ten selected films as well as secondary data to provide a broad picture of the representation of national identity in independent films of Bangladesh.

References

Anderson, B. (2006). *Imagined Community: Reflections on the Origin and Spread of Nationalism*. London: Verso.

Appadurai, A. (2001). Disjuncture and Difference in the Global Cultural Economy. In S. Seidman and J. C. Alexander (eds.), *The New Social Theory Reader: Contemporary Debates* (pp. 253–265). London: Routledge.

Bhabha, H. K. (1990). Introduction: Narrating the Nation. In H. K. Bhabha (ed.), *Nation and Narration* (pp. 1–7). London: Routledge.

Bhabha, H. K. (1994). *The Location of Culture*. London: Routledge.

Bordwell, D. (1985). *Narration in the Fiction Film*. London: Methuen.

Braningan, E. (1992), *Narrative Comprehension and Film*. London: Routledge.

Casetti, F. (1999). *Theories of Cinema: 1945-1995*. Austin: University of Texas Press.

Chatterjee, P. (1993). *The Nation and Its Fragments: Colonial and Postcolonial Histories*. New Jersey: Princeton University Press.

Chakravarti, S. S. (1994). *National Identity in Indian Popular Cinema 1947–87*. Austin: University of Texas Press.

Chatman, S. (2005). The Cinematic Narrator. In T. E. Wartenberg and A. Curran (eds.), *The Philosophy of Film: Introductory Texts and Readings* (pp. 190–197). Oxford: Blackwell Publishing

Chow, R. (1995). Primitive Passions: Visuality, Sexuality, *Ethnography and Contemporary Chinese Cinema*. New York: Columbia University Press.

Chowdhury, A. (2020). *Sheikh Mujibur Rahman and Bangladesh: the Quest for a State (1937–1971)*. Dhaka: Shrabon.

Chu, Y. (2003). *Hong Kong Cinema: Coloniser, Motherland and Self*. London: Routledge.

Culler, J. (1980). Foreword. In G. Genette (ed.), *Narrative Discourse* (pp. 1–9). Oxford: Basil Blackwell.

Davis, D. W. (1996). *Picturing Japaneseness: Monumental Style, National Identity, Japanese Film*. New York: Columbia University Press.

Genette, G. (1980). *Narrative Discourse*. Oxford: Basil Blackwell.

Gellner, E. (1983). *Nations and Nationalism*. London: Blackwell Publishing.

Hall, S. (1997). The Work of Representation. In S. Hall (ed.), *Representation: Cultural Representations and Signifying Practice* (pp 1–4). London: Sage Publications.

Hall, S. (1999). Culture, Community, Nation. In D. Boswell and J. Evans (eds.), *Representing the Nation: A Reader* (pp. 33–44). London: Routledge and The Open University.

Hayat, A. (1987). *Film History of Bangladesh (Bangladesher Cholochitrer Itihas)*. Dhaka: BFDC.

Holloway, J. (1979). *Narrative and Structure: Exploratory Essays*. Cambridge: Cambridge University Press.

Hossain, A. H. (2016). Islamism, Secularism and Post-Islamism: the Muslim World and the Case of Bangladesh. *Asian Journal of Political Science, 24*(2), 214–236.

Hussain, N. A. (2010). Religion and Modernity: Gender and Identity Politics in Bangladesh. *Women's Studies International Forum, 33*(2010), 325–333.

Jameson, F. (1986). Third World Literature in the Era of Multinational Capitalism, *Social Text*, 15: Autumn, pp. 65–88.

Kabir, A. (1979). *Film in Bangladesh*. Dhaka: Bangla Academy.

Khoo, G. C. (2005). Art, Entertainment and Politics at www.criticine.com/feature_article.php?id=20,. Accessed 13 April2009.

Khoo, G. C. (2006). *Reclaiming Adat: Contemporary Malaysian Film and Literature*. Vancouver: UBC Press.

King, G. (2005). *American Independent Cinema*. Bloomington: Indiana University Press.

Lee, H. (2000). *Contemporary Korean Cinema: Identity, Culture, Politics*. Manchester: Manchester University Press.

Levy, E. (1999). *Cinema of Outsiders: The Rise of American Independent Films*. New York: New York University Press.

Levy-Strauss, C. (1998). *Myth and Meaning*. Toronto: University of Toronto Press.

Lu, S. H.-p. (1997). *Transnational Chinese Cinemas: Identity, Nationhood, Gender*. Honolulu: University of Hawaii Press.

Merritt, G. (1999). *Celluloid Mavericks: A History of American Independent Film Making*. New York: Da Capo Press.

Mokammel, T. (n.d.). Problematics of Alternative Cinema in Bangladesh: An Introspection. In N. A. Atique (ed.), *From the Heart of Bangladesh*, Dhaka: Bangladesh Short Film Forum, pp. not numbered.

Mokammel, T. (2006). Twenty Years of Alternative Cinema: Experience and Achievement' (Bangladeshe Bikalpo Cinemar Bish Bochhor: Oviggota O Prapti). *Drishshoroop: Annual Compilation, 1411–1412*, 7–20.

Murad, M. H. (2006). Alternative Films of Bangladesh: Present and Future' (Bangladesher Cholochchitrer Bikolpodhara: Bortoman O Vobishshot). In F. Haq and S. Moon (eds.), *The Age of Film: The Film of the Age (Cholochchitrer Somoy: Somoyer Cholochchitro)* (pp. 30–39). Dhaka: Oitijyo.

Raju, Z. H. (2008). Madrasa and Muslim Identity on Screen: Nation, Islam and Bangladeshi Art Cinema on Global Stage. In J. Malik (ed.), *Madrasas in South Asia: Teaching Terror?* (pp. 125–141). London: Routledge.

Raju, Z. H. (2015). *Bangladesh Cinema and National Identity: In Search of Modern?*. London: Routledge.

Renan, E. (1990). What is a Nation?. In H. K. Bhabha (ed.), *Nation and Narration* (pp. 9–22). London: Routledge.

Smith, M. (2005). Engaging Characters. In T. E. Wartenberg and A. Curran (eds.), *The Philosophy of Film: Introductory Texts and Readings* (pp. 160–169). Oxford: Blackwell Publishing.

Stam, R., Burgoyne, R. & Flitterman-Lewis, S. (1992). *New Vocabularies in Film Semiotics*. London: Routledge.

Todorov, T. (1969). *Grammaire du Decameron*. The Hague: The Mouton.Tremois

Tremois, C. (2003). Cinema: 'Keep Love in your Heart. In A. B. M. N. Huda (ed.), *Rediscovering Bangladesh: Foreign Press on Matir Moina* (pp. 7–9). Dhaka: Audiovision.

Tzioumakis, Y. (2006). *American Independent Cinema: An Introduction*. Piscataway: Rutgers University Press.

Virdi, J. (2003). *The Cinematic ImagiNation*. Delhi: Permanent Black.

Woodward, K. (2000). *Questioning Identity: Gender, Class and Nation*, London: Routledge.

2 Identity Approaches of Bengali Muslims

If Bangladesh is such a homogeneous nation with 98% of its population identifying themselves as Bengali, the question arises 'why is ethnicity so important to Bangladeshis'? Hindus, Buddhists, Christians and Muslims are all Bengalis. It is Bengali culture that allows Muslims to claim Rabindranath Tagore, a Hindu poet and humanist, as their own. At the heart of this dilemma is a complex history that is coupled to political issues. Between Clive's 'victory at Plassey' in 1757 and the creation of Bangladesh in 1971, Bengal has been ruled, often unwillingly, by foreigners. Associated with the creation of Bangladesh is a sense the superiority of Bengali culture has been vindicated but is always vulnerable. In the past, it was vulnerable to colonialism, in the present to global television; it is thus always in need of protection, hence the recurring emphasis on Bengali culture and the clinging to its classic expression in the works of Tagore. However, as nearly 90% of Bengali is Muslim we would argue, as Eaton (1993), Ahmed (2001) and Van Schendel (2009) have observed, that the central defining fact of Bangladesh is the ongoing tension between Bengali culture and Islam. It shapes everyday life and lies at the heart of the films we examine in this book.

To investigate the issue of ethnicity and identity we adopt four major themes that have shaped the debate around the question of Bengali Muslim identity over the course of Bengali history. These are: (i) the ethnic and historico-cultural approach, which places great emphasis on language and literature; (ii) the religious approach, which asserts that Islam has the greatest influence in forming the Bengali identity; (iii) a popular approach, which emphasises the syncretic nature of Bengali religion and society, arguing that the Sufi tradition of Islam, Baulism and the *bhakti* tradition of Hinduism with a fair dose of secularism account for identity formation; and (iv) transformation in the form of hybridity, which is found in recent time while the people of Bangladesh were negotiating two major external forces – neoliberal economic and cultural globalisation (which includes the globalisation of Jihadist Islam). Other approaches exist but they tend to be marginal to the discourse of ethnicity. This chapter examines in detail

DOI: 10.4324/9781003271093-3

the claims made about Bengali Muslim identity in the context of these themes – showing how, over time, the various political, societal and historical characteristics of the time have constructed differing narratives. We will also argue that Bangladeshi identity is fluid and responsive to a number of competing factors.

To define and analyse the ethnicity of Bengali Muslim identity, historico-culturalists resort to antiquity, looking back to ancient times and the medieval history of Bengal after the Muslim conquest in 1204 (see Murshid, 2006). According to these accounts, mere historical description is not enough to analyse identity; in addition to chronology, one must analyse political, religious and cultural events as well as elements emerging from them, conflicting and synthesising with each other. All of these factors directly and indirectly are responsible for the formation of identities.

This historical analysis of the culturalists asserts that what distinguishes the formation of Bengali identity from other, competing accounts is its focus on a singular culture. However, a cursory look at the historical claims underpinning the concept of Bengaliness rests on precarious grounds. For example, the Bengali language does not become a distinctive language until the 13th century; a united Bengal was not formed until the 14th century, and the ethnicity of the people of this geographical area was not known as Bengali before the 18th century (Murshid, 2006: 26). On the other hand, Islam, which came to Bengal through the activities of wandering saints before 1204, only became a political force in the 15th century. The Muslim identity, with its inclination towards orthodoxy, became prevalent among Muslims quite late, in the 19th century. Popular religion had evolved from the liberal sub-religions and cults that were themselves derived from Buddhism, Hinduism and Islam and were rooted in the ancient period. Thus, the frequent claims that Bengali Muslim is an ancient identity, wilfully ignores or disguises the complexity of the historical forces contributing to this identity.

However, Hinduism, Buddhism and Islam have all contributed to the formation of the Bengali Muslim identity we wish to explore, although Bangladesh is now a predominantly Muslim country. According to the website of 'world population review'[1], 98% of the Bangladesh population are ethnic Bengalis with the remaining 2% made up of Biharis and other ethnic tribes. Ethnic minorities include indigenous people in northern Bangladesh and the Chittagong Hill Tracts. Muslim comes in with 89.1% of the population, Hindu with 10%, and other religions make up the remaining 0.9% (including Buddhist and Christian) of the population. However, the nature, characteristics and traits of the identity of the country were formed via the influence of all three major religions, and by the cults and sub-religions derived from these mainstream religions. For the sake of convenience, we will look at this issue in a simple before-and-after model – Bengal before the Muslim ascendancy and Bengal after the dominance of Islam.

Bengal before the Muslim Conquest

It comes as a surprise to some that Islam did not dominate the Bengal region for a long period of its pre-history. Like most areas of the Indian subcontinent, Bengal (as we shall call it for convenience) was always subject to competing ideological and cultural forces. Bengal has a proximity to the Silk Road, which had a profound effect on its trading and migratory patterns. A tradition in which strong indigenous influences still surface in Bengal culture, especially in the rural areas and notably in the Baul tradition. Moreover, while we regard these factors as important to understanding the formation of Bengali identity, especially as it is expressed in independent films, many of the influences we discuss are not immediately apparent in the films. However, we will argue that when you dig deeply enough traces will be found, even in the contemporary films discussed.

Bengal has been inhabited by different ethnic groups, whose names became associated with the area inhabited by them and thus have endured over time. As Eaton (1993) points out, Bengal was divided into *janapada*s (smaller territories) that were associated with different ethnic groups, listing their names as *Varendra, Vanga, Smatata* and *Harikel*. The existence of these *janapada*s is known later from Vedic literature, as areas inhabited by non-Aryan people.

The Aryans conquered the northwestern parts of India in the middle of the second millennium BCE but it took a long time for the Aryans to reach Bengal, the eastern part of ancient India, an area populated by what they described as 'barbarians' (*mleccha*) (Eaton, 1993: 6). Thus, the people of Bengal felt the tide of Aryanisation quite late, which occurred sometime in the 5th century BCE. It is estimated that it took about one thousand years to Aryanise the whole of Bengal (Chowdhury, 2004: 254). Bengal was not only Aryanised later than the rest of India, but the region adopted Aryan customs in an altered form, by incorporating local cultures as a way of coping with the pre-existing cultures and religion. Thus, Bengal has always been a distinctive region of India, marked by particular cultural and religious norms.

The Aryan period, with its emphasis on Brahmanism, was succeeded by Buddhism as the dominant religion towards the end of the first millennium CE. The first and most durable of the Buddhist ruling forces was the powerful Pala Empire (750–1161 AD), founded by a warrior and fervent Buddhist named Gopala (Eaton, 1993: 11). The reign of the Pala Empire saw Buddhism flourish, reaching its peak in Bengal and co-existing successfully with Brahmanism. As commercially expansive states rose in Eastern India from the 8th century CE, Buddhism, as a state cult, spread into neighbouring lands such as to Tibet, Burma, Cambodia and Java – where monumental Buddhist shrines appear to have been modelled on prototypes developed in Bengal and Bihar (Rashid 1977 cited in Eaton, 1993: 12). Under the Palas, for the first time in its history, Bengal came to be reckoned as a powerful force in north Indian politics. When the Pala Empire declined and they were ousted in the area by Vijayasena (possibly a feudatory ruler who had owed allegiance to the Pala Empire) and Brahminism reasserted itself as the dominant religion largely because the ancestors of the Vijayasena were *brahmaksatriyas* originating in Karnataka in southern India. During the later Sena dynasty, Hinduism underwent a process of revival that emphasised Hindu orthodoxy, which was advanced by the Senas.

Bengal under Muslim Rule

Bengal was colonised slowly by Islam and always in conjunction with Hindu rulers or bureaucrats. Evidence of Muslims rule in Bengal date from 1204 when the Turk, Ikhtiar Uddin Bakhtiar Khilji, conquered the region and established a short-lived regime. However, long before this, Arab Muslims had contact with Bengal through commercial trade, principally in cloth. The spread of religion was a consequence of proselytisation on a small scale by merchants and limited to the coastal regions. By the 9th century, Arab traders settled in Chittagong, the ancient commercial and port city of Bengal. Historians (Eaton, 1993, Murshid, 2006) note that Islamic preachers arrived in Bengal before the Turkish attack to evangelise the region. Although the aim of the conquerors was not strictly religious in intent their cause was advanced by the power of the sword, which helped saints to spread Islam throughout Bengal.

Muslims ruled Bengal from the 13th to 18th centuries but their control was not total. Hindus still exercised power in partnership with the Muslims. The Muslim conquerors, saints and immigrants were outsiders and they had to depend on Hindu *Raja*s and feudal lords to rule. Thus, the spread of Islam was not cataclysmic, but gradual. According to Golam Murshid, the period should be characterised as a period of 'Indo-Muslim' reign (Murshid, 2006: 28) because the Turkish rulers could only hold authority over the population with the compliance of the Hindus and Buddhists. However, they established a tradition that has lasted to this day – the damaging and looting of both Hindu and Buddhist temples in periods of instability. Later Sultans tried to localise their rule by marrying local women, patronising Bengali culture and literature and adopting local customs, a process that occurred over the centuries.

In actuality, the earlier sultans ruling Bengal were vassals of Delhi but, by the latter part of the 14th century, they emerged as independent rulers. Bengal enjoyed increasing prosperity during the Muslim Sultanate with increased agricultural production and expanded external trade, which brought about a boom in architecture, literature and so on. However, the Sultans lost their independence to the Mughals in the 16th century when they reverted to a vassal state. Sultans had protected Bengal from King Akbar's attack in 1575, but after 33 years, Islam Khan, the friend of King Jahangir, completely conquered Bengal. He thereby incorporated it totally into north Indian polity, but without destroying its distinctive regional culture.

During Mughal rule, there was a tremendous improvement in the road and transport systems, which assisted the expansion of both local and foreign trade and commerce and made Bengal one of the most prosperous regions of the world. This in turn attracted more foreign traders. First, among these were the Portuguese who came to the region in the early 16th century. This was a period of great competition among the Europeans for control of commerce in India, which came to a head when trade in Bengal increased under the rule of the East India Company. During the Mughal Period, the rulers followed the policy of not favouring any religion. Even Muslim Sufi saints were not supported by the Mughals, despite the popularity of this group with the population at large, Hindu and Muslim alike. Significantly the Mughal did not support the Bengali language and literature, unlike their Sultani predecessors. One important step during this period, however, was the moving of the capital to Dhaka. As the Mughal power declined in the 18th Century, the East India Company began to assert itself, largely through trade but later by gaining political power through conquest. By 1757, Muslim rule in Bengal came to an end when the ruler of Bengal, Nawab Sirajuddoula, was defeated by the East India Company in the Battle of Plassey. Clive won a notable victory and Muslims lost their political power totally when Delhi was also conquered by the British invaders. British conquerors established the city of Kolkata and the capital of the sub-continent was transferred from Delhi to Kolkata. Despite the loss of political power, however, Muslims remained the majority social group in many parts of Bengal.

In examining the political, social and cultural conditions of the territory, from the ancient period until the 19th century only one influence shaping Bengali identity was continuous, namely, popular religion. Put another way, the fluidity of identity did not create an exclusive form of identity but rather it created a palimpsest with each period contributing certain elements of the Bengali identity, which when interrogated, can be teased out. It is not a simple question of inclusion and exclusion but one of recognising the complexity. Claims of a continuous Bengali identity starting in ancient times are suspect.

The rise of Bengaliness expanded through the literary intelligentsia of Kolkata in the 19th century and the later modernist culturalist contributions of Kolkata and Dhaka were not directed against the existence of popular religion. Rather they wove contributions into the narrative of Bengaliness, thereby constructing a more modern account that drew heavily on Bengali history and mythology and included both Hindus and Muslims. By contrast, also in the 19th century, some Islamic reformist movements like that of Faraizi contributed to the rise of Muslimness in Bengal by arguing, for the first time, that Islam was the major determinant of Bengali identity and had been so from the initial conquest in the 13th Century. From the early 19th century till the middle of the 20th century, proponents of Bengaliness did not feel threatened by the rise of Islam, largely because they were urban Hindu Bengalis. However, it would be fair to say that at this stage popular religion lost its hold on the popular imagination, as it was mostly exercised by the rural peasants.

The brief historical outline provided above reveals several elements we can apply when it comes to analysing Bengali Muslim identity. The first is the fluidity of the concept of national or even ethnic identity, as we have shown that identity changes with the times, reflecting the prevailing historical conditions dominant at the time. It is the prevailing conditions of the moment, when Islam is seemingly ascendant, that shape the current arguments around identity in Bangladesh.

In the 1950s and 1960s, when Bangladesh was part of Pakistan, the anti-Pakistani sentiment contained in the ethno-linguist nationalist approach appealed greatly to the urban Muslim intelligentsia. The intellectuals were very successful throughout the 1960s in conveying their message to the masses by utilising a sympathetic press and other means of communication such as film. Each of these two streams – the religious and ethno-linguistic – has a conflicting approach to identity, which continued to this day. One posits identity as a construct of history, language and culture while the other sees it as divinely ordained. Popular religion, on which we have discussed later in this chapter, in many senses, bridged the gap between these two opposing positions has lost its importance, especially in the urban areas.

Interregnum: The British Imperialism and Movement of Pakistan State

The battle of Plassey and post-Plassey era established very firmly the dominance of the East India company in the political and commercial spheres of India. Lord Cornwallis abolished the fiction of the nawabi rule in 1880 and reduced the Nawab to a pensioner of the company. To govern the state, Cornwallis created many institutions related to administrative procedures, the judiciary and revenue collection. These political impositions shaped the history of Bengal over the next 200 years and Bengalis still live with the consequences.

The later administrative measures of Lord Curzon (1899–1905) took a radical step, with the partition of Bengal in 1905 into Eastern (largely Muslim) and Western (largely Hindu) parts, a political decision that in many ways prefigures the partition of 1947. However, historians have long argued that the partition measure was aimed at weakening nationalist politics by dividing the Bengal people along communal lines. Bengal's partition gave rise to embittered Hindu–Muslim relations; another legacy of rule that has had a profound effect on the social, political and cultural dynamics of Bengals as a whole. Most educated Muslims of East Bengal had supported the partition for largely political reasons, arguing that it allowed for the expression of a Bengal Muslim identity through the gain of political power and at the same time an escape from the cultural dominance of the *bhadralok*. The *bhadralok* were mainly Hindus, middle and upper-middle-class absentee landowners who dominated Calcutta culture and society. The frustrations of the various groups with the reversion to a united Bengal in 1911, brought about by intense lobbying by the Calcutta *bhadralok* and the *zamindar* class, were reflected in the subsequent politics of Bengal.

In spite of many attempts made by nationalist Muslim and Hindu leaders to restore the amity between the two communities, the gap caused by the events between 1905 and 1911 continued to widen. The sense of inclusiveness that had shaped Bengali culture was irreparably damaged. This was exacerbated by the Communal Award of 1932, which further contributed to communalist politics by providing reserved seats for various communities and professions, and which in turn led to the formation of the Muslim-dominated Ministries in the elections in 1937. This election represented a watershed in the Bengal polity. As a result of the elections, Congress had the authority to govern all provinces with the exceptions of the Panjab, the North West Frontier Provinces and Bengal.

The provincial council election of 1946 was conducted when the British had made it abundantly clear they would be leaving India. The Muslim League (who advocated an independent Muslim state) won all seats reserved for Muslims except two in the Bengal parliament, proving beyond doubt that the Muslims of Bengal supported the idea of Pakistan and supported the partition of British India along communal lines. Indeed, Bengali Muslims were the most vocal advocates of the Pakistan movement (Ahmed, 1994: 18). Congress, which represented the Hindus primarily, was not initially prepared to accept the idea of partition. The dispute resulted in continued communal tension and occasional riots that culminated in the great Kolkata killing of August 15–20, 1946, followed by communal riots in Noakhali and Bihar. These events sealed the fate of the united Bengal. The Hindu Mahashaba, the activists in the agitations against the partition of Bengal in 1905, first proposed and started agitation for the partition of Bengal on communal lines in the early 20th Century. The idea of partition was finally accepted by the Congress Party and the Muslim League, as both parties reached the conclusion that the communal divisions were unbridgeable; Bengal was partitioned in 1947. East Bengal (now Bangladesh) became independent from Britain on August 14, 1947 as part of Pakistan. The trajectory away from inclusiveness towards exclusivity was now almost complete.

How does this complex history of politics, race and communalism impact the independent films of Bangladesh? Part of the answer can be found in the topics treated in the films, which have a particular trajectory from an unwavering focus on 1971 and rural Bangladesh to more recent films that explore metropolitan issues within a context of globalism. The other part of the answer lies in what is not said, what is absent. There is little reference to the British legacy, communalism, partition or wider world. The films look inward for explanations of events, which in itself reflects how Bangladesh has interpreted its role in the world.

Language Movement and Emergence of Bangladesh

The physical existence of a united Pakistan was peculiar insofar as it consisted of two parts separated by 1,200 kilometres of Indian territory. What united these two disparate parts was not politics or even culture, but religion. In all other respects, the two wings of Pakistan were separated by ethnic differences among various groups of Pakistanis, especially between the Bengalis of East Pakistan and the non-Bengali West Pakistanis (Punjabis, Sindhis, Baluchis, Pathans and other minority groups). The first protest from East Pakistanis came just one year after the formation of Pakistan. It was in 1948, when Muhammad Ali Jinnah, the President of Pakistan declared the Urdu would be the only state language of Pakistan in a meeting in Dhaka University. The protesters, the students of the University, then started a language movement with the demand that Bengali be declared as a state language, equal to Urdu. Bengali achieved linguistic parity in 1952 after a number of lives had been lost. The differences were intensified after the 1954 election where the Bengali language movement essentially sought to establish a distinctive Bengali identity quite separate from the Pakistani identity the Punjabis of West Pakistan were trying to create. At stake in the election, in the view of the East Pakistanis, was their identity, which was embedded in their language. In the 1960s, the idea of a nation for the Bengali Muslims shifted radically from the religious to the cultural domain.

This discourse of ethno-linguistic nationalism is based on the Bengali language and culture coupled with a secular and anti-Islamic worldview. This ethno-linguistic Bengali nationalism was fostered by economic discrimination by the central government of West Pakistan. East Bengal was the major contributor to national GDP, but the military government that ruled Pakistan from 1956 to 1971, developed the western part of the country and neglected the eastern wing, investing foreign currency in establishing a strong Army for a 'thousand year fight' with India on the issue of Kashmir. The cultural upheaval and economic discrimination by politicians with a singular West Pakistan vision created a movement for autonomy in the east. The dominant political party in East Pakistan, the Awami League (AL), led by Sheikh Mujibur Rahman put forward a 'six point' plan to rectify the political imbalance. The formula proposed a loose federation in which only currency and defence would reside in the hands of the central government and all other governance matters would be regionalised. Meanwhile, the most severe cyclone in its history hit East Pakistan in 1970, but the response of the central government was so poor that it directly affected the election of 1970. AL captured 167 out of 169 seats in East Pakistan (out of 313 seats of the united Pakistan), which was enough for an absolute majority in the national parliament. By contrast, the Pakistan People's Party (PPP) led by Zulfiqar Ali Bhutto won 88 out of 144 National Assembly seats in West Pakistan. Bhutto conspired with the President General Yahia Khan, forming an alliance that prevented Mujib from ascending to power. After a series of pseudo dialogues in Dhaka, the West Pakistani-controlled army moved to establish military law on the night of 25 March, which was a prelude to a bloody war. It is widely believed that as many as 3 million people were killed by the West Pakistani Army, which is regarded by the majority of Bangladeshis as an act of genocide. An estimated 10 million people were dislocated and crossed the Indian borders. The bold resistance of Bengali guerrillas with the help of Indian Army, Bangladesh emerged as a nation on 16 December 1971. This represents the first time Bengalis became independent of an occupying power since ancient times. The War of Liberation is the defining moment of contemporary Bangladesh history and has played a major role in creating a national identity, i.e. who is and who is not a Bangladeshi. In broad terms, the majority of the citizens of Bangladesh are Bengali Muslim and it is apparent that ethno-religious factors contribute to the determination of national identity, which is clearly stated in the constitution. Nevertheless, there are groups who have contested this view of identity from the outset. The films we discuss explore this issue with intelligence and skill, hence their significance.

Bengaliness as a Way of Being

The advocates of any antique Bengali identity expressed through language argue that the Bengali language is at least a thousand years old, but its definite linguistic shape came much later (Murshid, 2006). One stream of modern historians (e.g. Shah, 1993) argues that the concept of Bengali as a nationality or an ethnic or cultural group was rooted in the pre-colonial period. Other accounts (e.g. Eaton, 1993) draw on the contribution of the popular religious cults that synthesised Hindu and Islamic themes, which can be found in the Bengali literature of medieval Muslim poets. The 16th century poet Haji Muhammad identified the Arabic Allah with Gosai (Skt., 'Master'), Saiyid Murtaza identified the Prophet's daughter Fatima with Jagat-Janani (Skt., 'Mother of the world') and Syed Sultan identified the God of Adam, Abraham, and Moses with Prabhu (Skt., 'Lord') or, more frequently, Niranjan (Skt., 'One without colour', i.e. without qualities) (Eaton, 1993: 276). Eaton (1993) discusses the *Satya Pir* cult and indeed Bengali folk religion generally in terms of a synthesis of Islam and Hinduism in the term *Satya Narayan* refers to the Brahmanic god Vishnu. These syncretic and harmonious features still exist in some parts of Bengali society. Muslims and Hindus of the forests of Southern Bangladesh worship *Banbibi* ('wife of the forest'; 'bibi' is a Muslim term of the word wife) to get rid of the evil powers of the forest. This practice is limited to certain cults or practices;

ordinary peoples' approach towards people of other religions is inclusive in general. By contrast, Anisuzzaman claims, Islamic jingoism comes through political steps and measures, promulgated between 1940 and 1947 as part of the struggle for independence (Anisuzzaman, 1995: 32). The Muslim League resolution adopted in Lahore in 1940 demanded the formation of two independent, sovereign and autonomous states in the north-western and eastern parts of India where the Muslims were the majority community. However, this resolution did not demand that it be a religious or non-secular state. But later events provoked Muhammad Ali Jinnah to formulate a two-nation theory based on religion. The two-nation theory was the basis for the partition of India in 1947. This theory underpinned the proposal that Muslims and non-Muslims should be two separate nations. Upon this theory, British India was divided into India and Pakistan. The east wing of Pakistan was liberated from the west in 1971 through a war and Bangladesh was born as the new state.

Without this development, it is possible, although highly unlikely, that Bengal would have been an independent state starting in 1947, which was certainly an option preferred by many Bengali intellectuals and nationalist leaders.

Bengaliness rose to significance in the Kolkata-based Bengali renaissance or enlightenment in the colonial period of the 19th century, but there was almost no participation of Bengal Muslims in this movement. The Muslim Bengali middle class that was emerging became active after the British divided Bengal in 1905, a move highly opposed by Bengali Hindus. The agitation against the partition of Bengal again propagated a concept of Bengali identity in high-flown language that spoke of a united Hindu-Muslim Bengali, though very few Muslims seem to have participated in the movement. According to Mohammad Shah (1993), Bengaliness truly becomes a political force in Bengal under the anti-Bengali Pakistani government of the 1950s and 1960s. This version was largely driven by the Muslim middle-class intelligentsia of Dhaka who appropriated many of the ideas of the earlier movements. The language movement in 1952 proposed an ethno-linguistic nationalism based on the claims of a language under threat, which had wide appeal and led to the movement for autonomy in the 1960s. In this case, Bengaliness as an identity approach based on ethnicity and language would underpin the development of a modern, secular and democratic state. The autonomy movement claimed a cultural identity based on the Bengali language, literature and culture as its heritage.

At the heart of these claims was the rise of Dhaka as the cultural capital of Bengal displacing Kolkata. After 1947, Bengali Muslims from East Bengal seized the opportunity to create Dhaka as their own hub of culture and economy. On the other hand, the Bengalis of West Bengal, instead of looking back to the common Bengali language and culture, were eager to stake their claim to a national Indian context. In many respects, Dhaka has become the future capital of Bengali literature and culture, as the recent

Dhaka Literary festivals demonstrate. Kolkata-based writers like Samaresh Majumdar or Sunil Ganguly expressed the same idea on several occasions.[2] Moreover, the two different regions are separated by religion, which has contributed to creating two distinct versions of Bengaliness.

The Rise of Muslimness

Before the advent of British colonial rule, communal antagonism as we know it today seemed not to exist either in Bengal or in the other regions of the Indian subcontinent (Ahmed, 1994: 14). Even after Muslim conquest, immigrants Sufis were more influential than the rulers. Those religious preachers, as Ahmed (2001) suggests, adopted a policy of compromise and concession in an effort to propagate the Islamic message. Even after mass conversion to Islam, there remained communal harmony in the society, at least among the ordinary people. However, there were several policies that were initiated and applied by the British during the colonial period that further divided Bengalis into Hindu and Muslim communities and exacerbated communal tensions. As a consequence of these actions on the part of the British, the political importance of Muslimness as an identity marker increased, whereas previously it was almost solely a religious marker. The principal causes for this dramatic shift can be attributed to three factors; first, the Islamic revivalist movement which contained anti-British sentiment; second, the 'Divide and Rule' policy adopted by the colonial rulers; and third, the growth of an aggressive Hindu chauvinism in the 19th century.

Islamic Revivalist Movement

When the British conquered Bengal in the 18th century, they encountered a Muslim population that was almost entirely rural, whose lifestyle was not much different from their Hindu neighbours in almost all respects; in dress, manners, names, occupations, rituals and practices (Ahmed, 2001: 14). Many Indian Muslims intellectuals engaged with the Wahabi movement in the 19th century, an Islamic Jihad, against British rulers, because they thought that the British had wrestled power from them. In Bengal, the Faraizi movement, led by Haji Shariatullah, and other similar movements, had a greater impact in rural areas. According to Eaton (1993), Haji Shariatullah had a pilgrimage in Saudi Arabia in 1799 and subsequently lived 19 years there for Islamic learning where he was influenced by Wahabism. Returning to Bengal in 1818, the Haji found a 'grotesque' form of Islam in Bengal and engaged himself to reform 'Bengal Islam' to an 'Arabic Islam'. In the history of Bengal, he is considered as the 'saviour' of Islam. As Rafiuddin Ahmed argues, what was particularly important about the Islamic revivalist movements of the 19th century... 'was the demand for absolute conformity with an Arab-oriented Islam' (Ahmed, 2001: 15).

Thus, all syncretic practices such as Baulism and other popular religions were rejected. It imposed total purification on Muslims including dress and manners, rituals and practices, language and identity. In the 19th and 20th centuries, Bengali Muslims became increasingly aware of the beliefs and practices then current in the Arab heartland and tried to uphold their Muslim identity by adopting more rigorous Islamic codes. The reformist movement in the 19th century paradoxically created a permanent imprint of 'pure' Islam in the psyche of Bengal Muslims and at the same time aided the spread of syncretic Islam, especially in rural areas as an undercurrent cult. Indeed, it is this period that the divisions that have wracked Islam in Bengal were created, especially the differences between urban dwellers and the rural peasantry and their respective practices.

British Policy

Rafiuddin Ahmed points out that the British, '... continually treated the Muslims as a separate political entity,... and both through policies of state patronage and public as well as private rhetoric, encouraged and even invited, them to organise separately' (Ahmed, 2001: 19). The British policies, which sometimes favoured and sometimes did not favour Muslims, created a tendency within Muslims to think of themselves as different, with a distinctive political and religious identity. Three steps and policies have to be mentioned here, which contributed to the emergence of *Muslimness* in the subcontinent under British rule: first, the Permanent Settlement of the land revenue system in 1837; second, the partition of Bengal in 1905 and third, the communal award of 1932.

British historian W. W. Hunter described the 'Musalmans' as in all respect as '... a race ruined under British rule (Hunter 1871 cited in Ahmed, 2001: 19)'. The first blow came from the Permanent Settlement policy, which damaged the old structure of administration and seriously hurt the upper class or *Ashraf* Muslims. The lower class or *Atraf* peasants also became the victims of the new revenue system. For the new revenue system to work, the British created a new class of landlords or Zamindars whose role was to collect tax from the peasants of the leased lands and submit it to the British rulers. These newly emerged tax collectors were mostly Hindus and their income came through the increased rate of tax imposed on the peasants, who were mostly Muslims. Through this job of collecting tax, the Zamindars became rich enough to send their sons to Kolkata for Western education. Through a process of cultural assimilation and appropriation there emerged an educated, modern class usually referred to as the *bhadralok* class who contributed largely to the 'Bengal Renaissance' in the 19th century. While Chatterji (1994) calls them *bhadralok*, Murshid (2006) identifies them as *babu*. While Hindus gained Western knowledge and expressed themselves through literature and the press the Muslims tended to ignore the opportunities proffered by the British and turned inwards, towards their religion.

An unintended outcome of Hindus acquiring a western-style education was their tendency to criticise the British. They also sought to reform Hinduism through the creation of several social initiatives. By contrast, Muslims lagged in every form of an advanced discourse around political and ethnic identity that emerged in Bengal in the late 19th century. This situation was directly or indirectly attributable to the Permanent Settlement according to Muslim intellectuals who were starting to emerge at the beginning of the 20th century. At one point, Muslims found themselves deprived and exploited by both the British and the Hindus, which prompted Muslim leaders to advocate an engagement with modernity through education, government service and politics. Thus a Muslim middle class emerged in the early 20th century.

If the Permanent Settlement was a curse for Muslims, the first partition of Bengal in 1905 initiated by Lord Curzon was regarded by Muslim leaders as compensation to them by the British. Bengal was divided into two parts: one part consisted of East Bengal and Assam and the other parts were West Bengal, Orissa and Bihar. This division suggested to observers that the first area would be a land of Muslims and Dhaka would become its capital. The partition was contested by Hindus in the name of broader Bengali identity and the partition was withdrawn in 1911. However, the distance between the two communities had been created and was to remain in place until 1947. In 1906, the Muslim League was established in Dhaka to represent Muslim interests at every level of Indian politics. The Indian National Congress had been formed much earlier and claimed to represent all Indians irrespective of religion. Although the Congress had declared a secular world view, the communal force inside the Congress played a vital role in the second partition of Bengal in 1947.

Ramsey Macdonald's Communal Award of 1932 dramatically altered the balance of power in the province (Chatterji, 1994: 15). At the beginning of the 20th century, Muslims were a majority in Bengal, but civil society and politics were dominated by Hindu *Bhadralok*s. The communal award allotted Hindus fewer seats in the new provincial legislative assembly and in the 1937 elections, conducted under Devolution, the Muslim League-led Fazlul Huq formed the provincial government in Bengal with the support of the *Namasudra*s, a numerous, non-caste Hindu group who had followed a similar path as the Muslims in empowering themselves through education and government service in the early 20th century. A situation arose in which conflicts between the newly emerged Muslim middle class and the *Bhadralok*s dominated Bengal politics and society between 1907 and 1947 and culminated in the creation of East Bengal as part of Pakistan in 1947.

Hindu Chauvinism

Hindu intellectual attitudes toward a separate identity and political path for Muslims are complex and clearly shaped by prevailing social attitudes. As they advocated inclusiveness as a community, the Hindus tended to oppose the first partition of Bengal in 1905. The Kolkata-based intelligentsia, including Rabindranath Tagore, supported the discourse of (united) Bengali nationalism. Yet most nationalist thinkers tended to illustrate national identity in religious terms and to equate being an Indian with being a Hindu. There were clear differences between the way in which Hindu and Muslim intellectuals thought about partition. In short, there is evidence to show that the Hindu intellectuals opposed the 1905 partition but advocated the major divide of 1947. What unified the seemingly contradictory stances were religious differences dressed up in political rhetoric. Joya Chatterji's (1994) work has demonstrated that Hindu chauvinism worked to establish the second partition of Bengal in 1947. Evidence for this can be seen in the writings of Bankimchandra Chattopadhay, Arobindo Ghosh and Swami Vivekananda and in the brand of 'extremist' nationalism they inspired. Anisuzzaman (1995) recalled his surprise when he first read the famous novel *Srikanta* (1917) by Saratchandra Chattopadhyay, in which a football match placed between Bengalis and Muslims, was recorded in terms that are entirely anti-Muslim. This suggests that Muslims were excluded in the discourse of Bengaliness and it is true that in the 1920s, 1930s and 1940s the 'Muslim' identity (of Bengali Muslim)] gained currency over the 'Bengali' identity (Shah, 1993: 731) in the Muslim community. Indeed, it can be argued that *Muslimness* was not chosen by the Muslims but rather as the result of Hindu chauvinism, especially in the early 20th century. This chauvinism drove the Muslims to support the 'two-nation theory' that had been presented for political reasons by the Muslim League, leading to an India that was divided into two nations on the basis of religion. It is paradoxical that the *Bhadralok*s opposed the first partition of Bengal in 1905, but the same community supported the second partition in 1947. The principal reason was that Muslims had gained political power by the Communal Award of 1932.

It is evident to many Bengali Muslim intellectuals (see Murshid, 2006 as an example) that the Islamic reformation of the 19th century and the pre-partition politics in the early 20th century established Muslimness as an identity among Bengali Muslims. This view is reinforced by events in East Pakistan in the post-partition era. The language movement in 1952 and the autonomy movement in the 1960s perpetuated a strong sense of Bengaliness in the 1960s, which ended with a bloody war in 1971. The state of Bangladesh emerged on the basis of a dual identity in which Bengalinesss competed with Islam for the attention of the people. This duality remains to be resolved as we show in the next section.

Considering all aspects and developments of Muslimness we identify three types of Islam in Bengal – Scholastic Islam, Political Islam and Popular Islam. For Scholastic Islam, people are following the scripture of Quran and Hadith or are regular practicing Muslims who try to follow an Islamic way of life. They are the majority in the society. People practicing Political Islam try to grab power in the society, either through communal politics or through Jihad. Popular Islamists do not follow the scriptures; their practices are more theological and conceptual. Sufis express their love and devotion to Allah through poems and songs. We will apply these three forms of Islam while analysing films.

Popular Religion: The Syncretic Identity Approach

In the context of Bengal, popular religion is defined through religious practices derived from mainstream religions, but with the inclusion of local divinities; the synthesis often taking an obscure and mystic shape. Tantric Buddhism, Vaishnavism, derived from Hinduism and Islamic Sufism, contributes to the popular religions of Bengal. What is called popular religion may also be called 'obscure religious cults' (Dasgupta, 1976) or 'sub-religions' (Chaterjee, 2005). The aspect that is common to all is 'mysticism'. Popular religious cults are opposed to the orthodoxy of the major religions, seeking salvation through individual devotion rather than following prescribed practices and mantras. Sudhir Chaterjee (2005) identifies as many as 102 sub-religions in the late 18th century Bengal, which evolved by negating the orthodoxy of Brahminism and Islamism. Their influence has remained powerful within the Bengali imagination over the succeeding centuries having influenced literature and poetry (we would argue that mysticism has a significant place in the work of both Tagore and Kazi Nazrul Islam), popular music (the Baul tradition and folk tradition) and drama such as the *jatra*s (folk theatre). Thus, popular religion has played a significant part in identity formation in Bengal especially in rural areas and traces of these religions can still be found in popular culture, including the cinema. Even other cultural expressions (band music as an example) often use or manipulate the form and content of folk and popular religious resources.

Tantric Buddhism, Sufism and Vaishnavism

Bengal was the grazing ground of Buddhism from the third century B.C. to the 7th or 8th century CE. According to Dasgupta (1976), after the death of Goutam Buddha, Buddhists were divided into two traditions over the question of the 'true' way of Buddhism – *Mahayana* and *Hinayana*. Mahayana or the 'Great Vehicle' as contrasted with the ethno-religious rigour of Hinayana, or 'Little Vehicle', was a religion of progress and liberalism. Bengal Buddhists were the followers of Mahayana Buddhism, which later transformed into Tantric Buddhism. There were two important aspects of Tantric Buddhism, especially of *Sahaja-yana*, other than sexo-yogic practices – one was *Guru-vada* and other was the importance of the human body in the *Sadhana*. In Indian philosophy and religion, the obscurity and mystic nature of the philosophy makes a disciple apprehend and unable to realise the truth. So, he must depend on a guru or preceptor who has already realised the supreme truth. Truth is transmitted from the guru to the disciple just as the light from one lamp to other. On the other hand, in any form of yogic practice, the human body is considered as the epitome of the universe. It is thought that if perfection or *siddhi* of the body is accomplished, all kinds of perfection in the three worlds can be attained easily.

This sexo-yogic esoteric practice, *guru-vada* and the importance of the body of Tantric Buddhism have influenced Nathism, Baulism and other important cults of medieval and modern Bengal. Buddhism declined totally in Bengal, during the reigns of the Hindu Senas and Muslims. This is because they were converted to Hindu or Muslim practices or migrated to northern or south-eastern neighbouring countries. But the philosophical base of Buddhist Tantrism has not vanished from Bengal. It impacted all forms of popular religions of Bengal.

Sufism, the religious stream of Muslim saints, began to make its way in India in the 11th century CE; but Sufism as a religious school began to influence the minds of the Indian people on a large scale from the end of the 12th century (Dasgupta, 1976: 9). It is not because of Muslim rulers that there was mass Islamisation in Bengal, rather it was the contributions of the saints (i.e. their personalities and the social works among the ordinary people). In contrast to the caste system of Hinduism, Islam endorsed equality. Therefore, many lower caste people were attracted to Islam. Moreover, the Islam that arrived in Bengal was quite different from the original, Arabic Islam, via saints who came from Iran and Central Asia. Islam was disseminated here through Persian, not Arabic.

The original Islam is dualistic, in which the relation between the creator and the created is that of a master and servant. But Sufis believe in non-dualism, in which the relation between creator and the created being is one of love. According to Golam Murshid (2006), in Sufism, there is a stage of *sadhana* which is called *fana*, in which the creature can be merged with the creator. This concept of *fana* is quite similar with the concept of *nirvana* of Buddhism.

This was the dominant depiction of Islam in Bengal until the 19th century. Sufism had enormous influence among people and some Sultans were found as Sufi Sultans. Sufism had impacted the medieval and early modern literature of Bengal. Due to the reformation movement in the 19th century towards 'original' or Arabic Islam, it lost dominance. However, since then it has survived in popular religious practices – among Bauls and followers of various *pirs*. The dominant Islam of Bangladesh is still a little different from that in other countries; hence Bangladeshi Muslims are recognised as 'moderate' Muslims by the outside world.

Ordinary people in rural Bengal pay primary allegiance to one of two religions: Bengali Vaishnavism or Bengali Islam. Anthropologist Ralph W. Nicholas (2001) believes that Bengali Hindus are basically the followers of Vaishnavism, a radical and reformist stream of Hinduism. According to Dasgupta (1976), the Vaishnava Sahajiya movement of Bengal marks the evolution of the Buddhist Sahajiya cult along a different path that is strongly influenced by the love religion of Bengal Vaishnavism. Naturally, it had the ideal of devotion, love and equality among human beings which is not found in Brahmanism and traditional scriptural Hinduism. This devotion and love have been expressed through lyrics depicting the devotional relation between Krishna and Radha. Vaishnavism got its momentum through Chaitanya Dev at Nadia of West Bengal, and it was extended throughout India. Other than Bengal Vrindavan became the second hub of Vaishnavism.

The message of equality espoused by Chaitanya was against the principles of Brahmanism, which prefers the caste system in the society. Chaitanya was radical in another sense; he diffused his philosophy in the Bengali language and ignored Sanskrit. He established *namakirtana* as the formal religious programme instead of *mantra*s from scripts. Vaishnavism also includes yogic practices.

The mode of equality and devotion could make Vaishnavism very popular in Bengal. On the other hand, the relatively stronger challenge of equality thrown by Islam was successfully faced by Vaishnavism, which is in other forms, saved Hinduism in Bengal. But after the death of Chaitanya, within 50 years, the *Goswami*s of Chaitanya left Bengal, migrated to Vrindavan and rejected the equality of Vaishnavism. Thus, Vaishnavism was divided into two groups of followers – pro-caste system, Brahman Vaishnavas and anti-caste system, ordinary *Bostom*s. The dominance of Vaishnavism declined and was divided.

In conclusion, the three off-shoots of the major religions in Bengal discussed here, in their dominant period, were liberal and localised. They were unique in many respects and can be thought of as forming the indigenous religions of Bengal. All of them have subsequently declined or transferred their allegiances to orthodoxy. The philosophical standpoint of equality and humanism of the religions has become an undercurrent of Bengali culture and is embraced by popular religious cults, which have always existed on the periphery of Bengal society. Among these cults are the Bauls of Bengal who have appropriated the philosophy of all three liberal approaches to the religion – Buddhist Tantrism, Islamic Sufism and Vaishnavism – and synthesised them into a distinctive Bengali voice.

Ahmad Sharif (2003) says Baulism emerged in the middle of the 17th century. Baulism is the most celebrated popular religion in Bengal, especially in Bangladesh. The most prominent Baul lyricist, thinker and philosopher Lalon Shah (1774–1890) were stationed at Kushtia, a Northern district of Bangladesh. Yogic practices from Buddhist Tantrism, devotion and love towards God from Vaishnavism and *fana* concept from Sufism have made Baulism a unique amalgamation of devotional and liberal religious cults. Like Tantrism and Sufism, Baulism also includes the concept of *guru-vada* and emphasis on the human body as the epitome of the universe. Bauls worship human beings instead of God – 'He is Baul who search God in human being' or 'Our Lord appeared in the Prophet's form' are two examples of Baulist thoughts. Bauls have expressed their ideas in lyrics and songs that are popular in rural Bengal through direct contact between the Bauls and the peasants. These ideas have been welcomed in recent times among urban people through the music industry. Baul thought questions the status quo and initiate debates about social and cultural issues; for example, they raise questions about the *Shariah* (orthodox Islam) on behalf of *Marfat* (liberal Sufi Islam) and these may be found in the films. A particularly good example is *The Clay Bird* (2002) where the village festivals and popular religious thoughts are juxtaposed against the rigid orthodoxy of the father and a Jihadist character in the film.

Post-Independence Bangladesh: Two Major Identities in Conflict

It has become part of the mythology surrounding the foundation of Bangladesh that Bengaliness contributed to the country's formation, but the post-independence path for Bengaliness has not been smooth. The challenge of Islam remains, and the two concepts remain in competition for the allegiance of Bangladeshi. Rather than point to an either/or situation we argue that identity in Bangladesh exists on a continuum. On one end is the secular Bangladesh intellectual who sets great store on the rich history of the Bengali language and culture. At the other end, we find the strict Islamists who see Islam as the social glue holding the nation together and is committed to the *ummah*. Election data suggest that most Bangladeshis inhabit a territory between these two extremes, where they reconcile Bengaliness and Islam in their everyday life. The ongoing struggles confronting Bangladesh occur at the ends of the continuum, causing the majority to suffer in many ways. This volatility and vulnerability stems from the country's founding and in many ways constitute the core of the tensions explored in the independent films under analysis.

After the liberation, the Sheikh Mujib government found it difficult to reorganise the war-shaken economy. Moreover, the AL economic advisors adopted the Indian model of the economic path for Bangladesh, which meant the state was to play the dominant role in not only controlling the distribution of goods, but also controlling the means of their production. Discontent arose in the political and social spheres as well as in the economic sphere. In 1975, Sheikh Mujib dissolved all political parties to form a single national party called the Bangladesh Krishak Sramik Awami League (BAKSAL), through which he offered some reform programmes to quell the unrest. Before Sheikh Mujib could fully implement his new ideas, he was assassinated, along with his family members and some of his colleagues by a group of ambitious junior military officers on August 15, 1975. The assassination was followed by the killing of four jailed AL leaders who had led the Liberation War in absence of Mujib. The few days after the assassination were wracked by coup and counter coup in the Army, culminating in the emergence of Major General Ziaur Rahman as leader of the nation.

General Ziaur Rahman consolidated his position as a 'democratic' president with the formation of a political party named the Bangladesh Nationalist Party (BNP), which won an election and established him as the dominant figure. Mujib's killing and Zia's emergence as President confirmed a fracturing of the notion of a unified nation that Mujib and the AL had fostered. Zia was more inclined to a presence for Islam in the national polity than Mujib and he sought to incorporate the Islamic parties, including those that had opposed the creation of Bangladesh, into the political process.

The Constitution (Amendment) Order, 1977 issued by General Zia made remarkable changes by incorporating Islam into the constitution, which depreciated secular notions and inherent socialism. The changes were wide ranging. The identity of the citizens of Bangladesh was no longer Bengali but Bangladeshi. Zia also dropped 'secularism' as a state principle, substituting it with 'absolute trust and faith in Almighty Allah' and *Bismillahir Rahmanir Rahim,* both of which were inserted in the preamble of the constitution. The new president decided to change the economic principles guiding the nation's development, redefining socialism to mean 'economic and social justice'. Further, he sought to consolidate, preserve and strengthen fraternal relations among Muslim countries based on Islamic solidarity. Finally, he declared that nationalisation and acquisition of property 'would be duly compensated'. In the view of the secularists, Zia had subverted the founding principles of the nation and moved Bangladesh more towards the programme articulated by those who had opposed the country's founding. This is in a way going back to the communal principles in partition time set by the Muslim leaders.

Another dimension to Ziaur Rahman's formula is the view that Bengali nationalism did not accommodate the indigenous people of Bangladesh, who were largely confined to the Chittagong Hill Tracts. Although Zia was a prominent freedom fighter in 1971 and fought under Mujib's Bengali Nationalistic ideologies, his changes to the constitution essentially discarded the predominantly Hindu Bengalis of West Bengal and virtually disenfranchised the indigenous people who are either Buddhist, Christian or animist. This resulted in officially moving Bangladeshi identity more towards Muslim identity as the defining characteristic.

When discussing identity in Bangladesh, only two approaches are continuously addressed in mainstream discourse. These include Bengali Nationalism and Bangladeshi Nationalism which, for the purpose of this chapter, have been renamed 'Bengaliness' and 'Muslimness', respectively. Willem Van Schendel (2009) has described these two approaches as Bengaliness and 'Bangladeshiness'. On discussing Bengaliness, he says:

From the 1950s to the 1970s, the delta's [Bangladesh is often described as Bengal Delta] vernacular elite had imagined Bangladesh as the homeland of Bengalis who had been denied justice under Pakistan. To them the Bengali nation stood for much more than a linguistic community [hence subsequently they formed a nation state through Liberation War].

(Van Schendel, 2009: 202)

On the other hand, Van Schendel (2009) explains the narrative of Bangladeshiness as originating from the movement for Pakistan and the 1971 Liberation war. In this schema, the Bangladeshi nation was the ultimate manifestation of the delta's Muslim-Bengali identity, which had been maturing during the British and Pakistan periods (Van Schendel, 2009: 203). For the narrative, as Schendel suggests, 1947 (the partition of India and the emergence of Pakistan) had been necessary for 1971 (the liberation of Bangladesh) to happen: the creation of Pakistan enabled the birth of the nation of Bangladesh.

Schendel identifies the emergence of Bangladeshiness with the 1975 collapse of the AL's control of the state. During this period, a new narrative of the nation developed in order to justify the military regime of Ziaur Rahman. In creating a distinction between 'Bengalis' and 'Bangladeshis' the religious dimensions of the identities were once more accentuated. It was Ziaur Rahman's political move to bring back the predominance of Muslim identity from 1947 to counter the existing supremacy of Bengali identity that was culminated in the late 1960s and was established through victory against Pakistan in 1971. It held that the independent nation that emerged from the 1971 war was overwhelmingly and essentially Muslim (Van Schendel, 2009: 202). Schendel clearly states the essence of Bangladeshiness as a Muslim identity. Badaruddin Umar (1974) stated earlier by arguing that the principle of Bangladeshi nationalism is nothing, but communalism based upon religion. Considering the religious essentialism of it, we are translating here the approach of Bangladeshiness as Muslimness.

Zia was assassinated by army officers in 1983 and Lt. General H M Ershad assumed power after another period of instability. Ershad also patronised Islamisation in politics and made Islam a state religion. BNP, the propagator of Bangladeshi Nationalism, came to power again in 1991 under the leadership of Khaleda Zia, the widow of General Zia, after the fall of the autocratic Ershad regime, which had lasted for nine years. In 1996, the AL, the proponents of Bengali nationalism, won the election under the leadership of Sheikh Hasina, the daughter of Sheikh Mujib. However, at this juncture, the AL has moved away from its secular position by adopting policies similar to those of the BNP in their respective approaches to religion, secularism and foreign policy. In 2001, BNP again came to power, this time in alliance with an Islamist party, the Jamaat-e-Islam, which had collaborated with the Pakistan Army in the War of 1971. To date, the collaboration between the Jamaat and BNP is the greatest marker of difference between the political parties.

'Who am I first, a Bengali or a Muslim?' The question is still highly relevant, haunting the people of Bangladesh. Those who consider themselves Bengalis first are probably secular in customs and beliefs, whereas those who see themselves as Muslims first clearly place a greater emphasis on Islam rather than Bengaliness. The partition in 1947, threw this issue into stark relief. Religion divided the region, putting the end to a politically united and independent Bengal. But Bangladesh became independent in 1971 on the basis of a secular Bengali nationalism.

After a few years of independence, General Zia's Bangladeshi nationalism further confused the situation by redefining who was a Bangladeshi. Sheikh Hasina-led AL has worsened the confusion during three consecutive terms since 2008. She rules in a non-democratic manner and has been accused of huge corruption, growing authoritarianism, muzzling freedom of expression and compromising with newly emerged Islamic forces like Hefajat-e-Islami.

Transformation and Deterritorialisation

The term transformation might be slippery here, as the formation of identity itself a dialectic process and any kind of identity goes through a continuous transformation, yet by the approach transformation we mean the rapid changes that are taking place in contemporary Bangladesh society must be mentioned separately which is worth to be a new category of identity approach of people of Bangladesh.

If neo-liberalism is the 'liberal commitment to individual liberty, a belief in the free market and opposition to state intervention in it' (Ritzer, 2010: 110), this policy is the foundation of contemporary globalisation, the idea of which was born in the 1930s and implemented in the 1980s. After the fall of communism in 1990, it seemed neo-liberalism was the inevitable economic policy for most of the nation states in the globe.

Arjun Appadurai (2001) goes on to identify 'deterritorialisation' as one of the central forces of the modern globalised world because it brings labouring populations into the lower-class sectors and spaces of relatively wealthy societies. Bangladesh is a classic example of this trend, with a vast diaspora of workers in the Gulf States, Malaysia and Singapore, but it's important to recognise that the diaspora is not comprised solely of these workers. Large numbers of middle-class Bangladeshis gravitate towards the USA, UK, Australia and Canada. Thus, the diaspora may be underpinned by economic considerations, but it is also with class and ideological issues. Moreover, on their return these groups bring back different baggage; for the Gulf worker, it may be an admiration for the strict seclusion of women, while for the student returning from Boston, it may be a taste for alcohol (an allegedly unobtainable, illicit pleasure for some in a Muslim culture). On the other hand, the deterritorialisation of neoliberal consumer culture and Jihadist

Islam can be seen as external forces entering Bangladesh and influencing society in a way that builds a new identity approach.

Fahmidul Haq (2011) observes, in the early 1990s, democracy in Bangladesh returned after a prolonged autocratic military regime. However, at the same time, neoliberal policies were adopted. The election-centric, immature democracy was not against a free-market economic policy. Rather, the parliamentary democracy welcomed the free market economy with the imperialistic influence of the countries like the United States or alliances like North American Free Trade Agreement (NAFTA). In this global economic system, Bangladesh was at the receiving end. Other than the readymade garments industry (which was based on cheap labour) and the telecommunications sector (which was rooted in foreign direct investment), in the 1990s, there arrived a class of traders who mainly imported products from foreign countries. A country of 160 million people meant a big potential market. From the traders' point of view, there was a need to change people into consumers and a consumer culture became an essential prerequisite of the prevailing economic process. This responsibility of creating the consumer culture was given to the media.

According to a report of World Bank, the Bangladesh economy sustained strong growth in fiscal year 2019 led by rising exports and record remittances.[3] These exports are largely dependent on textile and readymade garments and the remittances come from the overseas labour market. In both cases, the availability of cheap labour is the cause of the steady growth. The London-based Centre for Economics and Business Research has reported that in 2019 Bangladesh was ranked 41st among the world's largest economies, moving up two notches from 2018. The country has become the second biggest economy in South Asia, and it is predicted to be the 24th largest economy in the world, by 2033.[4] Bangladesh's gross domestic product is projected to grow at 7.2% this fiscal year and 7.3% the following year, according to the latest edition of the 'South Asia Economic Focus, Making (De)centralisation Work'.[5]

However, this economic progress has resulted in rapid urban growth, and rise of an ultra-rich group.[6] The benefits of the growth are limited to the privileged class due to a corrupt politico-commercial nexus among elites and through labour exploitation and Social and economic disparity have remained intact. This globalised reality is characterised by the prevalence of telecommunication technologies and mushroom growth of supermarkets in both city centre and periphery. The urban skylines are covered with high rises and flyovers. Peoples' moral values are shaped by consumer culture rather than solely by traditional Bengali culture.

Jihadist Islam

Other than neoliberal economic and cultural globalisation, Jihadist Islam is a major influence on contemporary Bangladesh. Through the internet and social media young people are recruited by global Jihadist organisations like Islamic State (IS) and some violent extremist incidents have recently taken place in Bangladesh. The backlash from 9/11 contributed to the rise of Jihadist Islam globally. Subsequent attacks in Afghanistan and Iraq as well as recent attacks in Libya and Syria have fuelled the global phenomenon; Bangladesh is not far from the influence of these global politics. The Middle-east policy of western powers is directly or indirectly responsible for this globalisation of Islam.

The first big militant Islamic organisation, Jamaat-ul-Mujahideen of Bangladesh (JMB), was founded in 1998. It was banned in 2005 when it committed a series of bombings in almost every district at the same time. The Bangladesh government later tried and hanged two leaders of JMB. Harkat-ul-Jihad al-Islami (HUJI) was responsible for the Dhaka grenade attack of Sheikh Hasina, the then leader of opposition and bombings in 2001. Mufti Hannan, the leader of HUJI, was sentenced to death in 2008. Since 2013, Bangladesh has experienced an increase in Jihadist attacks targeting religious minorities, secularist and atheist writers, bloggers, LGBT rights activists and university professors.

Parvez (2018) argues that after the relative decline of the IS in Syria and Iraq, the organisation has shifted from a centralised and globally coordinated effort towards local and regional struggles, exploiting grievances in various local contexts and conditions. Thus, Bangladesh became a priority. In November 2015, the IS magazine *Dabiq* published an article calling for the 'revival of Jihad in Bengal'. Press reports suggest that at least 20 militant organisations were active inside the country (Riaz and Parvez, 2018: 2). Jihadists have murdered at least 40 writers, publishers and activists, foreigners and members of minority faiths since 2013. Between 2013 and 2017, there were 50 incidents involving violent extremism resulting in 255 deaths and 942 wounded (Parvez, 2018: 54).

The attack on July 1, 2016 by a group of youths connected to the IS on the Holey Artisan café in a diplomatic zone of the capital Dhaka was the biggest militant attack in the country and drew international attention. The IS claimed responsibility for the attack, which killed 24 people. The casualties included nine Italians, seven Japanese, seven Bangladeshi and one Indian. A joint operation killed five attackers and caught one of them alive and 13 hostages were rescued. Subsequent country wide raids by the joint security force killed the mastermind of the attack and some other militant leaders. Violent extremism is seemingly under control in Bangladesh in the last two years.

Violent extremism and the rise of political Islam in Bangladesh has two stages – first one was the rise of JMB in the early 2000s and the next was target killings in the post Shahbag-movement period (2013–15) that also includes Holey Artisan attack. Shahbag movement took place in 2013 in demand of the capital punishment of the war criminals. But anti-Shahbag force propagated that some atheist bloggers were leading the movement which resulted in the rise of Hefajat-E-Islam, a network of Qawmi madrasa people. In the post-Shahbag chaotic climate, the target killings were taking place. JMB was a local militant organisation, Hefajat though not a militant organisation, was also a local political Islamic network. But in post-Shahbag period, global networks like IS intervened in Bangladesh. In this period, these killings by local and global networks got legitimacy by many Bangladeshis suggesting those who demean Allah or the prophet they might be worth killing. Even the government officials condemned killed bloggers for writing defamatory words. Later it was seen the AL government was compromising with the Hefajat-E-Islami to continue holding power. Prime Minister Sheikh Hasina has been honoured with the title 'Mother of Qawmi' by Hefajat-E-Islami in 2018.[7] The advent of Jihadist Islam in Bangladesh and other forms of political Islam have resulted allowing the government as well as general public an overall rise of political and Jihadist Islam in Bangladesh what was once a land of Sufi Islam. Some independent filmmakers have portrayed these realities in their films, especially which are made in recent times.

The tradition of Bengali culture is being transformed by encounters with global neoliberal ideologies and political or Jihadist Islam. In this chapter, we have tried to show that despite a tendency to posit extremes, whether you are either a Bengali first or a Muslim first, the situation is much more complex than these polarities suggest. We argue that even today traces of differing historical periods and antique religious movements have left their mark on what passes for a contemporary Bangladeshi identity. Ideologues of both persuasions tend to paint a strictly black and white scenario based on inclusion and exclusion, whereas we contend that it much more confusing than that. This can best be illuminated by reference to some observations of recent events.

Islamists go to the National Cricket Stadium at Mirpur and cheer the national cricket team to victory over visiting teams. Moreover, Madrassa students can often be seen playing cricket on the local fields. People who claim to be secular marry their children according to Muslim customs. Sometimes parents who have brought up their children to be humanists find a daughter suddenly turning up at home in a full *niqab*, much to their chagrin. It is her way, she says, of expressing her identity as a Muslim woman. In short, what we are saying is that the identity of Bengali (or Bangladeshi) Muslims is a remarkably fluid thing, occurring in a territory where the boundaries and the markers are constantly shifting, but always within a context of historical and religious precedents as well as social practices. Earlier popular religions or recent globalised transformations are also continuing to have impact. The filmmakers we will discuss have a remarkably rich palette upon which to work.

Notes

1 See 'Bangladesh Population 2020 (Live)' at https://worldpopulationreview.com/countries/bangladesh-population/. Accessed 31 May 2020.
2 See 'The Capital of Bengali Literature is Dhaka: Samaresh Majumdar (Bangla Sahityer Rajdhani Dhaka: Samaresh Majumdar)' at https://www.banglanews24.com/art-literature/news/bd/739790.details. Accessed 31 May 2020.
3 See 'World Bank: Bangladesh Economy Continues Robust Growth with Rising Exports and Remittances' at https://www.worldbank.org/en/news/press-release/2019/10/10/world-bank-bangladesh-economy-continues-robust-growth-with-rising-exports-and-remittances. Accessed 27 October 2019
4 See 'Bangladesh 2nd Largest Economy in South Asia' at https://www.thedailystar.net/bangladesh/bangladesh-ranked-41st-largest-economy-in-2019-all-over-the-world-study-1684078. Accessed 27 October 2019
5 See 'Bangladesh Second in South Asia in GDP Growth: WB' at https://www.thedailystar.net/business/bangladesh-second-gdp-growth-rate-country-in-south-asia-1813420. Accessed 27 October 2019.
6 CNBC reports on 16 January 2019: Bangladesh – which has seen the world's fastest growing ultra-wealthy population (those with a net worth of more than $30 million) over the past five years – draws its success from rapid urbanisation and increased infrastructure investment. See 'These Countries are Set to See their Millionaire Populations Skyrocket in the Next 5 Years' at https://www.cnbc.com/2019/01/16/countries-with-the-fastest-growing-millionaire-billionaire-populations.html. Accessed 29 October 2019.
7 See 'PM Sheikh Hasina Branded as 'Mother of Qawmi', at https://www.dhakatribune.com/bangladesh/dhaka/2018/11/04/pm-hasina-lauded-as-mother-of-qawmi. Accessed 29 October 2019.

References

Ahmed, A. F. S. (1994). *Bengali Nationalism and the Emergence of Bangladesh: An Introductory Outline*. Dhaka: ICBS.
Ahmed, R. (2001). Introduction – The Emergence of the Bengal Muslims. In R. Ahmed (ed.), *Understanding the Bengal Muslims: Interpretative Essays* (pp. 1–25). Oxford: Oxford University Press.
Anisuzzaman (1995). *Identity, Religion and Recent History*. Calcutta: Naya Udyog.
Appadurai, A. (2001). Disjuncture and Difference in the Global Cultural Economy. In S. Seidman and J. C. Alexander (eds.), *The New Social Theory Reader: Contemporary Debates* (pp. 253–265). London: Routledge.
Chatterji, J. (1994). *Bengal Divided: Hindu Communalism and Partition, 1932–1947*. Cambridge: Cambridge University Press, 1994.
Chaterjee, S. (2005). *In the Deep Isolate Path* (Gavir Nirjan Pathe). Calcutta: Ananda Publishers.
Choudhury, A. A. (2007). *In Quest of Lalon Sain* (Lalon Sainer Sondhane). Dhaka: Palol Publishers.
Chowdhury, B. M. (2004). Changing Class and Social Structure in Bangladesh: 1793–1980. In A. F. S. Ahmed and B. M. Chowdhury (eds.), *Bangladesh – National Culture and Heritage: An Introductory Reader* (pp. 253–266). Dhaka: Independent University, Bangladesh.

Dasgupta, S. (1976). *Obscure Religious Cults*. Calcutta: Firma KLM Private Limited.
Eaton, R. M. (1993). *The Rise of Islam and the Bengal Frontier: 1204–1760*. Berkley: University of California Press.
Haq, F. (2011). Selling Audience: The Role of Media in Creating Consumer Culture in Bangladesh. *Media Asia, 38*(4), 200–204.
Murshid, G. (2006). *One thousand Years of Bengali Culture (Hajar Bochhorer Bangla Samskriti)*. Dhaka: Protik.
Nicholas, R. W. (2001). Islam and Vaishanvism in the Environment of Rural Bengal. In R. Ahmed (ed.), *Understanding the Bengal Muslims: Interpretative Essays* (pp. 52–70). Oxford: Oxford University Press Limited, 2001.
Parvez, S. (2018). Explaining Political Violence in Contemporary Bangladesh. In A. Riaz, Z. Nasreen and F. Zaman (eds.), *Political Violence in South Asia* (pp. 51–59). Abingdon: Routledge.
Ritzer, G. (2010). *Globalisation: A Basic Text*. New Jersey: Willey Blackwell.
Riaz, A. & Parvez, S. (2018). Bangladeshi Militants: What Do We Know? *Terrorism and Political Violence, 30*(6), 944–961.
Shah, M. (1993). Social and Cultural Basis of Bengali Nationalism. In Islam S. (ed.), *History of Bangladesh: 1704–1971. Vol. 3* (Social and Cultural History) (pp. 691–734). Dhaka: Asiatic Society of Bangladesh.
Sharif, A. (2003). *Baul Theories* (Baul Tatwa). Dhaka: Parua.
Umar, B. (1974). *Politics and Society in East Pakistan and Bangladesh*. Dacca: Mowla Bros.
Van Schendel, W. (2009). *A History of Bangladesh*. New Delhi: Cambridge University Press.

3 The Making of Independent Cinema in Bangladesh

There is a steady growth of independent film culture although the length, format and characteristics of independent cinema have changed over time since its inception in the mid-1980s. Now independent *auteur*s are regarded as the most reputed filmmakers of the country. Along with five to seven independent feature films, some independent documentaries and short features are produced annually in Bangladesh. Though these films are often not popular among audiences because of their relatively complex form and content, it is important to study the independent cinema of Bangladesh for two major reasons; these films win awards in the international film festival circuit and they have become the backbone of national cinema of Bangladesh and these films create significant impact in the social and cultural domains.

Primarily these films are known as alternative films as the production and distribution systems operate outside the mainstream cinema. But the content and form of these films are often conventional, suggesting they are not alternative in the accepted international meaning of the term. Most of the films are made in a classical narrative style set by Hollywood and the subjects are either mostly about the Liberation War of 1971 or some contemporary issues. In recent times, the word 'independent' has replaced the term 'alternative'. However, film scholar Zakir Hossain Raju (2015) categorises independent cinema of Bangladesh as 'artisanal art cinema', distinguishing between the short films made in the 1980s and 1990s and the 'global art cinema' of the present.

Taking Raju's categorisation into account, this chapter discusses the emergence and growth of independent cinema in Bangladesh. It also discusses the nature of the independent cinema movement of Bangladesh and interprets the contribution of the film society movement made to its development. This interpretative discussion also includes the political economy and current challenges of independent filmmaking in Bangladesh and is organised around a number of themes; namely, the early characteristics, the different phases of production, the challenges faced by independent filmmakers in Bangladesh and the opportunities available to filmmakers. The

DOI: 10.4324/9781003271093-4

role of the government towards independent cinema is also discussed here, especially the issue of censorship gets an attention in the discussion.

Early Influences

According to Raju (2015), the film club discourse in the 1960s-90s served as the breeding ground for Bangladeshi independent cinema. This discourse worked for developing Bangladeshi independent cinema as a western-style art cinema as well as the normalisation of textual patterns of Euro-American classics as standard film language for Bangladeshi cinema.

Being influenced by the film society culture of India, especially the Calcutta Film Society which was established in 1947, by Satyajit Ray and others, the film society movement began in East Pakistan through the establishment of Pakistan Film Society (PFS) under leadership of Muhammad Khasru and some others in 1963. After liberation, a considerable number of film societies were established, both inside and outside of Dhaka. PFS was renamed the Bangladesh Film Society (BFS) in the post-independence period.

In the post-independence era, the general release (in local theatres) of selected European and American film classics stopped. The film societies became the principal way of accessing western filmic traditions for Bengali Muslims. Besides western films, film societies screened the Indian Bengali films influenced by Satyajit Ray, Ritwik Ghatak and other prominent directors as these Bengali films shared the same language and culture and helped to create the context for Bangladeshi independent films. After independence, most countries established an embassy in Dhaka, and film societies were able to collect foreign films for screening through the cooperation of the embassies.

In 1974, the leading film society BFS offered the first fully fledged film appreciation course which was conducted by Satish Bahadur, a teacher of Film and Television Institute of India (FTTI), Pune. BFS requested Bahadur to prepare an outline for a film archive and institute for Bangladesh. Upon Bahadur's draft, film society members moved and urged the government to establish a film archive in Bangladesh. In 1978, under the Ministry of Information, Bangladesh Film Institute and Archive (BFIA) was established.

We emphasise the film society movement and its influence on the Bangladeshi independent film movement for two reasons. It was in the ambit of the film societies that potential filmmakers were first exposed to the possibilities of alternative film discourses, their form and rhetoric. Therefore, it is no accident that Morshedul Islam, Tareque Masud and Tanvir Mokammel who are now leading independent filmmakers in Bangladesh, were all students of the first batch of the appreciation course offered by the BFIA and conducted by Alamgir Kabir. It was in this context that the idea of making low-budget independent films in 16 mm format in Bangladesh first emerged.

Other major film societies such as the Chalachchitram Film Society, Zahir Raihan Film Society and Rainbow Film Society also contributed to this process. Almost all the independent filmmakers were film society members at some stage in their careers, and the establishment of BFIA and the appreciation course it offered made a direct contribution to early Bangladesh independent cinema. The first short film Agami was produced by the Chalachchittram Film Society.

In 1986, the filmmakers, encouraged by the film society movement, established the Short Film Forum (SFF). SFF is a forum of makers and it organised its first International Short Film Festival in 1988. From then on, it became a regular event in the cine environment of Bangladesh. To date, 14 festivals have been arranged under the leadership of SFF and the current biannual festival is known as International Short and Independent Film Festival. SFF, however, provides limited support to filmmakers.

The rise of SFF and the decline of the film society movement occurred simultaneously. Some film society activists argue that the formation of SFF hindered the film society movement as many film society activists joined in the SFF. The president of Moviyana Film Society and the General Secretary of FSSB Belayat Hossain Mamun shared this opinion with the author(s) in personal discussion. Some people thought that arranging festivals should be the role of Federation of Film Societies of Bangladesh (FFSB) instead of the SFF. However, at least two film societies, Rainbow Film Society and Children's Film Society, arrange two regular international film festivals in Dhaka. Moviyana Film society organised many festivals sometimes individually and sometimes with the collaboration of Bangladesh Shilpakala Academy (Bangladesh Art Academy) with the entries of local independent features and short films among which 'New Films and New Filmmakers' festival got special attention nationally in 2015 and in 2016.

First Phase (1984–1992): Early Short Films

There is debate among film critics and historians about the starting point of independent filmmaking in Bangladesh. One noted film commentator and filmmaker Manjare Hasseen Murad (2006: 30) likes to count *Stop Genocide* (1971), the documentary made by Zahir Raihan, the great filmmaker in the 1960s, as the first independent film in Bangladesh. The film was one of the finest documentaries ever made in Bangladesh and created international sympathy towards Bangladeshis and built awareness among international powers about the genocide that occurred by the Pakistani army in 1971. In a critical sense, it was a propaganda film and it did not contribute in creating a trend of filmmaking immediately. Some other critics like Zakir Hossain Raju (2015) identified *The Ominous House* (Suryo Dighal Bari 1979) as the first independent [global art] cinema, which was the first film funded by Bangladesh Government after independence in 1971. It was made within the production and distribution network of the Bangladesh Film Development

Corporation (BFDC), the only studio in Bangladesh. Because the grant met only partial funding needs, producers involved in the project sought independent funds to complete the film, which was then distributed through mainstream networks. In that sense, it was not an independent film that could not create any impact of making some other films of the same kind. Then in the 1980s, a new kind of film was made, which may be called independent cinema. These films, which were short in length, were financed by the directors, shot outside of the studio system, distributed independently and exhibited outside of the cine-theatres. From an idealistic perspective these films can be called independent films. In that sense, *Towards* (Agami 1984) by Morshedul Islam was the first independent film as it was the first out-of-studio and self-financed film made in Bangladesh in the 1980s.

Early Characteristics

Independent filmmaking may be viewed as a 'counterculture' in its earliest phase of film production in Bangladesh as no 'full length feature films' were produced. However, in other countries like in the USA and Europe, independent films are made as full-length films in the 35 mm format. In Bangladesh, the first independent films were made in 16 mm format and the length was not fixed, largely for economic reasons as well as the lack of experience, and we would argue, the lack of confidence of the filmmakers.

The earlier short film movement created two major streams of independent filmmaking in Bangladesh; one is based on nationalist and melodramatic cliché (*Towards*) and the other based on experimental film, which was influenced by Sergei Eisenstein and Dziga Vertov (*Wanted*). Several short films were made in the late 1980s broadly followed these two streams. *The Cycle* (Abartan 1988) by Abu Sayeed was a departure from these repetitive works and it reinvigorated the evolution of the short film genre. The film was about the struggle of a lower-middle-class family. However, some other earlier independent films were *Inner Strength* (Adam Surat 1989) by Tareque Masud, *The return* (Protyabartan 1986) by Mostafa Kamal, *The Ring* (Chakki 1986) by Enayet Karim Babul.

Despite their short length all major genres produced in the sector, features, documentaries and even animation were made in either 16 mm or in video formats. In a wider sense, there was also an ideological aspect to this filmmaking; they possessed a secular, anti-communal ideology, inherited from the Liberation War of 1971, married to a leftish political bias, which is reflected in the films. All leading makers had a progressive background, either in the cultural sphere or on the political frontier. But interestingly, being left leaning and secular, all of them had a nationalist approach to their works, which was manifested in the various films' content. The dominant leftist politics of the 1960s, the sense of modernity and Marxism believed by the filmmakers were localised in the ideology of 'Bengaliness'. Tanvir Mokammel (2013) has this interpretation on this contradiction:

The reason seems self-evident as during the 1971 war most of these young filmmakers were in their boyhood, in their most sensitive and formative years. So, the trauma they had experienced, resulting in the 1971 war was to appear again and again in their films, almost like a – leitmotif.

Morshedul Islam (2006), the maker of the first independent film, comments on why he chose a subject, which addressed the Liberation War:

> I thought what the subject of my first film could be. I chose our Liberation War as the subject of my film and I tried to substantiate the Liberation War at the perspective of that time. General Ershad just took the power; we experienced earlier that there was a conspiracy in the state to down the spirit of Liberation War. The collaborators of the Liberation War were reorganised and our freedom fighters had to see this helplessly but could not do anything. I tried to portray this situation in my film. The film was ended with a hope that our next generation may bring back the magnitude of our Liberation War.

In the 1980s, the socio-political situation in Bangladesh was non-democratic and the filmmakers responded to it through their filmic expressions. The prevailing cine environment in the country was also a determinant factor in emerging independent filmmaking. In the early 1980s, when independent filmmaking started, the mainstream film industry was in relatively good shape though the content and form of the films were ordinary in standard. But there were a few exceptional efforts, which inspired potential young filmmakers. They thought about widening the perspectives of films that could be made within the studio system. Those few exceptional films were *The Ominous House* (1979), *The Kyte* (Ghuddi 1980) and *The Detective Force of Emil* (Emiler Goenda Bahini 1980). But these films suffered due to the non-cooperation of the distributors. Mainstream distributor-exhibitors primarily were not interested in screening the films in theatres because they judged them to be poor in box-office. *The Ominous House* was released on December 31, 1979, in the tiny town of Natore, only to later compete in the national film awards of that year. The film was released through the interference of the President of Bangladesh, Ziaur Rahman. The film was supported by the government and government-owned newspapers, but the film was denied wide release and the other 'exceptional' films were also a failure in the box office for similar reasons.

The critical success and popularity of both *Towards* and *Wanted* resulted in the beginning of the independent film movement in Bangladesh. Morshedul Islam says, these films were shown not only in Dhaka but also in every corner of Bangladesh. In many cases, these films were screened together (Islam, 2006). After the success of *Towards* and *Wanted*, a lot of

Table 3.1 Lists of selected early independent short films

Name of the Film	Director	Format and Length
Towards (Agami 1984)	Morshedul Islam	16 mm, 25 min
Wanted (*Hooliya* 1984)	Tanvir Mokammel	16 mm, 27 min
The Cycle (Abartan 1988)	Abu Sayeed	16 mm, 25 min
Inner Strength (Adam Surat 1989)	Tareque Masud	16 mm, 54 min

young filmmakers were attracted to make films outside of the studio system and the independent movement got its momentum which continued for at least a decade.

Some Limitations of Early Independent Films

Independent film culture, as we have discussed, may be considered a continuation of the film society movement. A major limitation confronting early independent films was their alienation from the Bangladeshi viewing public. Tareque Masud (2006) argues:

> We came from film society culture. What are the characteristics of this film society? It is an elitist culture; our film sense grew up by watching foreign films, to be more specific Western films.... You will rarely find any write-up on our films of that time. We arranged workshops, seminars on Eisenstein or Godard or Orson Welles. We were far from local film culture. At best we expressed contempt for local films in write-ups, we arranged demonstration against vulgarity of local films. We were neglecting local films and to be honest, those were worth neglecting. But we did nothing to improve the situation.

This alienation from the mass public was a major problem for early independent filmmaking, which continues to this day. Its selected audience was the educated, urban middle class who were in a sense a captive audience, who used to watch independent films on national days like *Pahela Baishak* (the Bengali new year), December 16th (the victory day) or February 21st (the international mother language day). Non-theatrical release was another limitation imposed by the mainstream industry. Moreover, the films were neither screened on television nor released abroad other than participating in international film festivals.

Another major limitation was that the films were often technically poor. In the early phase, being attracted to the charm of becoming a filmmaker, young people came to the industry without prior preparation and the production of low-quality films in terms of content and form were the result (Islam, 2006). Some of the early filmmakers did not have even any film society background and they did not participate in any appreciation courses

62 Independent Cinema in Bangladesh

or filmmaking workshops. Nevertheless, despite these limitations, this early phase was significant to the creation of an independent film sector in Bangladesh.

Second Phase (1993–1999): Thrust to Transformation

In the second phase, feature-length fiction films replaced short fiction films. Morshedul Islam made *The Beginning* (Suchona 1988, 62 minutes), again from the nationalist approach of the Liberation War. Tanvir Mokammel made *The River Called Madhumoti* (Nadir Naam Madhumoti 1995, 120 minutes); the film also explored the nationalist discourse. The next film by Morshedul Islam was *The Wheel* (Chaka, 1993, 65 minutes). There was a shift in the content as he had changed his topic. Based on the play of the same title by eminent playwright Selim Al Deen, it is a story of the struggle of two bullock cart drivers to bury an unidentified body. The next film of Tanvir Mokammel was *In the Bank of Chitra* (Chitra Nadir Pare 1999, 114 minutes). The film deals broadly with the historical background to the Liberation War – the partition of India/Bengal in 1947. Mokammel wanted to shoot it in 35 mm format, but he did not receive a government grant, so he had to shoot in 16 mm. However, aspiration was there among the directors to make films in 35 mm format. *Chitra* was later transferred onto 35 mm, enabling it to be released in cine theatres. *The Wheel* was also transferred to 35 mm, though not in Dhaka but in overseas where it got a theatrical release. At the same time, Tareque and Catherine Masud made a full-length documentary *Song of Freedom* (Muktir Gaan 1995, 78 minutes), originally shot on an intermediate technology – super 16, which cannot be transferred into 16 mm but may be transferred to 35 mm. The documentary was based on footage of the Liberation War shot by an American filmmaker, Lear Levin. The Masud duo assembled this footage and combined it with other archival clips from different parts of the world to make the film, which was successfully revived in 1995.

In the middle of the 1990s, independent films tried to overcome their limitations, by trying to reach to a wider audience. *Song of Freedom* was

Table 3.2 Lists of selected films of the second phase (1993–1999) of the independent cinema movement

Name of the Film	Director	Format and Length
The Wheel (Chaka 1993)	Morshedul Islam	16 mm, 65 min
Song of Freedom (Muktir Gaan 1995)	Tareque Masud and Catherine Masud	35 mm, 78 min
In the Bank of Chitra (Chitra Nadir Pare 1999)	Tanvir Mokammel	16 mm (later transferred into 35 mm), 114 min

transferred into 35 mm for theatrical release. However, at the last moment, the potential producer pulled out from the commercial release of the film. The makers were compelled to screen it in alternative exhibition centres like the Public Library Auditorium. After tremendous success in non-theatrical distribution, the film was released in cine theatres later. Morshedul Islam successfully made *Dukhai* (1997) and *Dipu Number Two* (1996) within the mainstream production and distribution system. *Dipu Number Two* got a government grant and attracted substantial revenue from mainstream theatres. *Dukhai* received funds from Japan Digital Lab and achieved moderate theatrical success. Being a leading independent filmmaker, Morshedul Islam made two consecutive full-length feature films in 35 mm format in the mainstream studio system and released them through mainstream distributing systems suggesting that independent filmmaking in Bangladesh was about to be transformed.

Industrial Cutting Edge

By the end of the 1990s, the independent film movement had consolidated its position. Independent films had started to be released in cinema halls. At that point, another platform was opened – television. State-owned Bangladesh Television was then the only television channel available in Bangladesh and it bought *Song of Freedom* for 0.7 million Taka (approx. USD 11,600) (Masud, 2006), which proved to be a substantial investment. *Song of Freedom* was also the first local film to be commercially sold through VHS cassette format. Till then local or foreign films were found in video clubs only for rental. Thus, a new market of independent cinema was created while the mainstream industry was struggling.

The budget of the film *Dukhai* by Morshedul Islam exceeded 10 million Taka (approximately USD 166,000), which was more than any other local industrial commercial cinema. *The Wheel* and *Dukhai* brought a certain quantitative and qualitative change in cinema practice and that impacted profoundly in the local industry. The best director award in International Film Festival, India in 1985, given to *Towards*, gave a momentum to the early short independent film movement in the 1980s. Again, the second phase of the independent film movement was inspired by the international awards given to *The Wheel* (1993) and both films were directed by Morshedul Islam. *The Wheel* did not only earn the best film award in Dunkirk Film Festival, France in 1994, it was also the first Bangladeshi feature film that received its first commercial distribution from a French company. When the film was sent to European festivals, it was shown in 16 mm format. But when the question of releasing in French theatres arose, it was transferred to 35 mm. No matter how limited or how artificially it was enhanced, the underlying significance ranks *The Wheel* as the first Bangladeshi film to ever receive a European distributor. Thus, independent cinema had become an industrial cutting edge.

In contrast, the short film movement declined in its importance because of the international success of *The Wheel* and the local success of *Song of Freedom*.[1]

We were Forced to be Independent

Tareque Masud (2006) describes, in an interview with us, how the film society and cine environment had forced him to remain an independent filmmaker. He interprets the situation by describing his experience in the making of *Song of Freedom*:

> We never possibly intended to be independent filmmakers, but we were forced to be independent. We started negotiating with mainstream distributor-producer Habib Khan[2] for *Song of Freedom*, but at last we failed to reach any consensus. We thought him even as the producer of *The Clay Bird*, but the unresolved deal of *Song of Freedom* compelled us to be independent. I was ready to lose my independence, since I was not given chance, I went ahead to produce my own film. The commercial success of *Song of Freedom* gave me enough money to almost produce the whole *The Clay Bird*. Only thing I could not afford French camera, French lab and French film stock.[3] The South Fund gave me the in kind support of hundred thousand dollar that gave me an extra edge that I could retain my independence by self-produced film and again I am getting an international quality. So, it is the society determining the fate of the nature of independent cinema. Unless Habib Khan pulled out, I would be produced by Habib Khan.

The background story of *In the Bank of Chitra* (1999) by Tanvir Mokammel can also be mentioned in this regard. Tanvir Mokammel had tried to shoot it in 35 mm format and he also sought a government grant but was denied. Despite the fact that there was a pro-liberation government in power and the subject of the film should have encouraged an AL Government, he was refused the grant, forcing him to make the film in 16 mm format thereby making it an independent film.

In this way, the energy was accumulated by the independent filmmakers. These makers did not have any other place to go. They were compelled to be independent and with the collective energy of Tanvir Mokammel, Morshedul Islam, Abu Sayeed, Tareque and Catherine Masud in the late 1990s, the strength of the independent film movement was established as they could not leave the platform of independent filmmaking.

Third Phase (2000–2010): New Challenges and Opportunities

Independent film gradually acquired maturity, both in content and form, by 2000. In post-2000 films the filmmakers chose different issues with a much greater diversity of subject matter than before. Especially, the new makers with digital format were trying to make subjective films rather than adhering to the old paradigm. Even the senior filmmakers are making new films where the issue on Liberation War no longer appeared as frequently as before.

Independent film reached its maturity in terms of techniques and technology with an increase in the number of filmmakers. All new cinematic technologies have been used in contemporary films, which included Cinemascope, digital sound with the latest digital cameras. Though most of the independent filmmaking follows classical narrative form, the experiments with film language in some films like *Shankhonad* (2004) by Abu Sayeed, *Aha!* (2007) by Enamul Karim Nirjhar or the digital film *Blackout* (2006) by Tokon Thaakoor were appreciated by critics precisely because of their formal innovation. However, contemporary films, even if it was made in a classical narrative style, exhibit greater visual beauty, the editing is smarter, camera movement is consistent with the situation, and in addition, the quality of the sound and picture had improved significantly.

Despite of its maturity, the greatest setback for the independent film remains limited distribution. Films tend to be released in a few theatres and are isolated from the mass audience. In this phase, an independent film ran one or two weeks in one or two theatres in Dhaka and then tends to be released on DVD leading to moderate sales. The maker's most important aspiration was to place their film to the international festivals circuit in order to gain an award thereby ensuring their reputation. In the 1980s and 1990s, independent films gained some audience from alternative distribution, but that network does not exist anymore. Independent films are now struggling to live up to their independent and alternative character, after the arrival of the corporate electronic media as a parallel industry.

Corporate Electronic Media as Parallel Industry

In its struggle to retain its independent character the 'indie' sector faces several challenges. The first is its problematic relationship with the studio cinema by which we mean the mainstream films made within the confines of BFDC, which still maintain a stranglehold on narrative cinema in Bangladesh. The second is the newly emerged corporate industry, which in many respects has become a parallel industry to the independent sector. This cinema occupies a space where corporate culture intersects with film culture. It relates to electronic media through corporate advertisement and has in effect swallowed the short film movement. The young filmmakers who want to make experimental short films must accommodate with this sector and produce films for television channels either as telefilms or soaps. The lure of corporate filmmaking has had a profound effect on the independent sector, greater than that of the mainstream cinema. Consequently, independent filmmakers have had to adopt different strategies in order to survive in the industry. The three principal strategies available are to either to work out of the country or to compromise their integrity and make more profit-oriented films or adjust the corporate electronic media. In order to maintain their independence in the face of the onslaught of the corporate electronic media, filmmakers must look for international finance. But international financiers have chosen selected areas for funding for filmmakers in the Third World as well as for Bangladesh. To get foreign funds the storyline must conform to the parameters set by the financiers. So, usually very few scripts are accepted and receive international funding. Bangladesh government provides five grants for feature-length films and five for short films which is a significant support for the filmmakers. But these funds are often given to unsuitable candidates. Consequently, in the current situation, independent cinema faces a real challenge in keeping its independent character because the corporate has been the most dependable source of funding for the independent cinema. A major player in this sector is Impress Telefilms, a sister concern of a leading private television company *Channel I*, who forward money liberally to aspiring filmmakers as long as they conform to the demands of Impress with product placement.

One crude example, in this context, of losing independence is the issue of product placement in the text. In the film *Bachelor* (2003) by Mostafa Sarwar Farooki, there is a scene where a character drinks a *deshi* cola (Euro Cola) and says 'no' to the American products in the context of post-Iraq aggression period. The film was 'presented' by Euro Cola. Through a pseudo political stand, the product Euro Cola is placed in the film. In the film *The Aienation* (Duratta 2004) by Morshedul Islam the main character Putul, a sick adolescent, usually does not like to eat, however, the housemaid is persuasive, and he agrees to eat only Maggi Noodles. The film was 'presented' by Maggi Noodles.

So, the political economy of Impress Produced films is as follows: after selecting the script they 'manage' a corporate sponsor for the particular film, the name of the sponsor (mostly not the name of the company but a product) goes in the publicity and title card as *nibedito* (presented by). Then the film is premiered in *Channel I*, the mother organisation, with a lot of commercial breaks (the sponsor's and others'). A common objection against this 'world premier' (*Channel I* is telecasted in Europe and North America for its Bangladeshi expatriate audience) from the audience is they cannot finish watching the whole film because of those commercial breaks. Then within some days, the film will be released in one or two leading theatres in Dhaka. It will run for one week or two and the story ends here if not it gets national or international awards. But of course, it feeds the 'filler' demand of the TV channel. For this formula, Impress developed, even a better film might be deprived of getting its audience. Tauquir Ahmed's film *The Unnamed* (Oggatonama 2016) got a limited theatrical release and only after it was uploaded on YouTube, it got popular and critical appreciation.

Forever Flows (Nirontor 2007) was produced by Impress Telefilm and earned three awards in two festivals in India, including the best picture award. The director of the film Abu Sayeed (2006) has an observation on the films produced by Impress, which is worth mentioning here:

> The output from that production house is not worth mentioning. They have produced so many films, but we got very few quality films. The reason behind it is they are not playing the role of the 'producer'. When it comes to the question of distribution, they release the film only in one or two cine theatres of the capital city. They are more interested in a television premier. They want to ensure their profit from the revenue of the advertisements of television premier. It can be also noted that the films produced by Impress lack the elements to be commercially successful. What they produce is neither commercial, nor artistic. They could plan to make five films targeting commercial success and five more to be award earners. They do not have different office or different work force. They produce film as a side venture of *Channel I*. Many prominent directors have made films under Impress, but there were very few remarkable works.

By contrast, another Impress-produced independent maker Morshedul Islam (2006) endorses the method developed by the production company in response to the prevailing cine situation in the country:

> We are compelled to do the premiere show in the TV channel. It guarantees around $30000, which may be 50% costs of making a film. Nowadays it would be very uncertain to get back this amount of money from cinema halls. For this, first, we do the premier show in the TV screen then we release it in the cinema halls. If I do not show the film in the TV, is there any guarantee that audience would go to the cinema halls to see the films?

Local Entrepreneur as Producer

To maintain their independence over the production, makers such as Tareque Masud and Tanvir Mokammel stay away from the corporate electronic media. Besides international funding, they have explored local entrepreneurs as a source of capital. As shown in Table 3.4, the source of the funding of several independent films is a combination of self and international funding and local producer. In this phase, there was a limited number of producing companies prepared to invest in independent films. There was only one producer-distributor with its own distinctive identity, different from both the mainstream industry and parallel corporate industry. It is Machhranga Productions backed by a leading local corporate company Square Group. By gratifying the profit and prestige of

Machhranga Productions, independent makers obtained funds from it. Machhranga provided partial funding of *Homeland* (Ontorjatra 2006) by Tareque Masud and Catherine Masud, *A Tree Without Roots* (Lalsalu 2001) by Tanvir Mokammel and *Shankhonaad* (2004) by Abu Sayeed and total funding of *Lalon* (2004) by Tanvir Mokammel. However, the rests of the films continue to be produced by television channels especially by Impress Telefilm. The absence of substantial number of local entrepreneurs as producers of independent film is a major constraint for the progress of independent cinema.

Digital Filmmaking in the 2000s

Digital filmmaking was a new option for independent filmmakers in the late 2000s in Bangladesh with the advantages of less expense and shorter time spent in production, easy management and more creative control for the director over the film. However, in Hollywood, digital filmmaking is not an alternative means of filmmaking but rather a chosen way of film production that offers endless imaginative possibilities for fantasy with special effects; as James Cameron, the master of special effect cinema, says, 'anything is possible right now if you throw enough money at it, or enough time' (Cameron 2002 cited in Allen, 2003: 210). For big-budget studio productions then, digital filmmaking may not be used to save money and time, rather it demands that producers throw 'enough money' and 'enough' time at it for creating fantasies like *Terminator*(s)or *Star War*(s), but for independent makers, who tend to represent reality instead of fantasy in film, it is really a chance to use a flexible and the latest technology. Peter Broderick (2000) says:

> [T]here are three things which indicate the extraordinary future for digital film-making: first, new cameras... which continue to improve and become lower in price; secondly, the availability of software for desktop computers to edit movies and do post-production at home; and, thirdly, the success of transfers from video to film.
> (Broderick 2000 cited in Allen, 2003: 219–220)

Broderick indicates three major technological changes in the digital age that have the potential to change the filmmaking process – newer digital camera that is improving day by day, digital editing and postproduction and transferring digital moving image into celluloid. Director Tareque and Catherine Masud have made three films so far in Bangladesh which were shot in digital format and later were transferred into celluloid. However, in the contemporary situation, with the digital projection technology, one needs not to transfer the digital image; it can be projected directly from the hard drive of a computer or optical disks or satellite and by using a digital projector. However, Bangladesh took much time to develop theatres with direct digital projection technology.

Table 3.3 Format, length and funding details of selected feature films (2000–2010)

Name of the Film	Director	Format and length	Source of Funding
A Tree Without Roots (Lalsalu 2001)	Tanvir Mokammel	35 mm, 110 mins	Self, International and Local (Kino Eye Films/ Montecinemaverite Foundation/The Hubert Bal Funds of the International Film Festival Rotterdam/ Proshika [Dhaka based NGO]/ Machhranga Productions Ltd.]
The Clay Bird (Matir Moina 2002)	Tareque Masud	35 mm, 98 mins	Self and International (Audiovision/South Fund, French Ministry of Culture and Communication)
Shankhonad (2004)	Abu Sayeed	35 mm, 102 mins	Self, TV Channel and Local (Aangik Communications/ Machhranga Productions Ltd./Impress Telefilm)
The Alienation (Duratto 2004)	Morshedul Islam	35 mm, 90 mins	TV Channel (Impress Telefilm)
Homeland (Ontorjatra 2006)	Tareque and Catherine Masud	35 mm (transferred from DV), 86 mins	Self, International and Local (Audiovision/The Hubert Bal Funds of the International Film Festival Rotterdam/British Council Dhaka/ Machhranga Productions)
Dollhouse (Khelaghar 2006)	Morshedul Islam	35 mm, 118 mins	Self, Friends, TV Channel (Manon Chalochchitro/4 friends/Impress Telefilm)
Forever Flows (Nirontor 2006)	Abu Sayeed	35 mm, 108 mins	Self and TV Channel (Aangik Communications/Impress Telefilm)
Transformation (Rupantor 2008)	Abu Sayeed	35 mm, 90 mins	Government grant, International (The Hubert Bal Funds of the International Film Festival Rotterdam)
Rabeya (2008)	Tanvir Mokammel	35 mm, 110 mins	Government grant and Self (Kino-Eye Films)
Love and Repulsion (Priotomesu 2009)	Morshedul Islam	DV, 140 mins	**Laser Vision**
Runway (2010)	Tareque Masud	DV, 96 mins	**Self (Srutichitro)**

70 *Independent Cinema in Bangladesh*

The first digitally shot significant film released in Bangladesh was *Homeland* (Ontorjatra 2006), which was an independent film, directed by Tareque and Catherine Masud. It was shot on digital video camera and transferred into 35 mm, an additional cost that many first-time directors would find exorbitant, especially with their background in television production. For this generation of filmmaker, the logical step would be to project the film directly from DVD or the hard disk of a computer, thereby ensuring that filmmakers could be really independent, as independent as a writer, who needs only a pen and papers for creation. But the real challenge for digital filmmaking was distribution. Tokon Thaakoor made his first digital film *Blackout* in early 2006 and by the middle of 2010, he was still unable to release the film because of the lack of a suitable projection facility for digital films in commercial cinemas in Bangladesh. However, when the projection facilities were developed in theatres, the version of the camera was already outdated.

In 2009, the government of Bangladesh had brought digital film under the censor certification process before it could be screened in the mainstream cine theatres. Even though Morshedul Islam projected his film *Love and Repulsion* (Priotomesu 2009) with advanced multimedia projector in a mainstream theatre, the whole question of digital projection remained a difficulty largely because there was no professional approach to this issue. However, until the commercial cinemas become professionally equipped with digital technology for screening the films, distribution and exhibition remained the largest obstacle confronting the digital development in independent filmmaking in Bangladesh. The discourse of digital filmmaking was initiated by independent filmmakers in the middle of the 2000s. Mainstream producers embraced the technological form later in the 2010s. Cine theatres were transferred to digital projection system in the 2010s.

Diverse Survival Strategies

Tanvir Mokammel and Tareque Masud are still trying to stay away from corporate control and have never taken funds from the Impress Telefilm. For survival, they have tried to raise finance from the international funding sources or Machhranga as producer-distributor. Tanvir Mokammel tried to make documentary films for survival, which were partly produced by others (NGOs, donor agencies or individual producers) because it is comparatively easier to get funding for documentary than fiction films. In an unfavourable situation, old private producers are no longer interested in the area and new producers have yet to emerge. Self-financing is the ultimate way to generate funding for independent filmmakers which is added by foreign funds or local entrepreneurs.

Independent cinema is seeking a way to reach to a wider audience in the country. The global release of Bangladeshi independent films, which adds revenue through distribution to foreign TV channels is an option, but their inexperience in the global distribution system, is a drawback. Several Bangladeshi independent filmmakers have been deprived of revenue because of this inexperience. Tareque Masud (2006) describes his experience on the global release of his first two feature films:

> After the experience of *The Clay Bird* I became careful about my creation. Now I do not want to spend my own money in my film and do not want to lose my control over my film. *The Clay Bird* is still selling every day. Initially for theatrical screening in France, UK or USA – I was to get $1000 per screening as the producer – but I lost it to my distributor MK2. In England, *The Clay Bird* was shown over one and half year in cine theatres. The whole money went to MK2. But now I am careful. For *Homeland*, I faced loss in Bangladesh... but it got more of an audience with one screening on *Channel 4*, which reached an audience throughout the UK. So, I spent much money in *The Clay Bird* but got little return and less audience and for *Homeland* I spent a little amount of money that returned huge sums of money and a bigger audience within six months.

The first globally acclaimed independent Bangladeshi film, *The Wheel* (1993) by Morshedul Islam was released in twelve theatres in France in 1996. Another film, *Shankhonad* (2004) by Abu Sayeed was released in Austria and Switzerland. Some films have been shown in foreign TV channels. *The Clay Bird* (Matir Moina 2002), *Homeland* (Ontorjatra 2006), *Shyamol Chhaya* (Grey Shadow 2004) and *The Alienation* (Duratto 2004), were shown in *Channel Four* in the UK in 2007, which opened new avenues for independent filmmaking. Morshedul Islam, the director of *The Alienation* (Duratto 2004) says, I got around 70% of the costs of my film from Channel Four. Now we have wide scopes of getting funds, both local and foreign. The commercial value of our films has been created outside of the country (Islam, 2006).

In the shrinking local market, Morshedul Islam (2006) emphasised the need to explore foreign funds for survival. Director Abu Sayeed does not want to mention a specific method for survival; rather he wants to remain positive to face uncertainties:

> There is no set rule in which way the fund will come. You must create your own fund. You will have to find your own path in the process of filmmaking. My life and my family have gone through this filmmaking process. Sometimes I have my own transport, sometimes I do not have. Sometimes I must sell my land or ornaments of my wife. And sometimes these are coming back. I may collect money from cooperative, one generous person or group of people jointly will give me money, or I may sell my property for managing funds. Which way will be applicable you never know? You must stay in the track, and you must be determined to make film. The money will come.
>
> (Sayeed 2006)

Abu Sayeed (2006) says he received (Indian) Rs 1,000,000 (approximately US$22,000) as award money from two festivals in India for his contemporary film *Forever Flows* (Nirontor 2006), which he dedicated to the production of his next film *The Flute* (Banshi 2007). This money was augmented by a grant of $38,500 from Vision Sud est, Switzerland to make the film *The Flute* (Banshi 2007). In the last project *Transformation* (Roopantor 2008), he received a $11,500 script grant from The Hubert Bal Funds of the International Film Festival Rotterdam. The film also received a government grant. The amount of the grant was BDT 1.6 million ($22,850) along with services up to BDT 1 million ($14,280) from the BFDC.

However, foreign funding is one of the options, but it is not considered as the only method of survival. For getting it, one must fulfil the agendas of fund giving organisations that results in the presence of Oriental gaze in the film. The local market was always the primary consideration. The problem lies in the distribution systems. In the early phase of the independent film movement in the 1980s and 1990s, the makers used the alternative distribution systems. After several years, Tareque Masud was screening his recent digital film *Runway* (2010) in districts all over the country through an alternative and non-theatrical distribution system with the help of the film societies.

Fourth Phase (2011–2018): Going Global

In more recent times, directors have begun to expand their breadth and depth of the field and encapsulate a wider range of perspectives. Here makers are more subjective – they are not obsessed with the Liberation War narratives only. They look at globalised and post 9/11 Bangladesh with different eyes than earlier filmmakers. We may count it as a new beginning of independent art cinema of Bangladesh. In the film, *Television* (2013) Mostofa Sarwar Foorki depicts how Muslim identity responds to modernity as well as new technologies in post globalised Bangladesh. The portrayal is sensible to the main protagonist who is the religious as well as an administrative leader in a peripheral village in Bangladesh. Some films are made recently to portray the identity of urban spheres. Dhaka, the capital of Bangladesh is one of the oldest cities in South Asia, but it was almost absent in cinematic depiction. But now Dhaka is regularly seen in independent films, such as *Ant Story* (Piprabidya 2015) by Mostofa Sarwar Farooki, *Under Construction* (2015) by Rubaiyat Hossain, *Aynabaji* (2016) by Amitabh Reza and *Live From Dhaka* (2016) by Abdullah Mohammad Saad.

The new growing trend is to present Bangladeshi cinema in global stage. And this is contributed by the independent sector. Either way, this has evolved as the survival strategy of the independent filmmakers. The young independent filmmakers are applying to the foreign agencies or film bazar or for festival grants by submitting the script and or project proposal, getting funds through competition and finding ways to participate in international festivals. Sometimes these films are screened in foreign television channels or commercially released in the theatres in other countries. Thus, gradually they are occupying a space on the stage of global cinema. Though these films are not widely screened in Bangladesh, but these are representing Bangladeshi people, society and culture to the global audience.

This recent trend was started through Tareque Masud's *The Clay Bird*. The film got South Fund award from France and a technically better film was made with French technologies. The film got FIPRESCI award at Cannes. A prominent distributing company MK-2 picked it and released the film in both sides of the Atlantic. It ran for weeks in USA, UK and France. Before this, *Chaka* (1993) by Morshedul Islam got limited release in France. The same happened to the case of *Shankhonad* (2004) by Abu Sayeed just after the *The Clay Bird*'s success. But *The Clay Bird* became ultimate influential film which paved a way for the next generation filmmakers to bring Bangladeshi films to the global stage.

In that process, Kamar Ahmad Simon's *Are You Listening!* (Shunte Ki Pao! 2012) was awarded by Jan Vrijman Fund from IDFA (International Documentary Film Festival Amsterdam) and got a grant from Vision Sud est from Switzerland. The film won the 'Grand Prix' in the 35th Cinema Du Reel in Paris. It also won golden conch as the best feature-length documentary in Mumbai International Film Festival (MIFF) in 2014. *Are You Listening!* visited several festivals in the different parts of the globe. Mostafa Sarwar Farooki's *Television* (2013) got German co-producer and bagged jury grand prize in 7th Asia-Pacific Screen Award in Australia. Rubayiat Hossain's *Under Construction* (2015) was released in France. Farooki's *No Bed of Roses* (Doob 2017) got co-producers from India and was released in several countries including India and Australia. Abu Shahed Imon's *Jalal's Story* (Jalaler Golpo 2014) won the best film award in Avanca Film Festival, Portugal. Abdullah Mohammad Saad's *Live From Dhaka* (2016) won the best director award in Singapore International Film Festival (SIFF). The distributing company Stray Dogs from France picked *Live From Dhaka* to distribute it globally. Saad's second film *Rehana Maryam Noor* (2021) competed in *Un Certain Regard* category at Cannes International Film Festival which is the best achievement of a Bangladeshi film so far in the international film circuit. Mostofa Sarwar Farooki's *No Lands Man* (2021) is a global film in a true sense which is set in India, Australia and the USA and performed by international cast and crew members. Amitabh Reza made *Rikshaw Girl* (2021), adapted from a bestseller novel published in the USA and funded and distributed by USA companies.

The 'Open Doors' programme of Locarno Film Festival, Switzerland has arrived as a great opportunity for Bangladeshi independent filmmakers to enter into global cinema stage. The programme is offered for those countries where the independent sector is struggling. The three years (2016–18) programme has focused on South Asian countries except India. Under this programme, the projects from Bangladesh got fund and guidance as well as

74 *Independent Cinema in Bangladesh*

Table 3.4 Selected global films

Title	Director
The Wheel (Chaka 1993)	Morshedul Islam
The Clay Bird (Matir Moina 2002)	Tareque Masud
Are You Listening! (Shunte Ki Pao! 2012)	Kamar Ahmad Simon
Television (2013)	Mostofa Sarwar Farooki
Under Construction (2015)	Rubayiat Hossain
Rehana Maryam Noor (2021)	Abdullah Mohammad Saad
No Lands Man (2021)	Mostofa Sarwar Farooki

potential producers to help them to catch good rated festivals and European markets where the films can be released. The projects of Kamar Ahmad Simon, Rubayiat Hoosain, Mahdi Hassan and Istiaque Zico have been selected for Open Doors. When all these films will be completed one after another, the films of Bangladesh will appear in global cinema with its own signature and character.

In fact, all upcoming projects of Mostofa Sarwar Farooki, Kamar Ahmad Simon, Rubayiat Hossain and some others will be made by foreign funds, will be screened in international festivals and will perhaps be commercially released in foreign countries. Most of these films are also getting the grants of Bangladesh government. Kamar Ahmad Simon's *Testimony of a Thread* (Ekti Sutar Jobanbondi, 2015) was his first television documentary which was co-produced by four leading Asian Broadcasters NHK (Japan), KBS (Korea), Mediacorp (Singapore) and PTS (Taiwan). This film won the Asian Pitch for its screenplay. Kamar's first fiction project *Iron Stream* (Shikolbaha) was the only non-European selection out of 24 projects which were invited to European Producers Workshop. *Iron Stream* received script development grant from Goteborg International Film Festival, Sweden. It was also invited to European Post-Production Connection (EP2C) and Produire au Sud a co-production platform of Festival of 3 Continents in Nantes, France. This script also won World Cinema Fund (WCF) from Berlin International Film Festival and National Film Grant of Bangladesh. Simon's *'day after…'* (Onnodin…) is the 2nd Part of 'Water Trilogy' after *Are You Listening!* The project was invited to La Atelier in Cannes 2017 as one of the 15 promising scripts. For this, Kamar was awarded 'Best Project Award' & 'ARTE International Prix' in Locarno Film Festival (Open Doors) 2016. Earlier the project also received grant awards from Sundance Film Festival and IDFA. It was the first Bangladeshi film competing at IDFA in the best film category. Farooki's under production project *No Land's Man* won Asia Pacific Screen Award (MPA Film Fund) 2014 and won the most promising project award from Film Bazar India and was selected as official project of Asian Project Market of Busan International Film Festival in 2014. International Film Initiative of Bangladesh (IFIB) established by filmmaker Samia Zaman is also contributing in connecting local filmmakers with global networks.

The international film critics as well as the audience generally cannot recognise Bangladeshi films in world cinema. Often, they mix it with Indian Cinema or Indian Bengali Cinema. But through *The Clay Bird, Television, Are You Listening!* Or *Kingdom of Clay Subjects* (Matir Projar Deshe 2016) by Imtiaz Bijon Ahmed – a rural Bangladesh is being characterised for global audience, and through *Under Construction, Live From Dhaka* and *Aynabaji* – an urban Bangladesh is being depicted. Though *Unnamed* (Oggatonama 2016) by Touquir Ahmed and *The Orange Ship* (Komola Rocket 2018) by Nur Islam Mithu could not create much impact in global stage, but these two films are honest in their attempts and portray two major areas of Bangladesh's economy – the remittance-oriented labour market (*Unnamed*) and export-oriented RMG industries (*The Orange Ship*). In both cases, the directors depict how the ordinary labours are exploited without providing them minimum safety and security. The storyline of both films is developed around a dead body which is a result of the system of labour exploitation. Thus, a shape of Bangladesh Cinema has been formed gradually through the projection of the unique cultural and social characteristics of the country. Nasiruddin Yousuf Bachchu's *Guerrilla* (2012) and Alpha (2019), Golam Rabbani Biplob's *On the Wings of Dreams* (Swopnodanay 2007) and *Beyond the Cricle* (Britter Baire 2009), Akram Khan's *The Cage* (Khacha 2017) and The Grass Flower (Ghashphul 2015), Zahidur Rahim Anjan's *Meghmallar* (2015), Giasuddin Selim's *Swapnajaal* (2018), Gazi Rakayat's *Passion for Clay* (Mrittika Maya 2013), Proshoon Rahman's *Her Own Address* (Sutapar Thikana 2012) Noman Robin's *Common Gender* (2012), N. Rashed Chowdhury's *Chandrabati Kotha* (2019) Mostofa Sarwar Farooki's No Land's Man (2021), Amitabh Reza's Rickshaw Girl (2021) and Rezwan Shahriar Sumit's The Salt in Our Waters (2021) are a few more contributory titles in that developing process.

Rubaiyat Hossain's *Made in Bangladesh* (2019) was a good addition to that process. The protagonist, a female RMG factory worker, despite management's disapproval, struggles to form a union in the factory for workers' rights, safe factory conditions and improved wages. The film was premiered in Toronto International Film Festival and was released in France, Portugal and Denmark. Criterion Collection included *Made in Bangladesh* in the lists of the 'hidden gems' of the decade 2010s.[4]

Abdullah Mohammad Saad's second film *Rehana Maryam Noor* (RMN, 2021) gets nomination in 'Un Certain Regard' category at Cannes Film Festival which is the first film of Bangladesh that got official selection in this major film festival. The film is about the struggling life of a 37-year-old assistant professor at a medical college who stands by a student who is sexually assaulted by a male professor. The film was internationally distributed by German-based sales and distribution company Films Boutique and produced by a Singapore-based producer. RMN's success has created a buzz among the independent filmmakers in Bangladesh.

During the global Covid-19 pandemic, Over The Top (OTT) platforms were established as alternative places for making and distributing films and web series. Bangladeshi independent films are not regular yet in the global platforms like Netflix or Amazon Prime. But the local platform Chorki arrived in 2021 and already have produced a few significant films and web series. Robiul Alam Robi's anthology series *Unoloukik* (2021) was the best production by Chorki. All five episodes of the mystery series were dark in nature and stunning in film aesthetics. However, before Chorki's arrival, Bangladeshi filmmakers started creating spaces in Indian OTTs. Indian Bengali OTT, Hoichoi started uploading recent Bangladeshi films already made and began producing Bangladeshi web series. Amitabh Reza's *Dhaka Metro* (2019), Syed Ahmed Shawki's *Taqdeer* (2020) and Ashfaq Nipun's *Mohanagar* (2021) are considered as some of the top-rated series from the Kolkata based platform Hoichoi. Mostofa Sarwar Farooki's *Ladies and Gentlemen* (2021) is also a significant series at the all-India platform Zee5. Mohammad Touqir Islam's web series *Shaaticup* (2022) was a surprise in the cine-scenario of Bangladesh which was independently produced in the northern city of Rajshahi with an authentic and raw style of a crime drama. The series was made distantly from the cine-center of Dhaka and later it was released on Chorki. Due to availaibility of Bangladeshi contents both in Indian and Bangladeshi OTT platforms, it is for the first time in the history, Indian spectators, especially the Bengalis located in West Bengal, India has started looking at Bangladeshi contents with surprise and amusement whereas the flow of content was largely one way – travelling from Kolkata and Mumbai, towards Bangladesh, both formally and informally.

In the other world, USA-based Bangladeshi engineer Nasif Bin Jafar won Scientific and Technical Academy Award in 2007 and 2015. He is credited for the development of 'fluid simulation' system in cinema which was first applied in *Pirates of the Caribbean: A World's End* (2007). His filmography includes several Hollywood productions such as *Madagascar 3: Europe's Most Wanted* (2012), *Kung Fu Panda 2* (2011), *Shrek Forever After* (2010), *The Croods* (2013) and so on. Also, Canada-based Wahid Ibne Reza was a member of OSCAR nominated visual effect team for *Guardian of Galaxy 2* (2017) and *Doctor Strange* (2016) and Spider-man: No Way Home (2021).

However, due to taking foreign fund and entering global distributing markets, a kind of self-censorship may occur among the makers and a trend of selecting the kind of story that might be liked by the financers. That might be flawed by representing own culture and society as an 'exotic commodity' to the western audience. Theorists (Chow, 1995; Raju, 2015) called it as 'oriental's orientalism', the idea was generated from the original works by Edward Said (1978). Rey Chow (1995) applied the idea for Chinese art cinema and Zakir Hossain Raju (2015) for Bangladeshi cinema. If we say *The Clay Bird* (which was released in 2002) was recognised as a 'cultural package' by the western audience from a 'Muslim filmmaker' just after the incident of 9/11 (that occurred in 2001), it might not be wrong, though the film was made before the incident. In many art house films made in Third World, 'poverty' was represented as a commodity for western audience. We have discussed this issue in Chapter 7 elaborately. The challenge is how an independent filmmaker can protect him/herself from this clout and create his/her space in global cinema at the same time.

Documentary in a Different Note

Documentary films in Bangladesh are largely produced by independent sector. However, many documentaries are commissioned by Non-government Organisations (NGOs), and a few are produced by television channels. Department of Film and Publications (DFP), a government department, produces many documentaries and news reels every year, but those are basically propaganda of the government and routine audiovisual productions with little creativity. The most important creative documentaries are initiated by independent filmmakers with a command on their films. The lists of creative documentary filmmakers include the following names – Tareque Masud, Tanvir Mokamel, Manzare Haseen Murad, Yasmin Kabir, Shaheen Dill-Riaz, Fouzia Khan, Shabnam Ferdousi, Kamar Ahmad Simon, Saiful Wadud Helal, Polash Rasul and so on. Among all, Tareque Masud's *Song of Freedom* (Muktir Gaan 1995) is the most influential film within Bangladesh and Shahin Dill-Riaz's *Iron Eaters* (Lohakhor 2007) and Kamar Ahmad Simon's *Are you Listening!* (Shunte Ki Pao! 2012) are most celebrated documentaries internationally. An NGO, Steps Towards Development established an Audio-Visual Centre and produced many documentaries largely on women rights issue. Society for Environment and Human Development (SEHD), another NGO, produced several environmental documentaries. 71 TV also produced a lot of documentaries. Some other NGOs occasionally produce documentaries based on their agenda from where some documentaries are made which carry creative values. *Home of Soot* (Kalighar 1999) is a documentary focusing on child labour.

Table 3.5 Selected documentaries

Title	Director
Song of Freedom (Muktir Gaan 1995)	Tareque Masud
The Unknown Bard (Achin Pakhi 1996)	Tanvir Mokammel
Rokeya (1996)	Manjare Haseen Murad
My Migrant Soul (Porobasi Mon Amar 2000)	Yasmin Kabir
Iron Eaters (Lohakhor 2007)	Shaheen Dill-Riaz
Are you Listening! (Shunte Ki Pao! 2012)	Kamar Ahmad Simon
Never Ending Story (Je Golper Shesh Nei 2014)	Fauzia Khan
Sacred Water (Jholmolia 2016)	Saiful Wadud Helal
Born Together (Jonmosathi 2017)	Shabnam Ferdousi
Blossoms from Ash (2019)	Noman Robin

78   Independent Cinema in Bangladesh

For documentary, due to the high number of productions, it is a bit difficult to discuss it historically; rather director-wise discussion might be easier to portray a picture of this arena. Some leading filmmakers (Tareque Masud and Tanvir Mokammel) have made documentary and feature film side by side, but some directors always made documentary, never tried for a feature film. Also, in documentary genre, a lot of filmmakers are females, which is very rare in feature film. In a patriarchal society, the feature film production climate is also patriarchal, but making documentary needs less crew members, less money and it gives the director much freedom on her film.

I have already discussed on *The Song of Freedom* in this chapter. However, Tareque Masud's *A Tale of Freedom* (Muktir Katha 1996, co-directed by Catherine Masud) tells us the story of the contribution of common people in the Liberation War, 1971 which was absent in *The Song of Freedom*. The film provides us the alternative historiography of Liberation War and tends to say it was a peoples' war as it explores the contributions of peasants, women and indigenous people in the war. Masud's *The Inner Strength* (Adam Surat 1989) is another significant documentary that focuses on S M Sultan, the great painter in Bangladesh and through following him Masud finds the peasants and their culture and philosophical thoughts are the inner strength of Bengal society.

Tanvir Mokammel made as many as 13 documentary films which depicted diverse unexplored subject matters that include garments workers (*Garments Girls* [Bostrobalikara 2007]), indigenous people (*Teardrops of Karnaphuli* [Karnaphulir Kanna 2005]), Baul philosophy (*The Unknown Bard* [AchinPakhi 1996]), Bihari – the stranded Pakistanis (*The promised Land* [Swapnabhumi 2007]) and also his favourite subject Liberation War of Bangladesh (*1971* [2011], *Tajuddin Ahmad: An Unsung Hero* [Tajuddin Ahmad: Nishshongo Sarothi [2007]).

Manjare Haseen Murad's *Rokeya* (1996) is based on the reformist and the writer Begum Rokeya who contributed a lot for educating Muslim women in the British Bengal. The feminist write is always an inspiration for women in Bangladesh even in the modern time. Murad is credited for leading the documentary filmmaking movement and inspiring young independent filmmakers to make documentary in Bangladesh. He established Bangladesh Documentary Council to work on different issues and aspects of documentary filmmaking in Bangladesh.

Yasmine Kabir made at least three significant documentaries which include *My Migrant Soul* (Porobasi Mon Amar 2000), *A Certain Liberation* (Shwadhinota 2003) and *The Last Rite* (Sheshkritya 2008). *My Migrant Soul* highlights the plight of the migrant workers and uses the story of one person to illustrate those of countless others. *A Certain Liberation* is a story of Gurudasi Mondol who gave herself up to madness during the Liberation War of Bangladesh, as she watched her entire family being killed by the collaborators of the occupying forces. *The Last Rite* is an allegorical portrayal of the agony of hard labour at the ship breaking yards in Chittagong. Unlike a traditional narrative, the film relies on its images and sounds to tell its story.

Berlin-based Bangladeshi director Shaheen Dill-Riaz's *Iron Eaters* (Lohakhor 2007) portrays the activities in the ship breaking yards and depicts workers' struggle in a hazardous yet low paid working environment. The film got prestigious German Grimme Award. Dill-riaz's ethnographic film *Sand and Water* (Jibon Jole Bele 2002) is a documentation of the life of *Chaura*s, the people who live in the *Char* (island) of a big river. Almost all his films have been released as feature-length documentaries in German movie theatres and most were broadcast on German national television as well. His other titles deal diverse subject matters – *Korankinder* (2009), *The Networker* (2011), *The Projectionist* (2012), *Bamboo Stories* (2019) and so on.

Fauzia Khan's *Never Ending Story* (Je Golper Shesh Nei 2014) deals with the sexuality of modern women in Dhaka with both expressive statements as well as metaphoric understatements. Women's subjectivity in the context of Bangladesh is evident in the documentaries of Fauzia Khan. *I Had Something to Say* (Amake Bolte Dao 2007) is another documentary by Khan that deals sexuality of adolescent girls.

Shabnam Ferdousi made nearly 20 documentaries among which *Spring of Desire* (Ichche Bosonto 2003) is made on the transgender community (locally known as *Hijra*) in Bangladesh. His latest film *Born Together* (Jonmosathi 2017) is a good addition to the documentary genre in Bangladesh where she embarked on a journey to learn the whereabouts and the struggles of her birth mates, who were born in the same hospital she was born, some of whom were the outcome of the ruthless rapes during the Liberation War.

Kamar Ahmad Simon's *Are You Listening!* (Shunte Ki Pao! 2012) feature-length observational documentary which is an ethnography of people in South-Western Bangladesh where defiant villagers were adapting to the situation after the area was severely hit by the cyclone Aila in 2009. His other documentary *Testimony of a Thread* (2015) explores the connecting worlds of hope and despair around the readymade garments industry in Bangladesh marked for man-made catastrophes like Savar Building Tragedy (2013), considered as the deadliest garment factory accident in history where more than one thousand garment workers died.

Ottawa based filmmaker Saiful Wadud Helal's *Sacred Water* (Jholmolia, 2016) emphasises on the need for rebuilding peoples' relationship with the nature, and questions how in the name of modernisation water crises are created in Bangladesh. His *The Heart of Bangladesh* (Bangladesher Ridoy 2014) narrates Shahbag Movement from a different perspective. Shahbag movement took place in February 2013 in the demand of the capital punishment of the war criminals.

Hilsha is the most favourite fish of the people of Ganges Delta and Polash Rasul's *A Tale of Hilsha* (Ilish Brittanto 2013) depicts the life cycle of the fish and the fishermen's views regarding their relationship with the fish.

According to the fishermen, the life of both Hilsha and fishermen is in frail condition.

Noman Robin's *Blossoms from Ash* (2019) tells the plights of Rohingya refugees from Myanmar living in the camps in South-eastern Bangladesh. The documentary chronicles the recent and previous history of a conflict that has gone on for centuries and the war crimes inflicted upon the Rohingya people. The camera follows three young refugee children, each of whom has lost everything due to the genocide and obliged to cross the border as they struggle to balance education, celebration and survival in a new unfavourable environment.

Some other names in documentary genre are Anwar Chowdhury, Bratto Amin, Farzana Boby, Humaira Bilkis and many more who have been making significant documentaries. However, making documentary is not an easy task in Bangladesh. Manjare Haseen Murad (2011) finds the perception of people towards documentary is a barrier:

> The problem of documentary film in Bangladesh is peoples' perceptions towards it. Documentary is not a strong genre in Bangladesh. The reason behind it, is the social perception of documentary. Everybody considers fiction film as only 'film form'. Documentary cannot provide entertainment; hence it is not commercially viable. That is why it is ignored.

Another problem lies in the distribution of the documentaries. Around the globe in most cases, television channels produce and broadcast documentaries. In Bangladesh, the channels are not interested in producing or even broadcasting independent documentaries. They have a tendency of broadcasting documentaries without paying the producer. Bangladesh has around 25 television channels but none of them has documentary production unit. Theatre based distribution for feature-length documentary is a very rare incident in Bangladesh. However, some positive signs are seen in the documentary arena. With the collaboration of international documentary networks Dhaka Doclab is established in the capital which is a platform for pitching and mentoring of documentary filmmakers in 2017. It was Nasiruddin Yousuf Bachchu's initiative to establish Dhaka Doclab which organises an annual event of pitching for South Asian documentary filmmakers which opened an avenue for local young and promising filmmakers as well. The organisation offers organising workshops, Master classes, seminars for documentary filmmakers through which the promising filmmakers get an opportunity to improve their project.

Government, Censorship and Independent Cinema

Since its inception, the Government of Bangladesh has shown a keen interest in the cinema for complex, social, cultural and political reasons despite its reluctance to invest in the industry. Over the years there have been innumerable calls for the government to establish a film school like the FTII in Pune and the independent sector has frequently sought government subsidies unsuccessfully. However, in recent time, government is providing grants for five full-length films and five short films. But often these grants are given to unsuitable candidates. Getting grants by lobbying in the political line-up has become a regular practice. In 2019, a writ petition was filed against government grants to films.[5] Nevertheless the Government of Bangladesh maintains a close eye on the machinations of the industry through three state institutions; Bangladesh government has three organisations related with film production and culture. They are BFDC, Bangladesh Film Censor Board (BFCB) and Bangladesh Film Archive (BFA). The government has recently established Bangladesh Cinema and Television Institute (BCTI) in 2013, but the institute is still struggling to be established as an ideal film school. These organisations answer to the Ministry of Information.

The BFDC is an autonomous studio and was established by the government in 1957 in the Pakistan era. It provides technological support to filmmakers by leasing its studios and equipment. The BFCB operates under the order no. 41, 1972 by the President, which is basically a modification of Film Censorship Act 1963, which emanated from the colonial Cinematographic Act, 1918 amended in 1920, and certifies all films for screening. The censorship act is a continuation of colonial censorship rules with some modifications. However, like India, if the board denies a certificate the film has little or no chance of success. BFA was established in 1978, with the function store prints, posters, photographs and other archival materials of films, organise workshops and short courses. It also publishes books relating to local film industry and provides grants to aspiring film scholars and authors.

The rationale for government interest in cinema is usually couched in terms of protection; it is the duty of the state to protect its citizens from harm and to maintain the moral values of the Bengal Muslim society and Bangladesh as a nation state. An aspect of censorship take very seriously by the cultural elite is the issue of vulgarity. Hindi cinema and its local derivatives are characterised as vulgar whereas classic Bengali culture is refined, and it is important to protect it from any taint of vulgarity through a mutually acceptable form of censorship. Local popular cinema is regarded as seriously tainted in two ways; through its direct appeal to the mass audience and complete focus on entertainment rather than elevated themes and its tendency to flout the censorship laws by inserting pornographic 'cut pieces' in already certificated films, a topic that Lotte Hoek (2013) has dealt in her book *Cutpieces: Celulloid Obscenity and Popular Cinema in Bangladesh*. She defined *cutpiece* as 'short strip of locally made uncertified celluloid containing sexual or violent imagery that appeared and disappeared abruptly from the reels of Bangladeshi action films' (Hoek, 2013: 1). The abrupt appearance and disappearance of the pieces come from the challenge of facing the censor board and local administrations hence she described this as 'unstable celluloid'. This was a trend in the mainstream industry especially in the early 2000s.

Every independent film must have a certificate from the BFCB before it may be released for screening. But it was not applicable for a video film. It was in the late 2000s when independent filmmaker like Morshedul Islam took an initiative to bring digital films under censorship so that the films could be released in theatres. This incident with its ambivalence, made a way to release digital video films in theatres, at the same time it shows an independent filmmaker's desire to be censored. However, the censor code in Bangladesh is a direct legacy of the colonial era. When cinema was introduced into British India the colonial masters had experience of the medium but instinctively feared its potential to appeal the 'illiterate masses'. Moreover, they thought they already had a satisfactory regulatory approach to the medium in the form of the Dramatic Performance Act, 1876, which was introduced to control the spread of nationalist messages through *jatra*s, a particular type of popular indigenous theatre that drew upon mythology and contemporary events in entertaining ways, which had mass appeal in Bengal. A protracted discussion took place between the central Government of India and the provincial governments on how best to control cinema. The British government became alarmed at the slow rate of progress in what they deemed a matter of the highest priority. The British had become the masters of propaganda in WWI and feared greatly the possibility that the Germans would match them, especially in India.

The discussion process uncovered several facts that alarmed the Government of India. Various provincial governments reported incidents of expressing anti-British feelings and significantly, making comments about European women during screenings. The result of all of this was the proclamation of the Indian Cinematographic Act (ICA) of 1918, which drew directly on the British censorship board. A central feature of the act was the creation of a central censorship board. However, in the post-war process of devolution film censorship became a provincial matter in the amended ICA of 1920 although controlled by a British minister in the provincial government. Initially, local boards of film censors were established in Bombay, Calcutta, Madras and Rangoon (Burma was part of the Indian Empire until 1937) followed by Lahore in 1922.

The new state of Bangladesh inherited the colonial approach to censorship and has applied it ever since with some modifications reflecting local sensitivities. Director Tanvir Mokammel (2013) says, though the Raj days have long been fossilised into memory, yet whether the Film Rules of 1972, the Film Rules of 1977 or the New Codes introduced in 1985, all these prevailing censor codes of Bangladesh are as anti-democratic as the rules of the British days and brazenly exclude colonial legacy. He had to go to the high court to obtain release order *The Name of the River Madhumati* (1995).

Independent filmmakers see the role of BFCB in an unfavourable light and sometimes the board appears to be their principal opponent as its activities have a negative impact on the success of films. Director Abu Sayeed (2006) argues that, instead of creating a cine-friendly environment, the government creates many constraints (such as) through the BFCB.

Morshedul Islam (2006) pointed out, that almost all independent films face problems with censorship and they were treated unfavourably by the BFCB. In particular, he referred to two aspects of independent filmmaking that the Board frequently had expressed their observations – the depiction of the Liberation War and social issues such as poverty, gender and the treatment of indigenous people.

The subject of many independent films is the Liberation War and the forces that opposed the separation of Bangladesh from Pakistan. The subject itself and portrayal of Islamist people in these films as villains (*Rajakar*s) created an uneasy situation for the pro-Islam governments such as the Bengal National Party (BNP) and its Jamaat-e-Islami allies in the 1990s and in early 2000s. Tareque Masud (2006) raises the question:

> What can you do when the Censor Board is formed with only ruling party people? This is more dangerous than Islamizing it. If you keep something which goes against their party, it would be shown as anti-Islam or anti state. If the political control and marshaling will be there, these problems will be there.

Morshedul Islam (2006), an ex-member of BFCB, thinks the policies and censor rules remain the same in every government; what matters is who applies these rules. For that, the respective government's approach may appear as peculiar. He referred to his experience with his first film *Towards*. Its release was held up by the Censor Board for several months in 1983 because they were uncertain how to interpret its message. The same government nominated it for a film festival in India in 1984. Not only that, he was given some money to transfer the film from 16 mm to 35 mm format and to sub-title the film for submission to the festival.

Tareque Masud (2007) believes in a censor-free film environment. He says, I am against the existence of any Censor Board and in favour of grading system for films. By which he means a system like that found in many countries where films are classified according to their audience, that is 'G' for General release and 'R' for restricted release. This point is vital because in a sense the early history of filmmaking in the world was pro-censorship. However, since the 1960s, most Western countries have liberalised their censorship systems and Masud would like to see Bangladesh follow suit the demand for gradation, that is films be given a rating before release, is an old discourse but the government declined to respond for complex reasons, at the heart of which is ongoing issue religious sensitivity.

According to Susan Hayward (2006), censorship tends to be imposed in three main areas: sex, violence and politics. Religion adds an additional layer of concern in Bangladesh and, is probably the most significant dimensions of censorship in the country. No government can allow a film that may offend Islamists, or for that matter the ordinary viewer. Thus, censorship is enmeshed directly in the secular/religion divide that has been central to the debates how Muslim identity is determined in Bangladesh. Outside of the country the first two have been the primary concern to groups lobbying for the welfare of minors; the third has been the concern of state institutions and governments almost universally. In Bangladesh, mainstream films representing graphic sex and violence got certificates through bribery, or other illegal ways (See Nasreen and Haq 2008), but it is the political and religious elements in the independent films that have always been found 'sensitive' by the Bangladeshi board.

Independent film has had very little interaction with the BFDC, both from choice and for technological reasons as they initially focused on out-of-studio productions shot in 16 mm. Independent filmmakers were very snobbish about studio productions and studio environment as they regarded the films produced under the BDFC banner as inferior and in bad taste. But lately many independent films have been shot in 35 mm and digital format, which has meant a developing a relationship borrowing cameras with the BFDC and the approach of independent makers is changing regarding the government established studio. The artistic success of independent films and gross decline of the commercial industry cinema have changed the approach of mainstream makers as well towards independent films. The gulf between the two tents has lessened in contemporary times.

The government has played a very nominal role in developing infrastructure in the BFDC or in developing some modern theatres. The films of independent directors, considering its global potential, are made in advanced technologies. But there are very few supports for that. Independent filmmakers, in most of the cases, rush to India for post-production jobs of the film. The film they make in better technology cannot be shown in most of theatres in the country due to their old exhibition system and bad theatrical environment. The government could take steps in establishing multiplexes in major towns of the country with the latest digital exhibition system. The government could not develop any internationally recognised film festival so far. However, the government has declared cinema as an industry, and they are working on finalising a film policy. But the freedom of expression situation under the recent AL led government is dissatisfactory. The government led by Sheikh Hasina has become authoritarian in recent time. A sense of fear is driving everybody. Arrest, abduction, killing are very much prevalent. Surveillance and censorship are regular weapons of the government. At the end of January 2018, a German organisation Bertelsmann Stiftung reports, Bangladesh is among five countries where minimum standard of democracy is absent. Along with Lebanon,

Mozambique, Nicaragua and Uganda, Bangladesh is among new five autocratic countries where democracy has been gradually undermined for years.[6] Also, the condition of freedom of speech is gradually decreasing here. Bangladesh ranked 151st in the annual World Press Freedom Index 2020 report published by Reporters Without Borders.[7] In this situation a filmmaker cannot choose a script that would be translated in an expensive media with scepticism of not getting a certificate. So self-censorship is prevalent among the filmmakers. Nasiruddin Yousuf Bachchu could make the film *Alpha* (2019) on extra-judicial killing perhaps due to his good relationship with the government. But Mostofa Sarwar Farooki's film *Saturday Afternoon* yet to get a certificate which dealt with the infamous Holey Artisan Bakery terrorist attack that took place in 2016. In a totalitarian sociopolitical environment, a director cannot make film independently. Haq (forthcoming, 2022) shows how existing censor codes limits the creative freedom of the filmmakers which is added with DSA 2018 and Bangladesh Film Certification Act 2019 (draft).

Notes

1 *Song of Freedom* did not have any international exposure but later it got international attention which came along with *The Clay Bird* (2002). After the success of *The Clay Bird*, *Song of Freedom* was released in England and Ireland.
2 Habib Khan is considered as the most prominent individual producer of art films. He produces films of Kolkata based Bengali filmmakers as well as some prominent joint productions of India and Bangladesh such as *The Name of a River* (Titas Ekti Nadir Naam 1973) by Ritwik Ghatak and *The Fisherman of the River Padma* (Padma Nadir Majhi 1993) by Goutam Ghosh.
3 *Song of Freedom* was released in 1995 and Tareque Masud and Catherine Masud were busy with distribution and exhibition of the film in following 4/5 years. In 1999 they submitted the script of *The Clay Bird* for South Fund of French Government.
4 See 'Hidden Gems of the 2010s' at https://www.criterion.com/current/posts/6738-hidden-gems-of-the-2010s. Accessed 5 June 2020.
5 *New Age* reports on 25 July 2019 a writ petition was filed with the High Court seeking postponement of the government's grant announced for 14 films in the fiscal 2018–19 amid massive irregularities and violation of policies. See 'Write Petition Filed Against the Govt's Grant to Films' at http://www.newagebd.net/article/79524/writ-petition-filed-against-govts-grant-to-films. Accessed 11 November 2019.
6 See 'Bangladesh Listed as New 'Autocracy'' at https://en.prothomalo.com/bangladesh/Bangladesh-listed-as-new-%E2%80%9Cautocracy%E2%80%9D. Accessed 31 May 2020.
7 See 'Tougher Politics, More Press Freedom Violations' at https://rsf.org/en/bangladesh. Accessed on 29 May 2020.

References

Allen, M. (2003). *Contemporary US Cinema*. Harlow: Longman.
Chow, R. (1995). *Primitive Passions: Visuality, Sexuality, Ethnography and Contemporary Chinese Cinema*. New York: Columbia University Press.

Hayward, S. (2006). *Cinema Studies: The Key Concepts*. London: Routledge.
Haq, F. (forthcoming 2022). Making Cinema Under Authoritarian Codes. In A. E. Ruud and M. Hasan (eds.), *Masks of Authoritarianism* (pp. 57–71). Singapore: Palgrave Macmillan.
Hoek, L. (2013). *Cutpieces: Celluloid Obscenity and Popular Cinema in Bangladesh*. New York: Columbia University Press.
Islam, M. (2006). Interview conducted by the author on 10 December 2006.
Levy, E. (1999). *Cinema of Outsiders: The Rise of American Independent Films*. New York: New York University Press.
Masud, T. (2006). Interview conducted by the author on 13 December 2006.
Mokammel, T. (2007). Interview conducted by the author on 26 April 2007.
Mokammel, T. (2013). Problematics of Alternative Cinema in Bangladesh: An Introspection. In N. A. Atique (ed.), *From the Heart of Bangladesh*. Dhaka: Bangladesh Short Film Forum, pp. not numbered.
Murad, M. H. (2006). Alternative Films of Bangladesh: Present and Future' (Bangladesher Cholochchitrer Bikolpodhara: Bortoman O Vobishshot), *Prokkhepon*. In F. Haq and S. Moon (eds.), *The Age of Film: The Film of the Age* (Cholochchitrer Somoy: Somoyer Cholochchitro) (pp. 30–39). Dhaka: Oitijyo.
Murad, M. H. (2011). Interview conducted by the author on 21 September 2011.
Nasreen, G. & Haq, F. (2008). *Film Industry of Bangladesh: Popular Culture in Crisis* (Bangladesher Cholochchitro Shilpo: Songkote Jonosongskriti). Dhaka: Shrabon.
Raju, Z. H. (2015). *Bangladesh Cinema and National Identity: In Search of the Modern?* London: Routledge.
Said, E. (1978). *Orientalism*. New York: Pantheon Books.
Sayeed, A. (2006). Interview conducted by the author on 15 November 2006.

4 Textual Analysis: Foundational Films

We have divided 10 selected films into three categories (foundational films, transitional films and contemporary films) and textual analysis of those films is organised according to that categorisation. As we mentioned in Chapter 1, this categorisation will help us to understand the broader aspects of the depiction of identity through cinema by independent filmmakers. For writing the analysis, we will follow the 'film narratology' model that is derived from Gerard Genette's (1980) notion of *Narrative Discourse*.

All three foundational films are based on the rural life of Bangladesh. Though only one film, among three, deals with the Liberation War, many other foundational independent films, which are not selected here, depict the grand narrative of the Liberation War. This grand narrative is developed according to the historiography built by the dominant middle class – the aggression and brutality of the Pakistani military, women as the primary victims, the heroism of the resistant *Mukti Bahini* (liberation army) and war crimes done by the local Islamists who collaborated with the Pakistani military. We have included *Dollhouse* by Morshedul Islam for analysis from this grand narrative, but there are many other films made by Tanvir Mokammel (*The River Named Madhumati* [Nadir Naam Madhumati 1995]), Morshedul Islam (*Towards* [Agami 1984]), Nasiruddin Yousuf (*Guerilla* 2011) and others that can be classified similarly.

The foundational films also look at the Muslim identity of Bengalis. If it is a film about the Liberation War, the collaborators (*Rajakar*s) will essentially have a Muslim archetype – an oldish man with beard on his face and *Tupi* on his head, committing all types of war crimes. If it is not a film about Liberation War, the Muslim is portrayed as a bigot, affects and victimises the lives of all other people – women and the defiant as well as weak men. We have analysed *A Tree Without Roots* by Tanvir Mokammel as a representative film of that kind. The foundational films also portray rural Bengal – the simple peasants and the exploitative feudal system they live under. They show festivity and rich cultural forms as well as a poverty-ridden people on the verge of extinction. *Kittonkhola* is analysed in this chapter as that type of a narrative.

DOI: 10.4324/9781003271093-5

Kittonkhola: Struggle with Identity in the Rural Bengal

Based on a play by eminent playwright Selim Al Deen, *Kittonkhola* (2000) is essentially a tale of the transformation of low-status people who are facing struggle of identity – the struggle ranges from the ethnicity to religiosity. Within a limited and short spatial and temporal situation in a village fair in the bank of the river Kittonkhola the story portrays a larger picture of Bengal society in which struggle and exploitation of ordinary people, the transformation of ethnicity and of extinct professions, the afflicted traditional theatre troupes and the mystic philosophy of popular religion have been captured through the camera lens. The film received National Film Awards in nine categories including the best film and best director in 2000.

It is the first feature film directed by Abu Sayeed which was shot in 16 mm format. The primary distribution of the film was non-theatrical, but later it was transferred in 35 mm and got a theatrical release. The film was jointly produced by Impress Telefilm and Aangik Communications.

Selim Al Deen was considered one of the best playwrights of post-Tagore Bengali literature. Most of his plays were produced by Dhaka Theatre, a leading theatre group in Bangladesh. His plays have been translated into English and Swedish. The major contribution of Selim Al Deen to Bengali theatrical performance is that he has tried to reestablish the ancient and medieval Indian/Bengali theatrical forms in contemporary group productions in Bangladesh with an epic approach. Other than *Kittonkhola*, his play *The Wheel* (Chaka, 1993) has been adapted to celluloid by another independent filmmaker, Morshedul Islam. The play *Kittonkhola* was written in 1978–80 and was later produced by Dhaka Theatre in 1981 (Zakaria, 2008) under the direction of Nasiruddin Yousuf. It has been considered as one of the best productions of Dhaka Theatre. But the distinctiveness of *Kittonkhola* is that it was from this play that Selim Ali Deen developed his unique style of playwriting. Selim Al Deen himself (Deen, 2006) and critics like Arun Sen (2008) thought it in the same way. The early works of Selim were influenced by Western forms of theatre and were metaphorical and satiric. Despite being successful in those plays, he explored local and indigenous forms of theatrical elements on an epic canvas that basically tell the tales of peripheral people and the traditional culture of Bengal.

Histoire

There was a village fair on the bank of the river Kittonkhola. Vendors have brought different kinds of products for their temporary shops. The girls from the gypsy tribe *Bedey* have anchored their fleet of boats near the fair to sell items like bangles, ribbons and offers of herbal medicines. The main attraction of the fair is a *jatra* troupe 'Adi Mahua Opera'. Gambling and local narcotics were brought as the part of the fair. Idu Contractor, the richest and most powerful man of the village, was the organiser and owner of the fair. The story of ordinary people from different professions and backgrounds evolves through mutual contacts and conflicts among the organisers, participants and visitors.

On the other hand, Idu Contractor wants Banasreebala, the actress of the *jatra* troupe in his bed. The owner of the troupe, Subal Das agrees with Idu to send Banasreebala, who has joined the troupe from a brothel for a better life. He threatens Banasree if she does not do as dictated the troupe will split up which means that Banasree will have to go back to brothel. The actor, Rabi Das, protests against this and asks Subal not to send Banasree to Idu. Chhaya is another *jatra* troupe member who was an orphan, picked up by Subalwhen he was a child. He has been sexually abused by Subal himself. Shattered by his life, Chhaya wants to forget everything by drinking alcohol and taking narcotics. Both the actors love Banasreebala and the actress also dreams to settle in a family. But an actress with brothel and *jatra* background has no way to find a better life. She commits suicide after failing to live an honoured and dignified life because of Idu's lust and Subal's consent.

Meanwhile, a simple villager, Sonai, is roaming in the fair when he falls in love with one of the Bedey, Dalimon. However, his love life is unhappy as well, because of the rigid caste system maintained by Bedey leaders. Sonai also loses all his money and lands by gambling according to the plan of Idu who wants Sonai's mortgaged lands.

A critical situation of misery and despair rises for every oppressed character who, in turn, wants to transform his or her identity and profession. *Jatra* troupe member Chhaya, who is Hindu in religion, wants to convert to join the majority Muslims so that he has better subsistence. A *Bedey* youth Rustam, who also loves Dalimon, want to leave his boat-life for a better life. Sonai's friend, the oil-seed grinder, Bashir, wants to crush his grinding machine because it does not provide enough support for him to survive. However, Dalimon is the only person in this story who does not want to change her identity as she wants to uphold her caste.

Recit

The film *Kittonkhola* conveys the message that ordinary people of Bengal struggle and try to survive. It describes how they are exploited by the powerful and how they struggle with their cultural tradition and their fatal attraction to tradition. The film also portrays the patterns of womanhood in traditional Bengal society. The film uniquely depicts why and how the people are engaged in the process of transforming their identity.

A Tale of the Transformation of Identity

Kittonkhola is basically a tale of the transformation of ordinary people whose existence is constantly threatened by the miseries of life. The playwright Selim Al Deen says, we have identified transformation as the

Figure 4.1 Rabi Das (Jayanta Chattopadhyay), Banasreebala (Naila Azad Nupur) and Subal (Mamunur Rashid) in the green room of the *Jatra* stage.

all-encompassing entities of traditional Bengal. This transformation is the change in identity and sometimes in the profession. The struggle in life compels people to change ethnicity and religion even. The life of Sonai goes through a lot of transformations (Deen, 2006: 352).

At the fair, while drinking local wine Sonai sings a song: 'Guru, I wish to go to *Shantipur* (the land of peace)'. Rustam, a youth from the *Bedey* caste, says, 'There's a tiger in *Shantipur*. Better get drunk and go for *Dukhaipur* (the land of sorrow)'. Rustam wants to leave his 'ill-fated' gypsy life to go to *Dukhaipur*, although he knows it is a land of sorrow. Yet he wants to settle in a land instead of roaming for his whole life in a boat. He is ready to alter his ethnic identity by any means. He wants the *Bedey* girl Dalimon with him, but Dalimon refuses to change her identity. All members of the *jatra* troupe are Hindus who are minorities in Bangladesh. Among them, Chhaya Ranjan has a lot of miseries in life. So, he sometimes thinks of changing his religion and he wants to migrate to Kolkata. This is to note here, since 1947, minority Hindu people of Bangladesh have been migrating to Kolkata or other parts of India, and this migration process is continuing now, although at a slower pace. The film ends with an open-ended scene where Sonai, Rustam, Chhaya, and Bashir – talk about their uncertain future. In that scene, Bashir, who grinds oilseed by profession wishes to torch the oil-grinding machine. He also said that he would request the King of Djinn to transform him into a stone, because he had no cattle to grind oilseed.

The central theme of continuous transformation process has been enhanced by a *Panchali* song. The *Panchali* is a local play form that is a combination of some other genres: song, music, extempore versifying, poetic contests and dance which is also a repeated theme song of the film:

> Oh my mad horse
>
> You ride men from place to place…

Other than ethnic identity, the film depicts the popular religious practices of ordinary people. Mystic songs are sung by mystic characters like *bayati* and *palakar*. The *jatra* performance from Mangalakavya is represented in such a way in the film that proves its ties to the popular religion. Just before Banasreebala's suicide, she recites some verses from *Manasamangala,* a story of the contest between Behula and Manasa. Manasa is a non-Aryan deity, who is worshipped by non-Aryan people of East Bengal. Banasreebala prefers to perform the character of Manasa Devi instead of virgin Behula. The traditional popular religious elements provide entertainment as well as thoughts, philosophy or mental food for ordinary people during the Kittonkhola fair.

In the film *Kittonkhola*, a large range of traditional cultural elements is portrayed in a relatively small space and time in the village fair. The cultural routes explored include *jatra*, *panchali* song, Baul song and fairy tales that prove the rich cultural patterns of traditional Bengal. The essential elements of the fair – the colourful masks, bioscope play, clay toys, balloons, garments, ornaments, local wine – all attract village people. If poor villagers do not have money, merely visiting the festive fair is a charming experience. Sonai did not have enough money to buy anything from the fair, but since childhood, the fair has always been an intense attraction to him.

Portrayal of the Power Structure of Peripheral Bengal

Idu contractor is one of the most powerful men in the human settlement on both sides of river Kittonkhola. Other than his contracting business, he is also a landlord who wants to snatch land from simple and poor people like Sonai. As Sonai refuses to give up the land permanently, Idu did not hesitate to prepare a blueprint for stealing it from Sonai. Idu is the organiser of the fair and the profits from the fair will go into his account. His power enables him to think of a way to get Banasreebala into his bed. He has forged connection with Shafiq Chairman, the head of the local government, to enhance his power. Idu has money, land and connections with other powerful people. Thus, this story illustrates the situation in which a very few powerful figures exploit the majority of people in the peasant society of Bengal who are poor and landless.

Bazlul Mobin Chowdhury (2004) classifies the post-colonial peasants of rural society in Bangladesh as *Jotedar*s (landowner), rich peasants, upper-middle-class peasants, lower-middle-class peasants, poor peasants and landless workers. In the film *Kittonkhola*, Idu represents the rich peasant category and Sonai as the poor peasant who will soon be landless because of Idu's application of power. Idu is not a *Jotedar*, the top peasant category, because it indicates to a family tradition. Idu has no such background; he survived by working in a rich peasant's house and later became a rich peasant himself.

Behula or Manasa: Feminine Dichotomy

The name of the mythical character Manasa was mentioned several times in the film. The *jatra* troupe has a popular production, *Pala of Lakhindar*, which is the other name of *Manasamangala*, in which Lakhindar's wife Behula shows her love and devotion to her husband, who has been bitten by a snake. The film introduces a critical reference when Banasreebala prefers the character Manasa (the name given to the curse of Devi of the snakes), but Subal Das asked her to perform as virgin Behula. In other words, a feminine dichotomy has been placed in the film.

The story of *Manasamangal* begins with the conflict of a merchant Chand Sadagar with Manasa. Chand is a worshipper of Shiva, but Manasa hopes that she can win over Chand to her worship. But, far from worshipping her, Chand refuses to even recognise her as a deity. Manasa takes revenge upon Chand by destroying seven of his ships at the sea and killing his seven sons. Finally, Behula the newly wed wife of Chand's youngest son Lakhindar makes the goddess bow to her love for her husband through her strength of character, limitless courage and deep devotion. Behula succeeds in bringing Chand's seven sons back to life by rescuing their ships. After that, Behula returns home and Chand becomes an ardent devotee of Manasa.

According to Dulal Bhowmik's (2004) analysis, *Manasamangal* is basically a tale of oppressed humanity. Chand and Behula have been portrayed as two strong and determined characters at a time when ordinary human beings were subjugated and humiliated. The conflict between human beings and the goddess brings out the social discriminations of society, as well as the conflict between Aryans and non-Aryans. Shiva, whom Chand worshipped, was probably originally not an Aryan god, but over time was elevated to that position. Manasa's victory over Chand suggests the victory of the indigenous or non-Aryan deity over the Aryan god. However, even Manasa is defeated by Behula. The verses not only suggest the victory of the non-Aryan deity over the Aryan god, but also the victory of the human spirit over a powerful goddess. *Manasamangal* is also remarkable for its portrayal of Behula who epitomises the best of Bengali womanhood, especially the Bengali woman's devotion to her husband.

In a scene, while the *jatra* show was running, Rabi Das asked Banasree not to perform at night in front of Subal in protest against being forced to satisfy Idu's lust. In reply, she says, 'We aren't chaste like Sita or Behula. Even if we were, nobody would treat us so'. In another scene when

Chhayaranjan asked Banasree whether she loved him or not, Banasree replied, 'It's no good to love me Chhaya. I'm like Manasa. She was born destitute. Her wedding night was disastrous too'. Banasree believes she is powerless and not only has to please Idu's lust but has no right to love Rabi or Chhaya. The irony is that the same society that produced Behula (the icon of ideal Bengali womanhood) also produced destitute like Banasree.

Narration

While adapting *Kittonkhola* into film, the director had tried to 'keep the integrity of the original work' (Beja, 1979). The changes he made in the text shortened the storyline and introduced a slight change at the end of the story. The director Abu Sayeed (2006) claimed that Selim Al Deen liked the ending of the film even after these modifications. He especially liked the use of the theme song – 'Oh my mad horse, you ride men from place to place'. Through the theme song, the main premise of the play has been achieved.

There is no distinct major character in the film. Rather it can be said that there are several major characters in the film. Sonai, Banasree, Chhayaranjan, Dalimon, Rustam, Rabi Das and Subal – all of them face agony, struggles and limitations. Their misery has been increased by Idu, who is the principal villain of the film. But the playwright Selim Al Deen says:

> Idu can be said a villain in the traditional way of tagging a character, but he is not like that.... He gets the reason of victim and victimiser in this culture. Untimely draught, storm, and rain give him the eternal power to exploit.... I have tried to build the character in a classical form. There is a classical form of exploitation in our culture.
> (Deen, 2006: 337)

Within the 'classical form of exploitation', Idu can find the justification for his criminal acts through the background of his hardships in early life. The suffering and hardship in the early life had made Idu ruthless, merciless and cruel.

Critics noted that the vibrancy of the village fair was not felt in the film. More wide-angle shots or crane or tracking shots could have made the film livelier and the indigenous theatrical forms could have been better be merged in the film. The cinematographer at best chose some good camera angles, i.e. when Sonai and Dalimon were talking in the fair, the low angle camera includes the moving merry-go-round in the background. One excellent shot was when Dalimon and Rustam were talking in the daytime in the boat: there is a quiet stream in the background, and a dam in the other bank of the river with fair-people walking on the dam, but these are only seen through the reflection in the river. Thus, some intelligent frame compositions enriched the language of the film. However, there was a lot of opportunities to create some in depth shots, because the fair is situated near a wide river that goes out to the horizon of the sky. But the opportunity was not fulfilled, as the film was shot in 16 mm. If it had been shot in 35 mm and for widescreen, with better depth of field, the film would have been even more magnificent.

The film ends with a good open-ended shot in which Sonai, Chhaya, Rustam and Basir were sitting next to each other, and the camera pans from one character to another, as they were sharing their uncertainties of the future. In the play Sonai killed Idu, but after losing everything he does not know what is going to happen next. By bringing the characters together at the finale, the film created a much stronger ending.

Abu Sayeed emerged as an *auteur* in the film – he has directed, co-written the screen play and the dialogues, and also composed background music. He was completely dependent on musical scores from *jatra* Although the instruments made the musical scores easier for him, it lacked creativity. However, local dialects in the dialogues e made the story seem natural and trustworthy.

The climax of the story was found at the ending of the film when Sonai lost his money and assets in the gambling and when Banasree committed suicide. But these climaxes have been arranged in some beautiful conflicting scenes. Banasree's suicidal scene was too long and slow, but just after the suicide the charismatic and meaningful theme song 'Oh my mad horse...' was performed. This scene is followed by the heartbreaking scene of burning the dead body at the bank of the river. Subal did not want to continue *jatra* that night but Idu disagrees. The cremation scene was followed by some *jatra* dancers on the stage who sings an old Hindi song with enthusiastic dance movements. For the first time, the audiences including Idu have become frantic to see the dance. Banasree's tragic death does not stop anything, life goes on. Only in the last scene, Chhaya says, 'Banasree is no more, yet the *jatra* will go on...' The arrangement of these conflicting scenes reveals the competent editing technique of Sujan Mahmud.

A Tree Without Roots: Portrayal of Muslimness of a Peasant Society

The film *A Tree Without Roots* deals with religion and its impact on Bengali-Muslim peasant society. Although the film does not deal with political identity directly, it portrays the social identity of rural Bangladesh, and especially how Muslimness worked in that society.

In a remote agrarian village, a haggard-looking Mullah named Majid appears suddenly. He cleans up an old dilapidated grave, declares it to be the shrine of a famous *Pir* (saint) and begins to worship it. The shrine, over the years, provides Majid not only economic solvency but psychological domination over the community as well. He marries Rahima, an obedient and hard-working peasant woman. Childless with Rahima and because of his polygamous sexual desire, he marries Jamila, a teenager who will revolt at the end of the film against Majid.

The film received eight Bangladesh National Film Awards including Best Film and Best Director in 2001. The film also received special mention in the 1st International Film Festival, 2003, Dhaka and was shown in London (UK), Rotterdam (the Netherlands), Montreal (Canada), Quebec (Canada), Cinenouvo (Belgium), Jeonju (South Korea), Fukuoka (Japan) and Delhi (India) International Film Festivals. The film is considered one of the best creations by independent filmmaker Tanvir Mokammel.

Before making *A Tree Without Roots*, the director Tanvir Mokammel studied the novels of Syed Waliullah and published the book *Syed Waliullah: Sisifas and the Question of Heritage in Novel* (Mokammel, 2000) in which he emphasises discussions of the novel *Lalsalu* on which the film was based.

Lalsalu and Syed Waliullah

The novel *Lalsalu* was published in 1948 by Comrade Publishers, Dhaka by the writer himself. The response to the first edition of the novel was very poor, but later it became one of the most widely received Bangla novels. The book has been in the syllabus of higher secondary schools for many years.

Syed Waliullah was born in Chittagong in 1922. A radio news broadcaster turned diplomat, Waliullah ended his career in UNESCO, Paris and died there in 1971. He wrote four novels, two books of short stories, and three plays. Among all his creations *Lalsalu* became most famous and internationally acclaimed. The novel was first translated into French and later into English. The title of the French version *L'Arbre Sans Racines* was published by Editions Du Seuli of Paris in 1961 – the blurb of the English version claims, it was the first Pakistani novel to be translated in French. In 1967, the novel was translated into English from London by Chatto and Windus Ltd and UNESCO jointly entitled *Tree Without Roots*. It was also translated into Urdu, Czech, and German (Amin, 2003). Recently, the book has been translated to Japanese also (The Daily *Prothom Alo* 2008). The author was conferred the Bangla Academy Award for this novel.

Histoire

A remote place named Mahabbatnagar is a comparatively solvent village peasant. Suddenly a stranger appears, who seems to be a Mullah and is named Majid. He came from the part of the country where there was scarcity of food and job and where 'little food means more religion' (Waliullah, 1967). Majid's Koranic school background could only be used in mosques and tutoring Koranic lessons, which does not make him fit for the modern job market.

After arriving as a stranger in the village, he cleans up an old dilapidated grave and declares it as the *majar* of a Muslim saint named Modasser Pir and begins to worship it. The villagers, of course, have no clue who the saint was, and driven by religious beliefs, started believing in the myth. An aura of religiosity was created by the mystery of the grave, the red fabric (*Lalsalu*) spread over its oval shape, the glowing candles and the Koranic chants that Majid recites beside the grave. The simple peasants completely surrender to Majid's dramatic activities. They start to bring rice, vegetables, chickens, goats and money as offerings to the 'holy shrine'. The shrine, over the years, provides Majid economic solvency. It gave him psychological domination over the community as well. From entering the village as a stranger, he became a man well rooted in society.

The shrine covered by *Lalsalu* becomes a symbol of fear, power and unquestioning respect. As a worshipper and caretaker of the shrine, Majid himself started enjoying power, money and respect from the ordinary villagers. The feudal lord of the village, Khaleque, joined with Majid as both of them wanted to apply power and fear among people from different aspects. Empowered by the *majar*, Majid punishes everyone who was disrespectful to him, even Khaleque's wife. Majid feels insecure when a live saint, with so-called heavenly power, comes to a neighbouring village and people started rushing after him. He was able to agitate the villagers of Mahabbatnagar and send them to fight with the followers of the saint.

He marries Rahima, a hard-working peasant woman with a robust body who becomes a submissive wife. But Majid was never honest with Rahima. He became sexually aroused by gazing at his housemaid, 'mother of Hasuni'. And then takes the second wife, a teenager named Jamila. But soon it was discovered that Jamila has no fear either of either Majid or the *majar*. She refuses to follow every order Majid imposed. Jamila, inadvertently, becomes Majid's nemesis. Jamila's denials make Majid powerless and vulnerable. A flood and storm finally strike the *majar* and the power structure built by Majid.

Recit

The film *A Tree Without Roots* deals with Muslimness, which is the major *recit* of the text. Muslimness represented in the film delineates the role of religion in agrarian Bangladesh – how religion makes people fatalistic, how fear is created among people through the means of religion, and how ordinary people can be cheated by the promoters of religion. The film also portrays the status of women in rural Bengal. Above all, it is a story of Majid, a fraudulent and cunning person who uses religion for his economic solvency and own establishment in the society.

A Fatalistic Society

In *A Tree Without Roots*, peasants in the village Mahabbatnagar have a highly fatalistic approach to live a life. The primary reason may be that

Figure 4.2 Majid (Raisul Islam Asad) in the shrine.

peasants depend on nature. The traditional agricultural system of Bengal – sowing seeds, irrigation and harvesting – fully depend on nature. Both draught and flood can harm the system and hence affect the village economy. Thunderstorms or hailstorms can destroy the crops while waiting for harvesting. This dependency on nature, in another sense, is dependent on religious beliefs and on God.

Majid heard about this old grave of Mahabbatnagar at *Garo Hill* from a forest officer whose ancestors were from this village although his family does not have any current connection with it. The dramatic appearance of Majid with the false story of a holy man's grave was entirely believable to the villagers. Even the village headman and feudal lord Khaleque uttered – 'What a shame! We don't even know!' – to himself after hearing such a story from a stranger. Subsequently, Majid started worshipping the *majar* along with the villagers. Because their hearts were weak and vulnerable, villagers started offering money, vegetables, chicken, goats according to their abilities at the *majar* in hopes of greater good fortune through the false *Pir*. After making their wishes, every incident, whether positive or negative, were considered to be messages from God. Being the caretaker of the *majar*, Majid got all the offerings and became not only solvent, but the most powerful person in the village.

Manufacturing Fear

In the name of Islam, Majid rules Mahabbatnagar through Islamic rituals; he discards diversified traditional or popular religious elements. Traditionally, villagers had followed rituals of Buddhist Tantrism and Hinduism, but Majid stopped everything and established a monolithic Islamic culture and ritual system. For that, he had to establish fear inside the villagers – fear of God, fear of death, fear of punishment in eternity, and above all, fear of the *majar*.

In the novel *Lalsalu*, the words 'fear' or 'related to fear' were used 70 times (Hossain 1982 cited in Awwal, 2007). In the film, it is seen Majid trying to establish fear in his wives, Rahima and Jamila, and the villagers. The concept of *gunah* (sin) helps him to do so. One must be punished in eternity if he or she commits *gunah* by not following Islamic rules. Therefore, he forbids Rahima from making any sound while walking and forbids her to stand in the open when her dress was wet after a bath and even at home. He forbids Jamila to laugh loudly – because the laugh of a Muslim woman should not be heard from outside. Majid rebukes Jamila in the film:

> It is not proper for a Muslim woman to be heard laughing. No one is to laugh that way in my house again.

He asks the village boys in a village court, 'Can you recite the holy scripture?' He orders, those who could not do the recitation, to come to his *maktab* (a non-formal Koranic class) and learn Islamic scriptures. He asks the young guys 'Are you circumcised?' He circumcises both father and son together in front of the villagers. This brutal scene was also enjoyed by women by peeping from a house near to the village court. In the novel it is said:

> He knew that it was sometimes necessary to strike hard at people, to terrify them, roar out in denunciation: Those who believe not, theirs will be a fearful doom.
>
> (Waliullah, 1967: 100)

Previously, villagers had only been afraid of evil powers. After the arrival of Majid, they became afraid of God, death and *majar*. When Jamila begins to revolt against Majid by not following his orders, Majid shouted: 'She has no fear of God, that's what wrong with her'.

During the harvesting, while the wind blows across the fields, the peasants share jokes and stories with one another, playing guessing games, shouting and laughing. They sang too and the songs were carried by their robust voices that flood the fields. The songs and laughter of the peasants created deep anger within Majid. For Majid, the songs and laughs of the peasants are like disobeying the *majar* built by him. He wants to quell this natural liveliness of villagers. His sermons: God is the provider. Seeing rich harvest who feel worshipping land are idolaters, sinners.

The peasants stopped singing. Thus, Majid introduced a religious system that does not permit killing anyone but annihilates the inner 'life' of the people. Villagers traditionally and occasionally listened to Baul music at night after a long day's working. Majid stopped that by stating it was anti-Islamic.

Women: Victim, Labourer and Rebellious

The prime victims of the aggressive and authoritative nature of Muslimness portrayed in the film were women. The expression of basic and natural feelings became forbidden to Rahima and Jamila. They should not talk and laugh loudly, go outside the house, walk naturally, stand in an open place after a bath. Rahima used to massage Majid's legs regularly, which symbolises her slavery to Majid. The housemaid 'mother of Hasuni' is another oppressed woman left by her husband who then stayed with her father and brothers. Once she was beaten brutally by her father because she complained about her quarrelling parents to Majid and subsequently the father was scolded by Majid. Majid punished the defiant Jamila at the end of the film, by tying her alone inside the feared *majar* during the stormy night. She was found senseless and nearly dead.

Aside from being the victims of religion and patriarchy, women of *A Tree Without Roots* can be categorised as labourer and rebel. If Rahima and the 'mother of Hasuni' fall into the labourer category, Jamila is rebellious.

We never see Rahima in prayer or involved in spiritual activities, we find her only processing crops or feeding cattle or serving Majid – massaging his legs, cooking and serving food for him, preparing *Hukkah*, the smoking tool of Majid. Rahima is always accompanied by the 'mother of Hasuni'. While they work, they do it in silence. We see peasants taking care of paddies, harvesting in the field. But at home, harvested paddies are processed and preserved by housewives. Those peasants can be easily recognised as workers, but the contribution of the housewives in agriculture has never been recognised. Thus, we find Rahima as a labourer, but unpaid and unacknowledged.

Jamila 'the baby doll', wife of the middle-aged Majid, is rarely seen at work. But she becomes the nemesis of hypocrite Majid. Her rebellion makes him vulnerable and helpless. At one point, the most powerful person of Mahabbatnagar, and blessed by the *majar*, Majid had to seek help from the silent and obedient wife Rahima. Jamila continued her rebellion until the end of the film. When she was found senseless in the *majar* at the end of the film, Jamila was found lying on flooded water and keeping her leg on part of the grave of the *Pir*, which is, symbolically, an ultimate rejection to the false grave of a saint.

Anti-Islamic Text?

The film, *A Tree Without Roots,* tells us a story of how religion is used to exploit ordinary people for economic gain. The film delineates the picture of Islamic rules and Muslimness prevailing in the rural peasant society of Bengal.

A rigid and monolithic Islam is depicted in the film Here, the caretaker of Islam (Majid) is a very shrewd, heartless and rude person. The Majid of the film is more monstrous than the Majid in the novel. In the novel, he commits fraud only to live. The novelist narrates:

> Sometimes he frightens while looking at the so called *majar*. But he has also the right to live – this thinking becomes prominent in his transient thoughts. He becomes terrified when he remembers the hard life of Garo Hill. He thinks he is the subject of almighty; he is stupid and blind for living. Allah must forgive his mistakes. His mercy is immense and endless.
>
> (Waliullah, 1967: 7)

Hayat Mamud, who was the editor of the book *Collected Novels* by Syed Waliullah, wrote in the introduction of the book:

> Though we do not support the hypocrisy of Majid, but our hatred does not rush to him; because his poverty and helplessness makes his fraudulence forgivable and makes him an ordinary and person of sorrow like us... gradually we are captured by a hidden sympathetic pain raised for Majid.
>
> (Mamud, 1996: xi)

Both the writer and the editor of the *Collected Novels* portrayed Majid as a human being with limitations. His fraudulence arises from the society in which he lives and throws him in spiritual dilemmas. But in the film *A Tree Without Roots*, Majid is not a man with human limitations. He has no misgivings about committing fraud; we always see his shrewd eyes and his aggressive ruling with a flag of Islam in his hand. This projects the image of a monolithic Majid and a monolithic Islam in the film.

Narration

While adapting *A Tree Without Roots,* director Tanvir Mokammel followed the first approach of adaptation as described by Morris Beja; he tried 'to keep the integrity of original work' (Beja, 1979). But there are two versions of the original works by Syed Waliullah, and the question is which version did the director follow? The novelist added five chapters to the Bengali novel *Lalsalu*, in the English version *Tree Without Roots*.

In the interview conducted for the purpose of this research, the director (Mokammel, 2006) claimed that he followed the English version, especially at the ending. However, his film had a distinctly different, the third version of the ending.

In the Bengali novel *Lalsalu*, there was a hailstorm and the crops of the villagers were destroyed. Majid was worried about the paddy during the storm, but Rahima was worried about Jamila, who had been tied at the *majar* a by Majid. Rahima asked Majid to bring Jamila back. Jamila was found in a faint and was brought back home. In the morning, Majid went to the paddy field and met the frustrated villagers beside their destroyed crops. The villagers expressed their grief, but Majid advised them to keep faith in God.

In the novel *Tree Without Roots*, the storm was followed by the flood and Majid's house and the *majar* were swept away. Majid found that people were no longer consulting him anymore about their immediate future after their fields were ravaged. Majid was astonished to see villagers seeking Khaleque's suggestions and help after the disaster. Jamila revolted, Rahima was no longer obedient, villagers were not depending on him, his house and paddy fields had been destroyed, and above all, the *majar* had also been swept away. He decided to leave the place. During the flood, he kept both his wives at Khaleque's house and decided to leave them behind. 'With a firm, quick stride, he started on his way' (Waliullah, 1967: 233).

In the film *A Tree Without Roots*, the storm was immediately followed by the flood. Villagers came to Majid's house with the bad news that the paddies had been destroyed; Majid advised them to keep faith in God. Rahima asked him to bring Jamila. Both found Jamila fainted at the *majar*. Majid lifts Jamila from flooded water and the film ends with an open-ended freeze shot in which Jamila is in Majid's arms, Rahima is behind him and both are looking at the sinking grave.

In the adaptation, there is an additional character who is Majid's assistant. Film critic Sajedul Awwal (2007) described the assistant, created by the director, as the extension of Majid, the soul image of Majid. The assistant suddenly arrived at the *majar* and provided an impression that he knew the secret behind the establishment of such a *majar*. Majid made him his assistant and they together continued the activities.

In the novel, Majid's internal world is described elaborately. His thinking pattern, his psychology, and his dilemma has been described with novelistic narration. But in film, it is not easy to describe one's internal world. Rather the expression of his thoughts within the narrative events can only be portrayed. The whole of internal Majid was unknown in the film.

The character was performed by Raisul Islam Asad, as art film directors always depended on for complex characters. Only problem for the audience, who read the novel, may appear about his height and health. In the novel, Majid was described as short with a thin physique. But Asad, unlike Majid, was tall and healthy.

One must recognise the visual beauty of imagery made and captured in *A Tree Without Roots* by eminent cinematographer Anwar Hossain. The colour and the magnificence of rural Bengal has been delineated with much efficiency. This beauty was not described by the novelist but can be considered as an additional narrative to the film.

When Majid failed to control Jamila, he asked for suggestions from Rahima. For the first time, Rahima got her importance in the narrative and Majid was rendered powerless. This situation was described elegantly by the cinematographer by an over-the-shoulder and high angle shot of Rahima in which Majid was seen sitting in the veranda, a position lower than that of Rahima.

The conflict was also well-portrayed in the scene in which Khaleque divorced his first wife by the order of Majid. In the first shot, she left her husband's house in a boat and then Majid was immediately seen to enter the same *ghat* by a boat with his second wife. This juxtaposition of the two conflicting shots hints at the irony of the events and the cruelty of Majid.

Despite its direct effect on the audience, however, there is general critical agreement on one point: the role of music in film should be a subordinate one (Boggs and Petrie, 2000). But the musical score of the film is non-subordinate. The musician Syed Sabab Ali Arju used some traditional instruments of the period and extensively used popular folk musical scores. Some musical tracks have been cleverly selected from Islamic songs, which create an Islamic environment throughout the film. However, it is accurately said that 'music that calls too much attention to itself at the expenses of the film as a whole is not effective' (Boggs and Petrie, 2000: 250).

Some shots were well taken, and the director tried to use some cinematic techniques to make the film language rich. This is especially true for the freeze shot at the end which made it an open-ended film that was different from the Bengali or English version of the novel. However, the storm at the end was poorly arranged and visualised.

Ratan Paul also did a good job in sound. Other than dialogue, both ambience and added sound effects have made the film lively. The calm and quiet village life was complemented by the sounds of animals and birds. Out-of-screen sound, such as someone calling from a far place, also made the surroundings livelier and realistic.

Dollhouse: Love in the Time of War

Set in the backdrop of the Liberation War of Bangladesh, the film *Dollhouse* (2006) tells the story of a female war victim. Rehana was sent to a village by her brother during the war. In the village, she builds a 'dollhouse' in an abandoned house with a young man. Adapted from a novel of the same title by eminent writer Mahmudul Haque, the film does not describe the war directly but narrates a special kind of casualty of the war – the psychic disorder of a war victim.

The audience response to the film was lukewarm but it received moderate admiration from the critics. Although it did not achieve awards at home or abroad, the film was exhibited in international festivals such as Fukuoka International Film Festival (Japan), Kolkata Film Festival (India), London Film Festival (UK), Singapore International Film Festival, Seattle International Film Festival (USA) (Islam, 2006). The film has been included in the syllabus of Film Studies Department in Hawaii University, USA also under the course 'South Asian Films' along with *Mr. and Mrs. Iyer* by Indian director Aparna Sen and *Khamoshi Pani* by Pakistani director Sabiha Sumar.

Histoire

There lived two friends, Yakub and Mukul in a far-flung village of Bangladesh in 1971. They were teachers by profession Yakub in the Village College and Mukul in the elementary school. Bangladesh was under attack by the West Pakistani military and guerrillas were resisting the occupation. Yakub by nature is a coward and confused person. When young people were joining the *Mukti Bahini*, the guerrilla force, he did not join them. Mukul, in contrast, involved himself indirectly with the war. By giving assistance secretly, such as delivering arms from one place to another, he contributed to the resistance force.

Rehana comes to the village along with other refugees from the capital city Dhaka. She is the cousin of Yakub's friend Tunu, who requested by letter that Yakub provide her shelter in the village for a few days. Yakub and Mukul decided to keep Rehana in an abandoned house, known as Adinath's Homestead, at the outskirt of the village where Mukul used to live. Yakub stays with her in the dilapidated, but palace-like, old house. Marooned by monsoon water and locked in by trees and bushes, a story of agony and love unfolds between them. They built a dollhouse by playing, gossiping, cooking together and acted as a pseudo-couple. Rehana was a talkative girl who liked to reminisce about her childhood. The quieter Yakub, had to listen to all her childhood stories. Yakub found it hard to understand Rehana because her laughs and cries appeared suddenly. She did not hesitate to denounce and tease Yakub without any significant reason. However, they loved each other, and they were happy with their dollhouse.

The dollhouse breaks down after three days when Tunu comes on the scene and tells the sad story. Rehana expresses his surprise at hearing that Yakub could not understand Rehana's abnormalities. In the army crackdown night on March 25, 1971, Rehana was staying in a student hostel of Dhaka university and was taken in an army camp. She was repeatedly raped and was released after a few days of captivity. Physical torture by the Pakistani Army resulted in her psychological breakdown. She was found senseless in a street and later was sent to the hospital. These traumatic

Figure 4.3 Yakub (Riaz) and Rehana (Sohana Saba) in a moment of despair.

experiences haunt Rehana and created her mental disorder. Since then, as Tunu says, she had behaved abnormally. Rehana comes onto the scene and hears her story being told. She reacts violently and decides to leave the place with Tunu. Yakub asked Rehana to stay with him, but she refuses to continue the relationship now that her history is known by her playmate of the dollhouse. At the end of the film, some guerrillas entered the abandoned house with the help of Mukul and Yakub wants to join them.

Recit

Dollhouse is a story that depicts an anti-war message through the sensible portrayal of the victimisation of woman. It also conveys the message that life goes on and relationships develop even in the turmoil of war. It upholds the importance of people continuing to resist an occupational army and it describes how some people become detached from the situation.

War Victimises Woman

Rehana represents over 200,000 women who were assaulted by the army of occupation during the 1971 war. The figure might be higher than that; according to Susan Brownmiller, during the nine-month terror,... a possible three million people lost their lives, ten millions fled across the border to India and 200,000, 300,000 or possible 400,000 women (three sets of statistics have been variously quoted) were raped (Brownmiller, 1975: 81). Her book delineates the horror created by the occupying forces:

Girls of eight and grandmothers of seventy-five had been sexually assaulted during the nine-month repression. Pakistani soldiers had not only violated Bengali women on the spot; they abducted tens of hundreds and held them by force in their military barracks for nightly use. The women were kept naked to prevent their escape. In some camps, pornographic movies were shown to the soldiers, 'in an obvious attempt to work the men up,' one Indian writer reported.

(Brownmiller, 1975: 83)

The film strongly stands against the war crime by telling the story of Rehana. *Dollhouse* tells the plight of a war victim woman sensibly. Her victimisation incidents were not pictured, as some films made in the 1970s tried to use the rape scenes as a selling component (see Kabir, 1979). Rehana symbolises Bangladesh which was shattered by invaders. In the Liberation War of Bangladesh, the invading army killed people, raped women, burnt houses and looted assets.

But the spectators come to know about Rehana's tragic history at the end of the film. The focus had been given to the days and nights Yakub and Rehana passed, played and gossiped together in the abandoned house.

War Can Confuse People

Occupational war may divide people into three groups: the victims, resisters and those who become confused and unable to choose a course of action. In the film, *Dollhouse* Rehana represents the first group, Mukul the second and Yakub the third group. A conversation between Mukul and Yakub reveals the individual's attitude towards the war. Yakub was sitting alone near a swamp and Mukul comes by a boat to Yakub.

Mukul: Sitting idle?
Yakub: What else can we do?
Mukul: Country is in crisis. How can we be inactive?
Yakub: Do you think Liberation Army can do something soon, Mukul?
Mukul: Sooner or later, since it has been started, no doubt we'll be liberated. Nobody can stop it.
Yakub: I love my country no less. I need to do something. But... everybody cannot do everything.

The contrast between the two characters is seen here. One wants to resist and the other wants to remain 'idle' because 'everybody cannot do everything'. In 1971, a lot of the Bengali youth joined the war, but many others remained confused. According to a Newsweek report, around 20,000 Bengali guerrillas fought against an Army of Pakistan comprising 60,000 well-trained members. The report entitled 'Bengal: Killing the people' was published on August 2, 1971 (though the war continued till December 16, 1971) and informed

106 Textual Analysis: Foundational Films

more 10,000 guerrillas who would join the following month and were being trained in India (Elahi, 1998: 380). Despite being concerned about the crisis of the motherland and the sufferings of the people, they either sat idle or fled from the city across the border to a remote and safe village. There were also a few people who collaborated with Pakistani Army who was known as *Rajakar*s.

However, one question was brought up why 'Yakub syndrome' does work among some people while others like Mukul show courage. The answer is given by the novelist Mahmudul Haque who has written at least two novels related to the Liberation War. For example, the protagonist Khoka is also seen as aloof from the events related to the Liberation War, *Jibon Amar Bon (Life My Sister* 1976). In an interview, Mahmudul Haque says, in every country and in every age, there are some people who remain aloof from the movements, who cannot mix with the mass people. If you tag them as insane you may not be wrong, but you cannot deny their existence (Haque, 2008). In the same interview, he (Haque, 2008) says, I wrote the way I saw the war. I did not join the war. I was a helpless man in the besieged city of Dhaka.

The writer of *Dollhouse* is not denying the role of Mukul, but he also endorses the existence of Yakub and thus he does not succumb to the high tone of Bengali nationalism by only writing the saga of Mukul. Portraying Yakub as a major character in the novel is an honest attempt to project reality by the novelist. This was not continued by the film director, which we discuss in the following section.

Nationalist Narrative of Resistance

The novelist portrays Yakub as an inactive person during the turmoil period of war, when everybody was involved either by participating as a guerrilla or by supporting them or at least by being concerned with the news of the war. This aloofness is a common portrayal of the main characters in the novels of Mahmudul Haque, but in the film *Dollhouse* Yakub was transformed into a potential guerrilla at the end.

Other than *Dollhouse*, Morshedul Islam has made several films related to the Liberation War of Bangladesh that include *Towards* (Agami 1984), *Autumn 71* (Sharat 71 2000), *My Friend Rashed* (Amar Bondhu Rashed 2011), *A Day in the Life of Anil Bagchi* (Anil Bagchir Ekdin 2015). In all of these films, we find the dominant narrative of the Liberation War – the repression of Pakistani Army, bravery of *Mukti Bahini,* and brutality of Islamist collaborators (*Rajakar*s). The storyline of *Dollhouse* was a bit different as the focus of the film was not on the bravery of *Mukti Bahini* and brutality of Islamist collaborators. But the imposition of the director to make Yakub willing to join *Mukti Bahini* is the construction of a nationalist narrative of resistance which was a deviation from the original text. Other than this transformation of Yakub, very few things have been changed from the original text. At the end of the novel, the narrator Yakub describes:

Mukul smacks on my back and says, didn't I tell you that I'll show you magic, didn't I? What are you seeing now, say what are you seeing?

I [Yakub] am seeing everything.

And in the film, the last dialogues between the two characters are as follow:

Mukul: Didn't I tell you I'd show magic? These boys did the operation in Taltola camp yesterday. This is Abul commander.
Abul: My regards sir.
Yakub: Abul, will you take me with you? In war?

A Dollhouse can be Built under Aggression

A series of questions may emerge in spectators' minds regarding the peculiarity and uniqueness in the storyline. How could Yakub and Rehana play a pseudo conjugal life in an isolated corner of the village? How could a war victim woman with a shattered body and mind meet a naive and detached man and develop a relationship? Why was the relationship so transient as Rehana left Yakub who requested her to stay back even after listening to her story?

Answers may lie within the questions and the cunning story settings by the author and his treatment of the devastating war. In a time of brutal aggression, when every corner of the country is affected, ordinary people begin to look differently at politics or patriotism. Life goes on, no matter how fatal the aggression is or how deeply it victimises people. The dollhouse makes the detached Yakub aware of the situation and made him think of joining the war; for the breaking of the dollhouse, he understood the degree of aggression and how ruthlessly the aggressors raped his beloved Rehana! On Rehana's side, meeting Yakub was a break from her traumatised life and she tried to find meaning in loving Yakub. But she cannot see herself as the appropriate partner for an innocent Yakub. So, she left him by breaking the dollhouse and it is unavoidable that what happened to Rehana will create a permanent imprint in her life. It is the war or aggression that shatters people, makes them resist, confuses them or creates new relationships.

Nature of Bengal: Additional Narrative

Although the main theme of the film has nothing to do with the nature of the war-shaken country, the beauty of Bengal is presented so strongly that it serves as an additional narrative to the film. In the novel, nature is present in the setting of the dollhouse, but the surroundings play a role in the narrative of the film. The Adinath's Homestead is a few hundred years old. It is surrounded by dense bushes and had been marooned by monsoon water. The period of the film is set in July–August of 1971, which is the time of the monsoon rain. Hence viewers see the film in a kind of wet and greenish context. In short, the presence of natural beauty is more evident in the film than the novel.

The way nature is portrayed can remind us of the complaints against the film *Distant Thunder* (*Ashani Sanket* 1973) by Satyajit Ray, which portrayed t the massive famine of Bengal in 1943 during the Second World War. Its countryside was pictured so beautifully in colour that it did not seem as a place of famine. Nature is represented in other Morshedul Islam's films like *The Wheel* (Chaka 1993) and *Dukhai* (1997), but not as much as in *Dollhouse*. In *Dukhai*, nature is powerful and the main character; nature is the annihilator and Dukhai was the victim. In *Dollhouse*, nature becomes predominant, although not physically as a character. It is Mother Nature who provides Yakub and Rehana a shelter to build up a dollhouse.

Narration

Other than the ending, no significant changes had been adapted in the film; hence, it can be said that the film director tried 'to keep the integrity of original work', as Morris Beja (Beja, 1979) has discussed. At best, characters and events have been shortened and little had been added other than capturing the natural beauty of the place in celluloid.

In the interview conducted for this study, director Morshedul Islam says:

> While adapting I did not divert the story from its original source. I thought there is no need to change the story. The narrative style in the novel was a bit complex; I have arranged the events in chronology in classical narrative style. I have shortened the character Tunu and detail descriptions of the abandoned house.
>
> (Islam, 2006)

In the novel, Yakub did not join the war, but in the film, he expressed a desire to the guerrilla leader to join the war. This is a difference between the filmmaker and the novelist in their approaches to the character and the nationalist war. In the novel, the character Tunu, the cousin of Rehana and the friend of Yakub, was portrayed extensively. But in the film, he was presented first through a letter by telling Yakub about Rehana's arrival in the village in the beginning part and he entered in the scene physically at the end to take Rehana away. In the novel, through Rehana's description, her grandfather's character was described elaborately. But in the film, the audience sees him only in one flashback scene.

Dollhouse is a film of three characters – Rehana, Yakub and Mukul. If the character Yakub is introverted, apprehensive and confused, Rehana is extroverted, friendly and mysterious. In a sense, she laughs for very little reason and cries without any relevance. Sometimes she seems very friendly and considerate to Yakub but the next moment she harshly abuses him. This makes it hard for Yakub as well as the spectators to understand her as a character. But at the end, the revelation of the attacks on her make everything clear.

Unlike Yakub and Rehana, the character Mukul is clearly portrayed in the text. He is brave, he is a dreamer and he supplies arms to the guerrillas. He is confident that one day the country will be liberated through the resistance of people. He hopes he will act in a *jatra* play again after the country's liberation.

But all three major characters are deprived of families, relatives and friends. Rehana's mother fled and married another man which was followed by her father's suicide. She grew up with her grandfather and grandmother. Cousin Tunu was her only guardian in the city while studying at Dhaka University. Yakub does not have parents either. He studied in Dhaka and he lived with his distantly related elder sister. Mukul, a member of the Hindu community, also does not have family or relatives in the village and stays in the Adinath's homestead with the permission of a powerful village leader. Having no family or relatives for all major characters in a text is a peculiar instance among any kind of art or literary piece.

The technique of *montage* – conflict between images, shots and events – was applied in the film. The setting of the film was a calm and tranquil place; the tireless talking of Rehana conflicts with this calmness. The war-drum played far away, which was conveyed through the appearance of refugees from the city also is in conflict with the calm life of the village (which is the central setting of the story). There are conflicting scenes as well – when Yakub and Rehana reached a consensus about their relationship. In the next scene, Tunu came into the story and the relationship was broken. Yakub's despair after Rehana left is captured by a melancholic song of Rabindranath Tagore, but the immediate ending of the song has been replaced by the alert and active showdown of the guerrillas.

Planning the composition of frames created some excellent 'frame within frame' shots. The dilapidated house consists of many frames on the walls – some look like windows, some look like doors – all are rectangular frames. The director places Yakub and Rehana on a frame or behind a frame and shoots them by placing the camera foreground – thus the camera frameworks within a frame. The space in front of the frame of the wall is relatively dark and the wall is covered and wet with moss. The back of the wall sheds abundant light on the frame and thus some beautiful 'frame within frame' shots are created. The palace-like old house and its high arches have not only enriched the *mis-en-scene*, it has created the symbolic spatial distance that shows male and female roles are within in dollhouse.

Cinematography is an asset in *Dollhouse*. The abandoned house was entirely quiet and is situated at the outskirts of a calm village showing a slow-moving life. For integrating that with the narrative techniques, the camera also moves very slowly; it is slow like a boat and boats are repeatedly used in the film as it is the only mode of transport in the village surrounded by a swamp. Thus, a common rhythm of is seen in the speed of life in the village, the speed of the camera movement and speed of the events in the film. The widescreen shots perfectly capture the wide space of the East Bengal village.

Music by Imon Saha was subordinate to the narrative and was used appropriately. He depended on Indian musical instruments – such as drum, sarod, tambourine, flute and western instrument like guitar – to create his musical scores. Two songs of Rabindranath Tagore have been used in the film and were sung by Rejwana Chowdhury Bannya and Azizur Rahman Tuhin. The song sung by Tuhin was used which conveys the solitude of Yakub when Rehana left him at the end of the film.

References

Amin, N. (2003). Lalsalu. In S. Islam (ed.), *Banglapedia: National Encyclopedia of Bangladesh* (Multimedia CD). Dhaka: Asiatic Society of Bangladesh.

Awwal, S. (2007). Interview conducted for the study on 02 February 2007.

Beja, M. (1979). *Film and Literature: An Introduction*. New York: Longman.

Bhowmik, D. (2004). Mangalakavya. In S. Islam (ed.), *Banglapedia: National Encyclopedia of Bangladesh* (Multimedia CD). Dhaka: Asiatic Society of Bangladesh.

Boggs, J. & Petrie, D. (2000). *The Art of Watching Films* (5th ed). California: Mayfield Publishing Company.

Brownmiller, S. (1975). *Against Our Will: Men, Women and Rape*. Toronto: Bantam Books.

Chowdhury, B. M. (2004). Changing Class and Social Structure in Bangladesh: 1793–1980. In A. F. S. Ahmed and B. M. Chowdhury (eds.), *Bangladesh – National Culture and Heritage: An Introductory Reader* (pp. 253–266). Dhaka: Independent University, Bangladesh.

Deen, S. A. (2006). On Kittonkhola (Kittonkhola Prosonge). In S. Zakaria (ed.), *Complete Works of Selim Al Deen-2* (*Selim Al Deen Rachonasamogro-2*) (pp. 350–356). Dhaka: Maola Brothers.

Elahi, M. (1998). Bengal: Murder of People – The Newsweek Special Report. *Assignment Bangladesh 1971* (pp. 374–386). Dhaka: Momin Press.

Genette, G. (1980). *Narrative Discourse*. Oxford: Basil Blackwell.

Haque, M. (2008). Interview with Mahmudul Haque: Ahmad Mostofa Kamal (Mahmudul Haquer Sakkhatkar: Ahmad Mostofa Kamal) at http://arts.bdnews24.com/?p=1772. Accessed 15 August 2008.

Islam, M. (2006). Interview conducted for the study on 10 December 2006.

Kabir, A. (1979). *Film in Bangladesh*. Dhaka: Bangla Academy.

Mamud, H. (1996). Introduction (Bhumika). In H. Mamud (ed.), *Complete Novels: Syed Waliullah* . Dhaka: Pratik, pp. not numbered.

Mokammel, T. (2000). *Syed Waliullah: Sisifas and the Question of Heritage in Novel* (*Syed Waliullah: Sisifas O Uponnase Oitijya Jiggasa*). Dhaka: Agami Publishers.

Mokammel, T. (2006). Twenty Years of Alternative Cinema: Experience and Achievement' (Bangladeshe Bikalpo Cinemar Bish Bochhor: Oviggota O Prapti). *Drishshoroop: Annual Compilation 1411–1412*, 7–20.

Sayeed, A. (2006). Interview conducted for the study on 15 November 2006.
Sen, A. (2008). Selim Al Deen: Personal and Beyond Personal (Selim Al Deen: Byektigoto Ebong Byektigotoke Chharie), at http://arts.bdnews24.com/?p=1842. Accessed 12 September 2008.
Waliullah, S. (1967). *Tree Without Roots*. London: Chatto and Windus Ltd.
Zakaria, S. (2008). Shrine Culture at Stake (Biponno Majar Sangskriti) at http://arts.bdnews24.com/index.php?s=saymon+zakaria. Accessed 20 November 2008.

5 Textual Analysis: Transitional Films

The readers might think that among the selected films produced between 2000 and 2015, all foundational films would be the earliest, transitional films would have been made in the middle period and the contemporary films would be the most recent. This temporal consideration is true in many cases, but not in all. Rather, the approach towards Muslimness and the perception of the Liberation War are important factors in characterising the films and characteristics of rural Bengal being described are also factors to be considered in categorisation. This means that *Dollhous,* which was made in 2006, is a foundational film but we propose *The Clay Bird*, made in 2002, a transitional film. This temporal discrepancy is true for transitional and contemporary categories.

The transitional films shift from the characteristics of foundational films – looks back to rural Bengal with fresh eyes and telling the story of its unexplored or unaddressed areas (*The Clay Bird* 2002 by Tareque Masud), challenges the dominant discourses of the 1971 Liberation War (*The Clay Bird* and *Meherjaan* 2011 by Rubaiyat Hossain), studies the religious people sensibly (*Television*, 2012 by Mostofa Sarwar Farooki) and depicts the varied versions of Muslim identities (*The Clay Bird*). The film *Television* also examines how religious people respond to and use modern technologies.

The Clay Bird: Plurality of Identity of Bangladesh

The Clay Bird is a film that predominantly deals with the many identity questions in Bangladesh. The film is autobiographical and as Zakir Hossain Raju says, it is also the biography of Bangladesh as a nation (Raju, 2002).

 The Clay Bird is a critically acclaimed cinema both at home and overseas. It was the first Bangladeshi film screened and given an award at the Cannes Film festival. It was selected as the opening film in the director's fortnight at Cannes 2002. It received the FIPRESCI award there and won the best screenplay award at the Marrakesh Film Festival in Morocco in 2002 and the best film award in Kara Film Festival, Pakistan, in 2003. It was

DOI: 10.4324/9781003271093-6

Bangladesh's submission to the Oscars, first time after the independence. It is also the first Bangladeshi feature film to be released commercially in cine theatres on both sides of the Atlantic through a renowned French distributor MK2; the film also was released as a DVD in France and USA.

However, release of the film was a problem at home because the BFCB banned it for being 'religiously sensitive'. The ban was lifted later after minor 'corrections' by the director. The protest against the ban by civil society and the intelligentsia of Bangladesh also put pressure on the censor board to lift the ban. The director's assessment of the reasons behind the ban was 'In retrospect, it was probably something to do with the backlash of September 11. They were just nervous' (Masud, 2004a). The film was made before September 11 but was released after the event that shook the world.

Histoire

The Clay Bird is set in the backdrop of the late 1960s, when Bangladesh – the Eastern part of Pakistan was rebelling against military dictatorship through a nationalist mass movement. The film tells us the story of Anu, a shy village boy who was sent by his orthodox father Kazi Majharul Islam to study in a madrasa, a Muslim seminary. Orthodox Islamist Kazi has sent Anu to madrasa because the boy goes to watch and participate in 'Hindu rubbishes' (religious and cultural events and festivals) along with his 'secular' uncle Milon. The father thinks the boy is moving away from his religiosity.

The film begins with a pre-dawn scene in the misty environment at a *ghat* of the pond situated in front of the madrasa where boys were brushing teeth, washing themselves and having ablutions for morning prayers. One of the madrasa teachers, Ibrahim, is showing Anu, a newcomer student, how to brush the teeth properly with the wooden branch traditionally used by the villagers.

In madrasa, Anu's contraband long hair had to be cut, he must wear madrasa uniform and even his name had been changed from Anu to Muhammad Anwarul Islam. Only Rokon became his friend. Rokon is not an ordinary boy, he has a 'special' friend whom we never see. He hears bizarre sounds and, above all, has his own imaginary world. Rokon has a hideaway place in the jungle with a lot of collections and is only visited by Anu.

Among the teachers of madrasa, *Baro Hujur* (senior teacher) is strict and rude while Ibrahim *Hujur* (junior teacher) is soft and loving to his students. This contrast can be found in their religious belief – *Baro Hujur* is orthodox, he thinks Islam is a complete code of life and if needed he prefers Jihad to uphold Islam in society. But Ibrahim *Hujur* thinks calling people into Jihad or other political extremism is not the job of a teacher of madrasa; rather he believes that giving Islamic lessons to students is the only job for the teachers.

Figure 5.1 Asma (Rimjhim) with a clay bird at her hand.

Anu's younger sister Asma dies without proper treatment. Homoeopathic practitioner Kazi's zealotry prevented the use of antibiotics brought by Milon. Asma's death makes Ayesha very silent and Kazi repentant. Kazi asks Ayesha to go outside or visit her brother's house. But Ayesha says she may go away forever. Back in the madrasa, Anu finds Rokon becoming sick from the sounds in his ear. One night he behaves abnormally, shouting and carrying with a stick to beat an anonymous enemy. He underwent exorcism by the pond in the cold water and was quarantined in a storeroom. Ibrahim *Hujur* and Anu continued feeding and giving him medicine.

Milon becomes involved in the nationalist movement. At midnight of March 25, 1971, the West Pakistani military attacked civilians in Dhaka. People fled and entered the villages. But villages were also attacked by the military. Milon died while resisting the army invasion. Kazi believes the military is coming to their village to keep peace and to protect Islam. But one day the sound of bullets was heard, villagers began to flee and (in the moment of climax) Anu reached home from madrasa. Anu's repressed mother Ayesha revolted at the end, taking Anu with her and leaving Kazi alone in the house which was set on fire by the 'Muslim military brothers' of Kazi. Anu and Ayesha passed a terrible night in a nearby jungle with other villagers and came back home in the morning to find the house destroyed by the military. They also found Kazi at the corner of their ravaged house, staring blankly, at the tiny homoeopathic pills that failed to save his daughter. Ayesha and Anu wanted Kazi to leave the area, but the defeated Kazi remained silent. More people have been seen fleeing after the fresh attack of the military in the morning. Ayesha tells Kazi, 'Look around, your Muslim brothers have burnt your sacred cloister to the ground'. Ayesha departs with Anu and the film ends. Though the story did not tell the results of the war, it is to be noted that the war took away three million lives and created ten million refugees, which led to the independence of Bangladesh on December 16th, 1971. This is not only the story of shy Anu, who looks at the world around him, but also the tale of the formation of the cultural identity of Bengali-Muslim.

Recit

The film *The Clay Bird* constructs all three kinds of identity – Bengaliness, Muslimness and popular religion. It also conveys messages of freedom – the freedom of expression, the spiritual freedom, freedom of a nation and so on. The film also advocates for cultural diversity and communal harmony.

Constructing Identity: Bengaliness, Muslimness and Popular Religion

Some important characters of *The Clay Bird* also represent either Bengaliness or Muslimness. Anu's father Kazi believes in Muslim brotherhood and he believes a Muslim (as found in the West Pakistani military) cannot kill another Muslim (whether they be East Pakistani rebellions or civilians). He also believes that the military is coming to keep peace and protect Islam from non-Islamic groups of secularists and nationalists. But Anu's uncle, the younger brother of Kazi, believes in Bengaliness and fought against the Pakistani military for the right of East Pakistani people. These two characters represent two opposite currents of the broader Bengali Muslim identity. Although these characters are not engaged in face-to-face conflict, their activities represent conflict in a broader political sphere. Milon is modern, liberal and believes in Marxism. But Kazi is a zealot in his Islamic beliefs. He does not like to let his son be in touch with other religious elements. He does not like to see his wife singing and sewing the image of a bird in a handkerchief and prefers homoeopathy to modern allopathic treatment. He would not even keep his windows open, out of concern that some un-Islamic elements might enter.

However, the director of *The Clay Bird* does not construct only two identities. He does not support Bengaliness directly, as do other independent filmmakers. He rather explores the third type of identity, i.e. popular religion and culture. The director (Masud, 2007) does not hesitate to say that *The Clay Bird* has endorsed popular Islam very clearly.

The pro-Islamic character Kazi was portrayed with much sensitivity in the film. This bearded man believes in a Muslim brotherhood; hence he cannot take the break-up of Pakistan easily. Kazi's belief in a Muslim brotherhood was contested by the secular and Marxist Milon (although, for the cultural reason, we never see a debate between the elder brother and the younger) and Milon was criticised by boatman Karim who believed in syncretic popular religion.

One can easily differentiate Kazi from the *Baro Hujur* of the madrasa who believes in Jihad to uphold Islam upon everything. His Muslimness is also criticised by Ibrahim *Hujur*, who also believes in popular and mystic Islam. *Baro Hujur* tries to inspire students towards Jihad, but Ibrahim *Hujur* believes opposite. He reminds the instructor Halim Mia that Islam in Bengal was not begun with a sword but because of the creative and poetic invitation to Islam by Sufi saints, which converted many to Islam.

A lot of *bayati*s are seen singing and debating in *The Clay Bird*. When Kazi went out for a religious meeting, Ayesha and Asma attended a village concert performed by a female *bayati*, in which the theme song of the film is heard. After the attack on Dhaka people were fleeing from the capital by boat, a blind *bayati* started singing a song that describes a 'fratricidal war' between the grandsons of the Prophet. In another song at the end of the film, two *bayati*s were engaged in *bahas* (debate), on the true way of Islamic life – *Shariah* (scholastic) or *Marfat* (popular) – the former is rigid and the latter is liberal *Marfat* won at the end of the *bahas* and again the director expressed his preference for popular religion and culture.

The first half of the film not only tells conflicting stories, but also describes the cultural and religious diversity that is prevailed in the Bengali peasant society. When Kazi leaves the house for pilgrimage, Ayesha goes to the concert of a female *bayati* with Asma at night. While returning home for Eid (Muslim festival), Anu goes to the village fair where he finds the *Charak* festival of Hindu believers and buys a clay bird as a gift for his sister. We see a traditional *Puthipath* (traditional form of reciting a ballad) on the *Qurbani* (sacrifice) of his son by Hazrat Ibrahim to Allah. This was later turned into the sacrifice of a beast to Allah, which became a major festival enjoyed by the Muslim community. The next scene *Qurbani* of a cow is seen at Anu's house. The Eid-day was enjoyed by Anu and his sister in wearing new clothes. Milon's friends, (which include a Hindu fellow) also visited the house. They also had special food which turned to a happy get together. At the early part of the film, there were colourful scenes of boat race and *Durga Pooja* (major religious festival of Hindus of Bengal) which were enjoyed by Anu and Milon. After this event, Anu was sent to madrasa.

The Clay Bird Symbolises Freedom

In one scene of *The Clay Bird*, Anu comes home from madrasa for a holiday, stops at a village fair and picks up a colourful clay bird to give to his sister. After coming home, he hands the clay bird over to Asma and tells her not to let her father see it. He knew Kazi would be angry because in Islam it would be considered a form of idolatry, which is prohibited. Asma replies, 'I'll hide it somewhere even you won't find it'. At the last sequence of the film, after the military onslaught, the clay bird fell from the inside roof of the devastated house. Without these two scenes, the physical existence of the clay bird was never seen in the film.

The term 'clay bird' was heard again in a song performed by a female *bayati* in a village concert, but this time in a thematic form. As Kazi's departure to a pilgrimage left her free to leave the home, Ayesha went to listen to the concert. In the song performed by the female *bayati*, the clay bird symbolises the main theme of the film in mystic metaphor. Masud (2004a) says, as Sufism teaches us, the human being is made of clay and the soul is always associated with a free bird. The soul is encaged in a body of clay and the body is very limited, very transitory, fragile and weak; the soul has an immense desire to be free. The *bayati* sings:

> The bird is trapped in the body's cage
> Its feet bound by the worldly chains
> It tries to fly but fails...
> The clay bird laments:
> 'Why did you infuse my heart with longing
> If you didn't give my wings the strength to fly?'

The theme of freedom versus different kinds of human limitations – social, political and religious – is clearly raised in the film. Ayesha wants to be free as a woman, as a human being; Anu wants to be free to do whatever he wants to do; Milon seeks national and territorial freedom which is his own narrow sense of freedom; the boatman Karim talks about a greater mystical and spiritual freedom. These characters are pursuing their own forms of freedom. The quest for freedom recurs even against the backdrop of the political movements depicted in the film. The whole nation is pursuing an identity that is supposed to be free. According to Tareque Masud (2004b), the overriding theme is limitation versus freedom, and the title reflects this and is also a tribute to Sufism, and its emphasis on the relationship between the soul and body.

Representing Cultural Diversity

In *The Clay Bird*, folkloric cultural elements from traditional Bengal were widely used. A few rural festivals and folk concerts were shown. The boat race, village fair, ballad of Qurbani in a *puthipath* programme, *bahas* in Baul song, and the Eid festival are portrayed and presented within the narrative. In every madrasacultural event, the protagonists were present as the audience. The boat race was presented in flashback when Anu told Rokon that he had come from a village. The boat race was not merely a race; it contained 'cultural shows' taken from Hindu mythology at the bank of the river. The boat race represents Anu's joyful village life before going to madrasa, the concert of female *bayati* can be thought of as a diversion for Ayesha in absence of Kazi. The song of *bahas* between two *bayati*s and the *puthipath* scene followed by Eid of Qurbani are just very loose elements as far as the narrative is concerned. Instead of focus in on the narrative, the director tends to represent a 'cultural package' of traditional Bengal. According to the director (Masud, 2003), 'I wanted to convey my own image of my country, that a moderate Muslim Bangladesh, and to bring out its social, cultural, and political diversity'.

It should also be noted that, in Bengal, the best medium of expression for expressing mystic thoughts is music. In contrast to the written tradition of Sufism in Iran, which is based on poetic texts, mysticism in Bangladesh took on the oral and musical forms of rural Bengali society. Although in the stricter sense of Islamic Shariah music is forbidden, mystical songs have become a powerful, yet subtle, form of protest. The lyrics of mystical songs are suggestive and restrained and, therefore, highly metaphoric in nature. This genre of local folk music is a convergence of Muslim Sufism, Hindu Vaishnavism and Buddhist mysticism.

Narration

It is not surprising that *The Clay Bird* has been compared with the masterpiece *Pather Panchali* (1955) by Satyajit Ray because of the similarity in their style of filmmaking. French critic Claude-Marie Tremois (Tremois, 2003) posits that those who like the work of one of the world's greatest filmmaker, Satyajit Ray, should like *The Clay Bird*, the first and most delicate film by Tareque Masud. In an interview, he (Masud, 2004b) says, the simplicity is something I borrowed from Satyajit Ray, I am indebted to him. He also said that he was inspired by the simplicity and economy of both Abbas Kiarostami, the Iranian filmmaker and of [Yasujiro] Ozu, the Japanese filmmaker. If *Pather Panchali* portrays the life of a lower-middle-class Hindu family of West Bengal, *The Clay Bird* is a story of a lower-middle-class Muslim family of East Bengal. But the theological dimension and the backdrop of birth of a nation of *The Clay Bird* represent a bit of a departure from *Pather Panchali*. The commonality is obviously the simplistic way of making a story of a lower-middle-class family.

But aside from being simple and linear like *Pather Panchali*, the narrative of *The Clay Bird* is not as tight. Instead, the scattered use of cultural and folkloric elements of traditional Bengal has made the narrative loose. The boat race, the song of theological *bahas*, the village concert and the *puthipath* ballad of Qurbani were not directly related to the narrative. Rather, they interrupt the natural flow of the narrative. It looks as the director does not want the audience to get involved entirely in the story. He wants to portray a picture and convey a message by standing outside of the story. Tareque Masud (2007) says:

When the story is crystallizing, suddenly we brought the attention of audience to other places. We expected the audience not to be involved in the storyline; we wanted to present *bahas* in front of them, which is main target of the film. Structurally there were some debates after regular interval. Instead of a cathartic and gratifying story engaging of the audience, we tried to bring back the audience in debates.

In *The Clay Bird,* the autobiography of Anu appears to represent the director's own experiences. But Anu is a dispassionate narrator and a passive observer of the world around him. In comparison to Anu, Rokon seems a stronger character. He is an orphan boy and the madrasa is his home. But he cannot cope up with the strict rules of madrasa. So, he builds his own secret world, which is a collection of odd materials: flute, drawings, handle of bicycle, mirror, etc. He does not need a real ball for play; he can easily play with invisible balls with Anu. He not only builds his own imaginary world by evading strict madrasa rules, but he also tends to protest at times in his own way. He likes Arabic lessons, but dislikes Urdu lessons. This can be easily connected with the Language Movement in 1952, when people of East Pakistan revolted against the enforced order by the West Pakistani President stating Urdu would be the only state language of Pakistan and demanded that Bangla be considered a state language. In another scene, when *Baro Hujur* was inviting his people to Jihad, the buzzing started inside Rokon's ears and he stopped listening to the sermon by putting his hands over his ears. The repressive *Baro Hujur* could see that he was behaving differently from the others and eventually he was punished and quarantined in the storeroom. No one knows what finally happened to Rokon.

Anu's father Kazi is portrayed with much sensibility. He is hard, tough, unkind and repressive. His external extremism covers his internal weakness. His weakness started to become apparent after Asma died because he understood that his zealotry led to her death. He asked Ayesha to go outside, and he started suggesting patients see a better doctor. If we analyse the context of the nationalist movement and Liberation War of Bangladesh, orthodox Muslims had collaborated with the Pakistani military as they could not accept the break-up of the Islamic state and emergence of a secular Bangladesh. They were also engaged in war crimes such as rape, loot and killing civilians by collaborating with the Pakistani Army. In addition, there were other Islamists, who were followers of scholastic Islam, who could not accept the break-up of Pakistan. This is because two decades previously, they worked for Pakistan as a Muslim state within the Indian sub-continent to fulfil their rights as Muslims and to deny the domination of Hindus. These Islamists did not collaborate with the army, but the break-up of Pakistan was heartbreaking for them. By portraying the character sensibly, Tareque Masud rewrote one aspect of the history of the birth of Bangladesh and the emergence of

120   Textual Analysis: Transitional Films

Bengali Muslim identity. Other independent filmmakers have essentially portrayed the Islamists in 1971 as anti-Liberation and collaborators of the Pakistani Army.

The character of Ayesha represents women who are victims of patriarchy and scholastic Islam. When modern Kazi turned religious, Ayesha became his prime victim. She had to go into *Purdah* – she lost her right to sing, draw pictures and to go outside. Later she had to lose her friend and brother-in-law Milon because he was deeply involved in the nationalist movement. But by the end of the film, she criticises Kazi, 'Look around, your Muslim brothers have burnt your sacred cloister to the ground'. Ayesha revolts at the end, she and her son Anu left the village and Kazi behind under military attack.

The characters of *Baro Hujur* and Ibrahim *Hujur* have been created to show the director's position against scholastic or orthodox Islam and his tribute to mystic or popular Islam. Milon is also a major character who represents the secular and leftist stream in the late 1960s in Bangladesh. His dream of revolution has been turned into a nationalist discourse. Milon is liberal; he introduces Anu with a diversified world and brings allopathic medicine for Asma. But his ultra-secular perspective cannot encompass the spiritual liberalism of boatman Karim. By the character, Milon the director criticises the limitation of secularists also.

Tareque Masud preferred non-professional actors to get the informal acting style. Other than Jayanto Chattopadhyay as Kazi and Rokeya Prachi as Ayesha, the rest of the major actors never acted before. But both professional and nonprofessional actors were successful in their performance. Many boys acted as madrasa students, and the director handled them with good care.

The use of details is a neorealist characteristic. Like Satyajit Ray, Tareque Masud also attempted to use details as symbols for the message. An excellent detail was used to indicate the death of Asma. While walking with Milon and Anu, she wanted a white flower instead of a red one from her Milon uncle. This preference for the white flower makes the audience psychologically aware of Asma's forthcoming death. At times, Anu or Rokon are seen walking through a veranda in the madrassa, bound by grills with spikes and through a narrow corridor bordered by high walls. This *mis-en-scene* symbolises how small and weak these kids are under the strict rules of madrasa. The window of the house was used as one of the main metaphors of the film. The sweets from the Hindu festival and the allopath for Asma's treatment get inside the house through this window. By opening and closing the window the audience can understand that Ayesha wants to open the window and Kazi wants to close it, hence this symbolises that Ayesha desires freedom but Kazi is resistant towards it.

Understatement is an important narrative technique of *The Clay Bird*. Only Kazi and *Baro Hujur* are aggressive in their approach. Other characters do not raise their voices. The audience never sees Milon protesting to his elder brother or Ibrahim *Hujur* against Baro *Hujur*. Their protest lies through their different activities. As a little boy, Rokon's protest is also indirect. Although the film is set against a backdrop of the nationalist movement and military attack on the village, but violence is never seen. This style of avoiding showing direct violence may lessen the intensity of the event, but it has ensured the director's intention to keep everything understated throughout the film. The director (Masud, 2004b) says:

> ... [i]t was a conscious choice to make a gentle film – the gentleness is the core of the film, an appeal for tolerance, harmony and peace. You cannot show it in a contradictory way by exposing violence.... It is important to show people being affected by violence, the devastating consequences it has. Whereas, if you show violence itself, you may make people more violent, and we have tried to stay away from that.

The influence of Sufism has set the simple and gentle nature of the film.

Visual beauty is an asset of *The Clay Bird*. The visual images of rural Bangladesh as well as its people and culture are elegantly captured by Indian cinematographer Sudhir Palsane. The stunning beauty of the landscape of rural Bangladesh as captured through Sudhir's camera has made *The Clay Bird* a spectacle of exotic Bangladesh, although the director's intention was bringing out the people and its culture, not nature. Tareque Masud (2004b) says:

> There are films that deliberately make an effort to show beautiful landscapes. This is a trap.... I do think we deliberately avoided getting into the trap of showing the physical beauty of the country. What we tried to capture was the inner beauty of ordinary people in villages, an inner beauty born of their culture. They are not stars with beautiful faces but ordinary hard working peasants with their own beauty.... We focused more on the culture – the festivities, the recitations, the village fairs, Eid – and inner beauty than the landscapes. In other Bengali films – with all due respect to great masters like Satyajit Ray – there is a tremendous tendency towards lyricism and romanticizing the village or rural Bangladesh and we consciously avoided that.

The movement of the camera was judicious. Most of the time the camera moves slowly in a way that resembles the slow life in the Bengal village. However, the camera was fast, as expected, in the boat race scene.

The use of a natural soundtrack made the film more attractive and trustworthy. The sound of driving the boat, the sound of heavy wind in the leaves of the mango tree, the sound of crickets – all made the film rich. Sound recordist Indrajit Neogi has shown his skill in these instances. The mixing of the boat race scene was skillfully done by Ratan Paul, the sound mixer. In music, both vocal and instrumental are assets of the film. It reveals the rich musical heritage of traditional Bengal.

Editing of *The Clay Bird* was done by Tareque Masud's America born wife Catherine Masud. She is also the co-director of some other films of Tareque Masud. She is also the producer of *The Clay Bird*. The film broadly follows a classical narrative style in storytelling, which does not allow continuity editing method. Rather, whenever the story is crystallised, a disruption occurs, by using a song.

Meherjaan: Challenge to the Grand Narrative of Liberation War

Meherjaan is very much the first film in which a talented director is struggling to find a voice. Rubaiyat Hossain certainly lacked a command of technique in this film as compared to her next film *Under Construction* (2015). *Meherjaan* begins with cross-cutting between past and present in an attempt to introduce the major characters and set the tone of the film. The result is confusion and it takes some time for clarity to appear. This was achieved through the development of a strong narrative and, paradoxically, through a degree of ambiguity. The different life experiences of the principle female characters are interwoven with skill and sympathy. Hossain clearly has something to say that is worth listening to, however, it seems that the Bangladeshi moral police did not like what they were hearing and ran a prejudicial campaign against the film. The film created a huge furor among a large part of the audience after its release in January 2011 and was pulled from theatres after only one week.

The War of Liberation has been sanctified and only the approved version is permissible. The film seeks to look at the great foundational myth of the nationalistic narrative of Bangladesh through a different lens. Anybody who challenges that view is vilified.

What is the official version? Simply all Pakistani troops were ravaging monsters, all *mukhijodha* (the freedom fighters) are heroes and/or martyrs, Bangladeshi women were vulnerable to the lust of Pakistani troops and unable to defend themselves, the *razakar* were evil, and the idyllic 'Sonar Bangla' (the golden Bengal) was destroyed only to be rebuilt through the efforts of the AL. Hossain addresses all of these aspects of the foundational myths but asks questions that can confuse the grand narrative.

Histoire

The setting is rural Bangladesh, more precisely in a village ruled by a benign despot – the grandfather. He is ambivalent about the revolution and his guiding principle is to prevent bloodshed. He witnessed the excesses of Partition and wishes to avoid them at all costs. Consequently, he is courteous towards all parties – the leftists who have come to the village to hide

Textual Analysis: Transitional Films 123

and rest, the Pakistani troops, the *razakar*s (who collaborated with the Army of occupation), and the *mukhtijodha*s. In many respects, his position is Gandhian, i.e. seeking to protect and resist through passive resistance. Indeed, in a key scene where the Pakistani officer tries to bully the Grandfather, the latter's serenity and courtesy turns the table and the officer leaves the garden setting showing respect for the Grandfather. Yet he is killed. The grand narrative demands that this be clearly shown as the action of the marauding Pakistanis, but Hossain's version is ambiguous. It could be the troops who have just arrived in the village who kill Khwaja Sahib, the grandfather but the murderer could also be Sumon, a local leftist who wishes to demonstrate his credentials to the visiting leader from Dhaka.

The film revolves around the women in Khwaja Sahib's family; his three surviving daughters and two granddaughters, Neela and Meher. Neela is a progressive woman. She was a member of a communist cell in Dhaka and clearly has a mind of her own. Like so many of her class, she fled Dhaka at the onset of hostilities to take refuge in her ancestral village. On the way 'home' she is picked up by the Pakistani troops and raped and subjected to extreme mental and physical torture. The details are never provided but hinted at through conversations of the women. As a result of her rape, Neela becomes pregnant. At a key moment, she confesses the rape was not her first sexual experience. Again, the ambiguity interrupts the grand narrative. In the eyes of her older female relatives, she is ruined beyond redemption and they oppose the marriage of Neela to a local activist and old family friend despite the wishes of Neela and Sumon. The grandfather reserves his judgement for the most part but ultimately supports the senior women in the family. Throughout all this, Neela remains distraught, angry and vengeful. She wields a large knife and frequently expresses her desire for revenge. Eventually, she joins the liberation forces and fights, but then dies in childbirth. Her daughter Sarah is adopted by Germans and grows upwesternised but dissatisfied with her lack of knowledge about her origins. It is her return to Bangladesh that triggers the narrative and leads to the revelations about her family.

Meher, the eponymous hero, is an indulged, seventeen-year-old beauty who roams the surrounding woods looking at plants and butterflies, or so it seems. She leads an idyllic, carefree life seemingly untouched by the war despite the presence of her refugee cousins. On one of her walks in the forest she is suddenly thrown to the ground and silenced by a handsome young soldier – in short, the fairytale unfolds. He is not seeking to ravish her but protect her from other Pakistani soldiers in the immediate vicinity. He, it turns out, is a deserter from the Pakistani army who has refused to follow orders and fire on a mosque. Moreover, he is a Baluchi (not a hated Panjabi), wounded, and in fear of his life. With the help of two peasants, Meher takes Wasim to a remote hut where he is nursed back to health. In the process, Meher and Wasim realise they have fallen in love. This affair creates a problem as described in the plot. Meher was slapped and rebuked

Figure 5.2 Meher (Jaya Bachchan) in prayer.

by the family. The decision was made that Wasim would have to leave the village. Meher's urging saved his life. She accompanied him until the waiting boat took away him to an unknown destination.

Recit

Meherjaan as a film arrived with a surprising message that shocked the audience. The sharp deviation from the grand narrative of the Liberation War in the film and Bangladesh society was not ready to accept the alternative discourse proposed by the film. The proposed narrative was rejected by the nationalists and a major part of the civil society.

An Absurd Affair?

The guardians of the grand narrative mounted a strenuous campaign against the film on the basis that it traduced the memories of the heroes and martyrs who died and suffered because of the war. Moreover, a good Bengali girl would never betray her heritage and love a Pakistani, even if he was Baluchi. However, the history of war and conquest is full of narratives depicting illicit and surreptitious love affairs between conquered and conqueror. The experience of the French in World War II illustrates this nicely but if examples from the West are offensive, we can always look at the Spanish conquest of the Aztecs or the Rajput princesses marrying the Muslim conquerors. Some evidence is also found in different films made about war. In Alain Resnais's famous film *Hiroshima Mon Amour* (1959), the female protagonist, in her youth in a French town, loved a German soldier and for that she was shamed and her head was shaved as punishment and also the soldier was beaten to death. Bollywood film *Veer Zaara* (2004) made by Yash Chopra is a love story between an Indian Air Force pilot and a Pakistani woman from a political family. There are many such examples in the history of world cinema.

Although there was rarely a reference to a love affair between a Bengali woman and Pakistani soldier in the time of war, the director Rubaiyat Hossain has at least one reference. She says, 'I researched the nationalist representation of the raped women of 1971, and during that time I conducted a few interviews with survivors. One of them gave me a very complex story of falling in love with a soldier while she was being raped by the others' (cited in Chowdhury, 2015: 770). While an aesthetic or creative experimentation can be done by a writer or filmmaker, especially when the creator wants to convey a specific message (loving others) through his/her piece, such experimentation has been taken as a distortion of historical truths.

Can a Birangana Speak?

Each of the major female characters is distinctive; among three sisters, Neela is embittered and cynical, Meher is innocent and compassionate and Salma is slightly dotty but determined to marry the freedom fighter of her choice. The older women are little more than background figures created to emphasise the strength and modernity of the younger women. The men are little more than cyphers apart from the grandfather. This portrayal of the characters shows the feminist approach of the director.

One of the most striking parts of the film is, that despite being a rape victim of war and mentally shattered by the experience, Neela is not ashamed about what happened to her. Unlike her aunts, she was not afraid of losing dignity or the possibility of marriage, she wanted to tell everybody about the incident, and she was adamant in her desire to take her revenge on the Pakistani soldiers. Eventually, she joined the female *Mukti Bahini* unit and fought for liberation.

In this film, the *Birangana* (rape victims of the 1971 war) is speaking and participating in the field at the frontline of fight, which is almost absent in the actual *Birangana* discourse. They are always found as passive victims and the literature on *Birangana* is full of their sacrifice and the torture and abuse stories. At least in most of the films on the Liberation War made in Bangladesh, women are represented as rape victims and in many cases for commercial purposes. Prolonged rape scenes are used to sell sex to the audience. Even in arthouse and independent films, the *Birangana*s were never speaking. In Morshedul Islam's *Dollhouse* (2006), Rehana was found traumatised and mentally imbalanced, but never talked about her experiences. A few documentaries have already been made in which the story of the *Birangana*'s pain, abuse and sacrifice have been described; no other perspective is found on those films. Neela, as a rape victim of war, talked about what she experienced for the first time in cinema and joined the war as a fighter. For the first time, a *Birangana* really spoke up with an agentic position and thus 'disrupted gendered nationalist narrative of male valor and female shame' (Chowdhury, 2015: 766).

Nationalist Jingoism and Moral Policing

From what we can gather, much of the opposition to the film came from people who had not seen it, but they knew it was subversive and derogatory. Critics who took the trouble to see the film opposed the censorship demanded by the guardians and practiced by the exhibitors but critiqued the film in cinematic terms. It is indeed interesting that the depiction of sex in the film, caused offense in Bangladesh more than any other aspect, suggesting the power of sex to derail the grand narrative and puncture the dominant discourse (which demonises the Pakistanis and their collaborators). It as a 'hyper-masculinist response' (Chowdhury, 2015: 760) of the normative masculine psyche found that 'the enemy' (Wasim) was winning 'our girl' (Meher) and because of that 'our boy' (Sami) is refused and eventually slapped by our 'derailed girl'. Apart from that, the response was predominantly a hyper-nationalist reaction that no space should be given to any member of the enemy of the Liberation War, even after nearly 50 years. Any sympathy or any drift from the grand narrative was considered pro-Pakistani and pro-*Jamaati* and anti-Bangladeshi. As the film did not show enough respect to the grand narrative, the film was criticised as pro-Pakistani and was assumed to be the result of a deep-rooted conspiracy against Bangladesh. The moral police characterised by nationalist deterministic individuals wanted to give a lesson to the director about what to say and what not to say regarding the Liberation War and relevant discourse.

The director tried to make the enemy soldier Wasim 'acceptable' to the audience by means of some logical progressions in the script. He was a Balochi soldier, supposedly less atrocious than Punjabi soldiers and, he was a deserter from the Pakistani Army as he refused to kill people in a mosque. Nayanika Mookherjee says, various Balochi and Pathan soldiers are often attributed with having helped East Pakistani civilians by aiding their escape.... [N]ine out of the 25 odd regiments based in Bangladesh in 1971 were Balochi and the 22nd Baloch regiment allegedly carried out unprecedented atrocities in Chittagong (Mookherjee, 2011: 25–26). However, while running away he saved Meher from a group of soldiers in a jungle of the village. In exchange, Meher helped unwell Wasim and while nursing him a love affair grew between them. But this progression in the narrative was not 'accepted' by the moral police and the film faced the furor.

An Untimely Deconstruction?

The deconstruction of the grand narrative of the Liberation War might have been untimely or a bit early when it was released in 2011. The International Crime Tribunal (ICT) was set to bring local war criminals under trial, an unresolved issue even after four decades of the war. Pakistan as a state had yet to seek forgiveness for their genocide in Bangladesh. Moreover, the status of the war had not been recognised yet from the international community, at least from the Bangladesh perspectives. Pakistan sees it as losing brothers and was caused by India's conspiracy. India sees it as the war between India and Pakistan in which India won. The international community also often describes it as a war between India and Pakistan. It is true that India helped greatly by giving shelter and feeding 1,00,00,000 refugees and trained *Mukti Bahini*, but *Mukti Bahini* and Bengali officers and soldiers also took part in the war. And they resisted the occupant army for nine months and only in the first week of December 1971, in the 9th month of the war, Indian air strikes confirmed the victory. In this context, Meherjaan's message might be untimely, especially when the war crime tribunal was a major political issue.

In addition, the leader of the Liberation War, Sheikh Mujibur Rahman was killed in 1975, just after four years of liberation. For the next two decades, the secular or pro-Liberation ideology was set back, and Muslim identity derived from Pakistan movement in the 1940s came to the forefront. The oscillation of the people of Bangladesh between Bengali and Muslim identities has created a great dealt of suffering for them. Also, after two decades, AL has come far from its secular ideologies and included religious components in their policies and practices. Ali Riaz says:

> [A]s the politics of Islamism became a legitimate discourse and the religio-politico force, with the patronage of the state [in prolonged Zia and Ershad regime], became considerably stronger, secularists were faced with dilemma: how to confront them, both in the short and long term. The AL's deliberate decision to join the bandwagon reveals either their lack of sincerity to engage the society in a debate on the role of religion in public life or and inclination to return to power at any cost.... The shift of the AL was also guided by the electoral equation. The unexpected defeat in the 1991 election convinced them to move to the right, vacating their centrist position.
>
> (Riaz 2010: 58)

The reactionary response of the country towards the film is to some extent understandable. But an artist's creative journey cannot be controlled by the desires of the state or a community. Meanwhile, 9/11 happened and Muslims were oppressed and the victim of the global politics. The approach towards Muslim identity shifted in both global and local political discourse. This shift has been evident, especially in Bangladesh art house filmmaking. Earlier in Liberation War films, the *razakar* character was essentially a bearded Muslim (all *razakar*s were not bearded in 1971). The secular director's present notion of portraying Muslim identity as unacceptable was applied to the Liberation War villains. But there were some changes from the representation of the grand narrative especially after 9/11. In *Dark Shadow* (Shaymol Chhaya 2004) by Humayun Ahmed, the bearded young Muslim was a freedom fighter. In *Clouds After Cloud* (Megher Por Megh 2004) by Chashi Nazrul Islam, a major character had a role of an Islamist who worked for liberation. In *Journey of Victory* (Joyjatra 2004) by Tauquir Ahmed, the first protest against the Pakistani Army was done by an Imam of a mosque. Before all these, in Tareue Masud's influential film *The Clay Bird* (2002), there was a major Islamist character who was hurt to see united Pakistan falling apart but did not collaborate with the Pakistan Army or do any fighting. In this context, Meherjaan came with a deconstructive narrative.

Is 'Loving the Other' Possible?

The premise of the film is as follows:

> Meherjaan is a film about loving the Other. Meherjaan gives away with the unitary masculine narrative in order to usher in an emotional multiplicity of feminine emotion and sensibility. This film critiques certain pitfalls of nationalism that create conditions to justify war, killing and violence. Finally, Meherjaan attempts to offer an aesthetic solution to war and violence by taking refuge in love and spiritual submission.

By loving the other, the director wanted to break the conditions that have been used to justify war, killing and violence. The medieval period of world history was full of war, killing and violence, and this is continuing in the modern world. Hossain emphasises a 'reckoning' with the 'Other', not necessarily at the state or judicial level, but through interpersonal relationships (Chowdhury, 2015: 763). However, as the events in the film indicate, loving the 'Other' is not easy and perhaps impossible. Hatred and jingoism are the norms of the members of the nation state who propagate hating 'others' to give the fuel for loving 'ourselves'.

Narration

Where the film really struggles is in maintaining a narrative pace. These are exciting times and people's lives are in danger. There is a possibility of a complete social breakdown and yet Meher and Wasim find time to wander through the forests and paddy fields unobserved and oblivious to events that will shape their lives forever. If this is meant to signify the power of love to transcend normality, it was established. The bucolic love scenes detract from the rest of the action, which suggests to us at least, that Hossain was unclear to whether her film was meant to be a commercial blockbuster, or an art house movie aimed at the intelligentsia. This confusion is emphasised in the penultimate scene, the burning of the village accompanied by the sound of the cry of the distressed people.

There is little to complain about with the acting. But conscious use of bright colours sometimes gives a feeling of magic to realist moments and sometimes appeared as mere commercialism. Through Wasim's gaze, Meher appears as a vision of beauty and in pink coloured dresses, which is a feminine signifier. Background scores and cinematography were consistent, but the camera presented the rural location as an exotic commodity. In a single film, the director wanted to deal with a lot of complex issues without a lot of explanations – the political trajectory of Bengal from 1947 to 1971, religion as spiritual as well as a means of resistance, the indicative same sex relations of Sara and the Sufi couple Arup and Rahi, the role of communists in the political landscape of Bangladesh and so on. However, we must say, credit can be given to the film as this is a rare piece in which the contribution of the communists was recognised.

Television: Religion's Negotiation with Modernity

The film *Television* studies how Islamic values are practiced in a peripheral Bengal society in modern times. The film shows how the religious orthodoxy deals and negotiates with external forces, especially media technologies. The film also shows, how the dialectic between these two apparently opposite entities affects and changes peoples' belief systems as well as how human relations are determined by the dialectic.

Television is considered to be one of the best films made by Mostofa Sarwar Farooki. The film received a grand jury prize at the Asia Pacific Screen Award, 2013. It was also the closing film at the Busan International Film Festival in 2012. The film was Bangladesh's submission to the 86th Academy Awards in the foreign-language category.

Histoire

In a remote village called Mithanupur, an orthodox village leader named Amin Patwari (alias Chairman Sahib) bans all kinds of images in his territory. Believing that the appreciation of images is *haram* (prohibited) in Islam. He reads the newspaper only after his assistant covers the images of women printed in it. Television is banned in his territory. However, being somewhat rational, he allows a Hindu man (Kumar Babu) to bring a television set at his home, as images are not prohibited to Hindus.

130 Textual Analysis: Transitional Films

Now Muslim villagers rush to watch television at Kumar Babu's house. The old man's efforts to keep people away from images were in vain. Moreover, the leader's young son secretly talks to his girlfriend through video chat. In an inspection at the Hindu man's house, Amin caught Kohinoor, the girlfriend of his son Solaiman, watching television with others. Amin punishes her in front of the public. Being humiliated in public she breaks up with Solaiman. She sends a message through Majnu, the employee of Solaiman who is also in love with Kohinoor, that if Solaiman could revolt against his father, they might be reconciled. Solaiman demonstrates this by organising the village boys into a rally, declares her marriage date through a microphone and promises publicly buying a television. The gang insulted the chairman and beat the chairman's assistant, Jabbar. Solaiman's rebellion hurts his father and surprises the villagers. Kohinoor asks Solaiman to seek forgiveness from his father. Solaiman's short-term rebellion ends by asking forgiveness and the father's initiation of marrying off duos. Amin decides to perform Hajj in Mecca, but while preparing his passport, capturing a picture becomes a big issue. He compromises in printing picture for passport though it makes him upset. On the way to his Hajj pilgrimage, Amin was cheated by the Hajj agents in the capital city Dhaka. While passing interim time in a hotel, the depressed and disheartened old man could perform his Hajj with the help of the television which was relaying the Hajj event live from Mecca.

Figure 5.3 Amin Patwary (Kazi Shahir Huda Rumi) in front of a *halal* television.

Recit

The film states that television is a great source of image and imagination. The film also shows the conflict between modernity and religious zealotry. But at the end, it depicts how religious rules and norms deal with the advent of modernity. In that process, religious characters and ideologies are addressed sensibly.

Television as a Vehicle of Imag(e)ination

It is difficult to conceive of how in the 'post-broadcast' time (Hartley, 2003) there was no television in a village. In the storyline, we see Solaiman purchasing a computer to video chat with his girlfriend even before Kumar Babu brings the first television in the village. We cannot imagine such a place, no matter how remote it might be where there is an internet connection but no prevalence of television. Of course, it is Amin Patwary's shadow governance that made it possible. At the beginning of the film, when a female television reporter had come to interview and questioned the legitimacy of Amin Patwary's shadow governance, there was no television in the village.

John Hartley (2003) says, in post-broadcast time, people are not only 'reading' television, they are also 'writing' on television. That means people are capturing video and uploading it on YouTube, Facebook and other streaming sites or social media. In Bangladesh, television sets had already reached every village by the 1990s except for some hilly areas. The script writers (Anisul Hoque and Mostofa Sarwar Farooki) created a fictional reality by sacrificing the actual one. However, the director has chosen a *Char* (a river island) that is separated by a long and wide river from the mainland. This isolation might have made Amin's governance possible, although it does not explain the reason of the prior absence of television there. They tried to place television as a signifier and the source of images through which the twists and turns of the storyline would take place.

Over the decades, television has created an alternate reality. Alternatively, the reality itself is determined by television, as Boorstin says, 'nothing is really real unless it happens on television' (cited in Wasko, 2005: 8). By living in a traditional society and following an age-old religion, Amin Patwary understands that watching television would attract his people to a that which is not preferred by Islam and hence by himself. He, therefore, puts forward a prohibition by Islam against drawing or watching images of living creatures. Being a true Islamist, he beliefs in a conspiracy theory that technologies like television are invented and marketed by the Jews and Christians to spoil the sanctity of Muslims.

Television is the ultimate vehicle for images and imagination. After seizing the Kumar Babu's television, villagers started crossing the river to watch television and film. Amin's assistant came with a new idea of *halal*

132 Textual Analysis: Transitional Films

entertainment for villagers. He introduced a *halal* television which is basically a big television-like stage where a drama was being staged. But Amin did not allow that either as some villagers while acting in different roles were imagining themselves to be those characters. According to Amin, imagination is very bad. Young people tend to fantasise about things while riding on the horse of imagination.

Amin was right as we see Majnu, the unsung lover of Kohinoor declares that it does not matter whether Kohinoor loves him or not, he will continue seeing her live in a 'private television' where he will do a lot of censored things with her in his imagination. While chatting over the phone Solaiman also asked Kohinoor to keep the call on so that Solaiman could feel and imagine her movements live through a 'mind television'. But where Amin was wrong was thinking that while sexuality is a biological process, nobody can prevent the minds of the young people from dreams and imaginations.

A Conflict between Zealotry and Modernity?

The film *Television* portrays the conflict between tradition and modernity. Amin wants to preserve the traditional values that are manifested through religion. He restricts people from birth control as he thinks life and death are acts of Allah, humans are nobody to control that. He allows men to use mobile phones without cameras but prohibits women from that.

Raymond Williams says, [...] television has altered our world. In the same way, people often speak of a new world, a new society, a new phase of history, being created – 'brought about' – by this or that new technology: the steam engine, the automobile, the atomic bomb (Williams, 2003[1974]: 1). However, Williams' optimistic notion to call television a tool for 'long revolution' can be contested in terms of the effect of its 'counter revolution'. Roger Silverstone argues,

> Technologies lead double lives, and television is no exception. They are both, as Williams argues, the 'contemporary tools for the long revolution towards an educated and participatory democracy' – a project of which he never lost sight; but they are also the tools of what he dubs the counter-revolution, in which the forces of capital successfully intrude into the finest grain of our everyday lives.
> (Silverstone, 2003: xiii)

Amin could see only the counter-revolutionary role of television as an agent of change in the society. However, he was only seeing reality through religious lens. Within the film, it is noted that one religious leader might disagree with his position, as his twin brother Razzab Patwary, who lives in Dhaka, talks on television regularly about religious issues and preaches to the nation. But Amin thinks Razzab is 'spoilt' and his path is not truly Islamic. Actually, Amin only follows scriptures that were introduced 1400 years before and he has not agreed to accept any interpretation given in modern context. But he had to allow almost everything he contested. He had to give permission to use all modern technologies. He himself had to use 'necessary evils, such as the picture for his passport and television for performing Hajj.

Religious Sense and Sensibility

The character Amin Patwari is driven by strict Islamic senses, yet he has sensibilities. He is orthodox and authoritarian. Religious bigotry is his method of governing people. He believes that taking interest from money is prohibited in Islam, so he drove away NGO representatives offering micro-credit programmes to the village. But he also loves his people, and his people respect him as well. He is not a monstrous religious leader, rather his strict attitudes are derived from his desire to keep people on the right path.

Amin himself was using a repaired mobile phone for his business needs. But he did not allow mobile phones in the village. He was concerned that by using the internet and Facebook in the mobile phone, the young generation would be spoilt. But with the help of his intelligent assistant Majnu, Solaiman could convince Amin that mobile phones are needed for the betterment of the business. Amin agrees to provide a mobile phone to his son and at the same time he announces that other villagers are also allowed to use it. But it must be used only for calling. Mobile phones with cameras would be prohibited. Solaiman buys a phone for himself and another for his girlfriend Kohinoor and thus his main purpose of buying a phone which is with Kohinoor was fulfilled.

After the raid at Kumar Babu's house, Amin discovered Muslim villagers were also watching television. So, he ordered that the television be thrown in the river. But before that he allocated Kumar the price of the television and the allocation was higher than the original price.

After the revolt of Solaiman, Amin realised that Solaiman and Kohinoor were deeply in love. So, he took the initiative to marry them. All these incidents prove that although Amin was an orthodox, but he was a sensible person at the same time. Be it good or bad, he chose a way of living directed towards the scriptures of Islam and he applies them to the villagers. His authoritarian approach and bigotry come from that belief system. The director has portrayed his character with much attention and compassion.

Love in the Time of Religious Bigotry

The norms and values in the Mithanupur society are set by Amin Patwary and are based on an Islamic value system where images are not allowed, let alone mixing between girls and boys. But the biological desire of the young men and women do not always follow these norms. Amin's own son is in an affair with Kohinoor, whose father lives in overseas. Kohinoor is a charming and smart girl but Solaiman is a simple young man who loves her and respects his father deeply. Solaiman's assistant Majnu is very intelligent and also loves Kohinoor. His poverty compelled him to be the subordinate to Solaiman. Solaiman gave up learning operating computer as it seemed difficult due to his poor learning capacity. It is Majnu who connects the internet with the computer. It was Majnu's suggestion that created a situation in which Amin had to allow Solaiman and others to have mobile phones. But it is very painful for Majnu to see how Solaiman and Kohinoor are having fun and carrying on long chats through the mobile phone or through video conferencing. Whenever the network is poor, and the video chat is interrupted. it is Majnu who had to fix it. When the marriage between Solaiman and Kohinoor was set, it is Majnu who must arrange everything for the wedding. After the marriage was fixed, this sad lover wanted to leave the place. But Solaiman's ordered fancy foods to be sent Kohinoor's place blocked Majnu at once.

The relationship between Majnu and Kohinoor has a different dimension. Having known that this relationship has no future, he still expresses to Kohinoor how deeply he loved her. Majnu knows that class difference is a barrier here. He also knew that if Solaiman had come to learn of Majnu's passion towards Kohinoor, he would lose his job, yet he could not resist. He asked Kohinoor not to tell Solaiman and Kohinoor kept it within herself. Kohinoor does not accept Majnu, but she does not tell Solaiman about Majnu's feelings towards her. Majnu's one-sided love and passion towards Kohinoor and his intelligence make him a strong character in the narrative, brighter than Solaiman.

Narration

Television is a content-based narrative film. Cinematic experimentation is not usually found in the film. But within the classical narrative structure, there are some interesting technical parts that are worth discussing.

The characterisation in the film is developed in an intelligent way. The character of Amin has been developed with much care and attention. Traditionally in Bangladeshi cinema and other cultural forms, Islamist men are not portrayed in a positive manner. The secular-minded authors think an Islamist person is against modernity and progress and should be portrayed as a villain. They usually do not show the use of morality and ethics of religion in the daily lives of people. From that point of view, the character of Amin Patwary is portrayed quite sensibly. The director also has shown the challenges that technological prevalence and progress pose for religious and that people like Amin Patwary were not ready to negotiate. Amin had to compromise with the challenges at the end. In that way, the film *Television* positively studies the representative character of religion at the same time providing a critique of the religious belief system Amin wanted to implement.

The triangular love relations among Kohinoor, Solaiman and Majnu are weaved intelligently. The social strata developed based on class make intelligent Majnu subordinate to Solaiman, who was someway stupid. For the same reason, Majnu does not get the love of Kohinoor. The characterisation process is an important aspect of the film. Even the small characters are developed with much attention. At the beginning of the film, after completing the interview with Amin, a young man (Jahangir) asked an odd question of the female journalist about the jeans she wore and thus tried to humiliate her. The same character was in the first group who rushed to watch television at Kumar Babu's home. He was caught watching TV across the river. He was ahead of everybody with a bamboo stick at the time of Solaiman's revolt. The same person was the most enthusiastic in asking people when a 'visa system' was would be introduced by Amin's people to cross the river. In rural Bengal, this kind of person is seen everywhere and active in everything.

The location of the film was carefully selected, and Golam Maola Nabir's camera used ample elements to capture the stunning beauty of rural Bangladesh. The village is situated near a wide river. The volume of water in the river and the wide-open sky and landscapes create a great and beautiful environment. In the midst of this overflowing beauty, the strict governance by Amin appears paradoxical. The cinematographer used several mirror shots to create the further space within the frame, which has been used by many great cinematographers previously. After the break-up, to reveal the loneliness of Solaiman, a lone boat in the river was used to symbolise the state of his mind. Colourful car toys of Kohinoor's younger brother were shown several times; the meaning of that was not clear, however, they gave some visual relief to audience. Solaiman's workplace and the walls of Kohinoor's house were also covered or painted by strong colours like pink, yellow and blue. The pink colour at Soaliman's workplace represents the mental status of the lover boy. The yellow and blue colours signify the warmth of the charming Kohinoor.

At least in one scene, Khaled Mahmud Rajan's editing was stunning. Solaiman wants Kohinoor to keep the mobile phone on so that he can listen to her sounds and movements and can imagine himself at her place. Afterwards, we see Solaiman was not only listening to the ambience of Kohinoor's place, his physical position was also shifted. We find Solaiman inside Kohinoor's home sitting the same way he had been sitting in the workplace in the previous scene. Thus, Solaiman's imagination was expressed visually by the editor's manipulation of the space.

References

Chowdhury, E. H. (2015). When Love and Violence Meet: Women's Agency and Transformative Politics in Rubaiyat Hossain's Meherjan, *Hypatia*, *30*(4), 760–777.

Hartley, J. (2003[1974]). Reading Television after Twenty Five Years: A New Forward by John Hartley. In J. Fiske and J. Hartley (eds.), *Reading Television* (pp. ix–xxii). London: Routledge.

Masud, T. (2003). Interview: *Le Monde Aden*. In A. B. M. N. Huda, (ed.), *Rediscovering Bangladesh: Foreign Press on Matir Moina* (pp. 21–24). Dhaka: Audiovision.

Masud, T. (2004a). The Clay Bird: Asia Source Interview with Tareque Masud at http://www.asiasource.org/news/special_reports/masud.cfm. Accessed 4 March 2008.

Masud, T. (2004b). The first Bangladeshi entry for the Oscars – banned in Bangladesh at http://www.indiacurrents.com/news/view_article.html?article. Accessed 15 February 2008.

Masud, T. (2006). Interview conducted by the author on 13 December 2006.

Masud, T. (2007). Interview conducted for the study on 11 February, 2007.

Mookherjee, N. (2011). Love in the Time of 1971: The Furore over Meherjaan. *Economic and Political Weekly*, *46*(12), 25–27.

Raju, Z. H. (2002). A Coming of Age: Tareque Masud's The Clay Bird. *Cinemaya*, *14*(2), 56–57.

Riaz, A. (2010). The Politics of Islamization in Bangladesh. In A. Riaz (ed.), *Religion and Politics in South Asia* (pp. 45–70). London: Routledge.

Silverstone, R. (2003[1974]). Preface of the Routledge Classics Edition. In R. Williams (ed.), *Television: Technology and Cultural Form* (pp. vi–xiii). London: Routledge.

Tremois, C. (2003). Cinema: 'Keep Love in your Heart'. In A. B. M. N. Huda (ed.), *Rediscovering Bangladesh: Foreign Press on Matir Moina* (pp. 7–9). Dhaka: Audiovision.

Wasko, J. (2005). Introduction. In J. Wasko (ed.), *A Companion to Television* (pp. 1–12). Oxford: Blackwell Publishing.

Williams, R. (2003[1974]). *Television: Technology and Cultural Form*. London: Routledge.

6 Textual Analysis: Contemporary Films

Unlike rural peasant society or *mufassil*-looking urban centres, recent Bangladesh is closely connected with the globe and affected by the neoliberal globalisation process. Even in the peripheral small towns and villages, there are many low-priced smartphones with internet connections and television sets. For this connectivity, Bangladesh society is experiencing all the virtues and vices of the global phenomena. On one hand, the abundance of information has supported people in developing new initiatives and entrepreneurships – both offline and online. In other ways it has contributed to an advent of global vices – consumer culture and moral degradation of people, financial disparity and labour exploitation, aggressive Jihadist Islam and so on. The onslaught of these positive and negative factors is changing the identity of the Bangladeshi people rapidly.

The contemporary films too, explore the present, drifting away from the Liberation War of 1971 as the centre of attention (although its presence is inescapable as a backdrop to contemporary Bangladeshi affairs) and focusing more on the transformation occurring in globalised Bangladesh. Recent Bangladesh is closely connected with the globe and affected by the neoliberal globalisation process. Even in the peripheral small towns and villages, there are many low-priced smartphones with internet connections and television sets. For this connectivity, Bangladesh society is experiencing all the virtues and vices of the global phenomena. On one hand, the abundance of information has supported people in developing new initiatives and entrepreneurships – both offline and online. In other ways it has contributed to an advent of global vices – consumer culture and moral degradation of people, financial disparity and labour exploitation, aggressive Jihadist Islam and so on. The onslaught of these positive and negative factors is changing the identity of the Bangladeshi people rapidly. This is very important in understanding how Bangladeshi filmmakers respond to these changes.

Under the contemporary films category, labour exploitation in the readymade garment (RMG) sector, the biggest industry in Bangladesh, has been portrayed in *Under Construction* (2015) by Rubaiyat Hossain. The rise of Jihadist Islam is being depicted in *Runway* (2010) by Tareque Masud. Mostofa Sarwar Farooki's *Ant Story* (2013) shows how the pressure of

138   *Textual Analysis: Contemporary Films*

consumer culture and moral degradation make a simple person a freak. All of these films cover a few more issues that are worth mentioning in this discussion such as the rapid urban growth, the misery of migrant workers, women's struggle to create their own space in a patriarchal society, the issue of privacy in the digital age and so on. However, ironically, in the globalised Bangladesh, there is a rise in the debate of nationalism. Both Bengali-Muslim and the 'other' identities are covered by the contemporary independent filmmakers. Aung Rakhine's *My Bicycle* (2015) portrays the culture and society of indigenous Chakma people in the CHT.

A *Runway*: Profiling Terror Network in Bangladesh

Runway is a story of a poor family living in a dilapidated house near the runway of the airport. However, it is more a story of socio-economic and political crisis in recent Bangladesh than a story of a family only. This is Tareque Masud's first film, which dealt with recent issues of Bangladesh and predominantly focused on religious terrorism; but it has also portrayed the exploitation of women working in the RMG industry, a critique of the micro-credit-based activities of NGOs as well as the exploitation of Bangladeshi labourers in overseas. The major contributing sectors to the increasing reserves of the Bangladesh economy are the remittances of migrant workers and export-oriented RMG. On the other hand, the economic and social conditions in rural Bangladesh are sometimes controlled by the micro-credit programmes operated by NGOs. In recent times, *Jongibad* (Jihadist terrorism) is another crisis that evolved in Bangladesh. The family members of Ruhul, who is in his early youth, are representatives of the large issues facing Bangladesh today; Ruhul's family is a small replica of recent Bangladesh.

Runway is one of the earliest films made in digital format in Bangladesh. In 2010, when the film was released, Bangladeshi cine theatres were not ready with digital projection systems. The self-financed film was screened countrywide by means of an informal distribution system at makeshift halls at university campuses and cultural centres in the different corners of the country. With the help of film society members and cultural groups, the director Tareque Masud initiated dialogues with the young generation at Q&A sessions, suggesting the crisis of terrorism must be met through dialogues with the young generation and through cultural manifestations.

Histoire

Ruhul's father had migrated to Middle East as a worker, his mother bought a cow by the credit she got from an NGO, and his sister was a worker in RMG factory. The other member of the family is his old paternal grandfather. A madrasa dropout, Ruhul is unemployed and naive. Often, he visits his maternal uncle's cyber cafe where he tries to learn how to operate a computer and how to browse the internet. He cannot handle managing the wonder machine and his uncle is unhappy with him. A young man Arif helps him and becomes Ruhul's friend. He started discussing the true path of Islam with the bearded and good looking young man Arif. Gradually Ruhul became involved in *Jongi* (terror) affairs with the guidance of Arif. He was trained in Jihadi militancy by 'Udru Bhai', the *Mujahid* who was back from Afghanistan and Kashmir warfare.

After joining the terrorist group, Ruhul's attitude changed. He forced his sister Fatema not to turn on television other than watching news. He had a yet-to-be-exposed romantic relationship with Sheuli, the friend of Fatema. While talking to her, he started maintaining a physical distance. He even asked his mother to stop taking credits from the micro-credit company, as any form of interest is *haram* (prohibited) in Islam. None of the family members allowed the newly adopted orthodoxy of Ruhul. Instead, he was rebuked by the family members. Ruhul started to be more outgoing.

On the Jihad frontier, Arif and his team planted bombs in the movie theatres, as movies were considered to be anti-Islamic. The leader of the team, Urdu Bhai, claimed that the un-Islamic cultures like the *jatra* play and the *Orosh* (the get-together of the followers in commemorating the death of the saint) in shrines were stopped due to their initiatives. He announced the area of their movement a 'free land' and started their own administration which followed Islamic *Shariah*. But an influential person from the government called upon them, rebuked them and warned them against excess, otherwise government protection would be taken away. He asked the Jihadists not to do any harm to the judges of the court. The *jongi* leader accused the influential personnel (suggesting a political leader in the government) that they supported Islamic nationalism in words only; in practice they were afraid of many things. They could not pass any *Shariah* law as the foreign donors opposed it.

However, there was a car bomb attack in the court and Arif was severely injured. The fellow *jongi*s saw injured Arif in the television and thought Arif would tell everything to the police after he recovered sufficiently. The militants ran away, but Ruhul did not. He started thinking differently and decided to go back home. At home, in the early morning, he left his bed and sat outside. Under the golden light of the dawn, he discovered the fresh natural environment and ongoing human life – the fisherman was catching fish, ducks were swimming on the water, ants were busy with their jobs, the butterflies were flying freely. He again found the meaning of life. His mother washed his mouth with milk as a ritual as he had come back to his previous life.

Recit

The film *Runway* closely studies the nature of Jihadist terrorism in post-2000 Bangladesh. The incident of 9/11 and subsequent attacks in Afghanistan and

140 *Textual Analysis: Contemporary Films*

Figure 6.1 Ruhul (Fazlul Haque) comes back home from the city.

Iraq were benchmarks of the global rise of Jihadist terrorism. Bangladesh also experienced some Jihadist attacks in the time period 2004–2005. *Runway* portrays this home-grown terrorism that had some global connections. In his earlier film, *The Clay Bird,* Tareque Masud dealt with Jihad theoretically. Here in *Runway*, he attempts to study Jihad in a realistic and authentic manner, because Bangladesh already had started experiencing Jihadist attacks.

Dealing with Jihadist Islam

Tareque Masud dealt with several issues of contemporary Bangladesh – RMG sector, Migrant workers, micro-credit – altogether these are giving the shape of an identity of recent Bangladesh, both nationally and internationally. However, the film *Runway* predominantly focuses on Jihadist Islam, which is a recent concern in Bangladesh society. What are the true ways of Islam – like Ruhul, most of the practicing Muslims in Bangladesh are confused while searching for answer to this question. The ultimate question has haunted the Bengal Muslims – primarily what are they, Bengali or Muslim? The rise of global Jihadist Islam is a result of a few complex but interrelated factors – global Muslim fraternity, a fight against imperialism, opposition to the aggression of 'harmful' Western culture, and attacks on

Muslim countries by the western military which is perceived as Judeo-Christian conspiracy by the Muslims. Some analysts see the war against terror is basically an imperialist aggression to take control of the energy sectors of the Middle East and Central Asia (see Rashid, 2001). Even after so many bombings, Jihadist terrorism was not eliminated – it was migrated from one place to other.

The rise of Jamayatul Mujahidin (JMB) and Harkatul Jihad in Bangladesh in the 2005–06 periods had a connection with this globalisation of Jihadist terrorism. JMB wanted to capture power through Jihad and to implement Islamic *Shariah* law and ultimately to form a government. The film *Runway* was made in 2010 and the film selected this rise of *Jongibad* in Bangladesh as the subject matter.

However, Jihadists believe in coercion and they wanted to stop popular religious practices. They attacked shrines, forcibly stopped the musical programmes of the Bauls and bombarded movie theatres considering the film is a polluted cultural form. For years, *jatra* plays had not been staged. They also killed Maoists in North and South-West Bengal. They set off bombs in the yards of the court, the pillar of the westernised democracy as well as a system developed by men which they considered to deny the justice system of God. In the film *Runway*, all of these issues have been portrayed with skills.

Geneology of a 'Jongi'

Who is a *Jongi*? The leader, Udru Bhai, was an extremist Mujahid who had experienced the war in Afghanistan and Kashmir. At the same time, a tech-savvy and smart young man like Arif was also there with him. This intelligent young man has reached here while he was having a journey searching for an ideology. After the fall of communism, when imperialist aggression was perceived as synonymous with the abuse of Muslims, the resistant Palestine militants or Taliban fighters became the inspiration for people like Arif. There is also Ruhul, a madrasa dropout, poor and unemployed. *Jongibad* provides him an ideology as well as money. The Jihadists are in a mission to implement *Shariah* in a coercive manner. Arif was inclined to *Jongibad* by choice and would not be expected ever to return to a normal life. But Ruhul might be brought back; at least the director's desire was to bring Ruhul back. Ruhul might not leave his quest for a true path of Islam but he came back to a regular life at the end. He at least understood the path he took was not right.

The director clearly has the opinion that the path taken by Ruhul and others were wrong, and they were needed to be brought back to a normal life. Anybody having modern democratic ideas, humanist approach and rational mind and who accepts the existing legal frameworks, would say the same. However, the director has portrayed the possible contexts of being *Jongi*. Hence the pro-Jihad *Hujur* (Urdu Bhai) has said, in Quran, there were only 82 verses on saying prayers but there were 681 verses on Jihad. This means there might be approval within the holy book for a person like Ruhul who is looking for a true path of *Dwin*, the ways of living that comply the divine laws. On the other hand, Arif was not happy with the major party representing political Islam, Jamaat-E-Islam. The reason for Arif's divorce with his wife was her party's policy of practicing Islam and democracy at the same time as he believed the two are contradictory to each other. This hypocritical stand allowed the party to achieve power. Administrative support was behind the rise of Islamic *Jongi*s in the 2005–06 time period as was also stated in the film. However, there was tension between the *Jongi*s and the administration – on how far the administration would continue supporting them. This was the reason for the *Jongi*s' 'excess' which was also addressed in the film.

Class Exploitations Everywhere

There are issues of labour exploitation and labour discontent in the RMG sector. Fatema's salary was suspended for two months. In the labour market of the Middle East, Bangladeshi labourers are exploited by the Muslim 'brothers'. The mighty NGOs apply pressure to the poor credit holders to return the instalment – the mother returns the credit from her daughter's salary, not from the milk of the cow, which was bought by the credit. The issue of the fraudulence of telecom companies towards users is also mentioned in the film. People like Ruhul are part of a non-privileged and oppressed class. Once, Ruhul's rickshaw puller was beaten by a car owner for a collision between the two transports. For protesting it, Ruhul was also beaten. Ruhul started thinking about this as class domination – although the rickshaw puller was not responsible for the collision, he was beaten. For opposing the oppressive behaviour of the rich man, Ruhul was also beaten. Immediately after this, while returning home, Ruhul saw that a little boy was trying to hit a plane leaving the runway with his catapult. Ruhul seemed happy to see this. Ruhul's sister is also a victim of class exploitation. She says that if there is oppression, there should be protest. The channels show only the unrest in the factories, but they do not show the exploitation of workers by the factory owners. The sister condemns the fact that everybody is in favour of the rich people. The owners give them only BDT 1500 ($18 [in 2018, it was increased to $95]) as a monthly wage but television shows do not reveal how much companies earn through exploitation.

These personal and societal realities are also responsible for driving Ruhul and others to be *Jongi*s. *Jongibad* provides them power and energy. Arif was a facilitator for Ruhul to be a *Jongi*. The information served by Arif was also an inspiration for Ruhul's realisation that the *Kafir*s in the world are controlling the Muslims. However, the director did not focus much on global politics, especially how the policy of western powers in the Middle East has contributed in the rise of global Jihadist Islam.

Narration

The end of the film is too unifying, which is not consistent with its central theme. This is not limited only to the return of Ruhul; Ruhul's uncle, who used to run a cyber cafe, was released from capture by the intelligence agency because he was reported to have a *Jongi* connection. After his return, Ruhul came to know that his lover Sheuli was living an independent life in a hostel and thus avoided a bad marriage. Even Ruhul's father returned from the Middle East, which was not at all necessary to the plot. He never contacted the family back home; a friend of his told the family that he was having a tough life in the climate of the Iraq war; his return as a happy person was not consistent with the story line.

A strength of the film was the cinematography. Misuk Munier's camera skillfully captured the arrival and take-off of the planes at the runway. After Ruhul's return to his house, he sat in the yard in the morning and the camera nicely described the details of the ongoing life around. During the first part of the film, when planes land in the morning, the tiny home shakes and the grandfather awakes from sleep; the shot proves how weak is the house and how helpless the family is under the gigantic planes.

The background music of the film appeared ordinary in comparison with *The Clay Bird*. But the use of Dolby digital sound was appropriate. In particular, the depth and pitch needed for the sound of the plane's landing and take-off were appropriate. The use of non-professional actors in the film rendered the film realistic and credible. Ali Ahsan in the character Arif was perfect casting. Fazlul Haq in the character Ruhul was also a good selection.

Runway is a film of contemporary issues. This film helped the audience to understand contemporary Bangladesh, especially the *Jongibad* phenomenon. There is no partial construction of *Jongibad* here, as other creative art pieces have done. The arguments on behalf of being *Jongi* were part of the film and then it was established why and how the committed acts were wrong, illegal and against humanity. This sensibility is the greatest strength of the film.

B *Ant Story*: Globalised Man's Descent into Madness

Mostofa Sarwar Farooki's *Ant Story* explores the issue of contemporary Bangladeshi sexuality from a psychoanalytical perspective. Briefly, the narrative is driven by the search to recover a sex tape made by an actress (a celebrity). The attempt to recover the tape allows Farooki to comment on other aspects of contemporary Dhaka City, making the film a powerful critique of Bangladesh in the age of consumption.

Ant Story was nominated for awards, participated in competitions or was selected officially in different film festivals that included the Dubai International Film Festival 2013, Shanghai International Film Festival 2014, Asia Pacific Screen Award 2014, Busan International Film Festival 2014, Singapore International Film Festival 2014 and so on.

Histoire

An intimate videotape featuring a film actress and her boyfriend in a compromising situation accidentally falls into the hands of an ordinary Bangladeshi youth, Mithu, who is struggling to come to terms with life in the big city. He has insufficient funds to meet his daily needs let alone his desires – for consumer goods that are representative of the move of Bangladesh into the global economy. Consequently, Mithu sees the tape in two ways as an opportunity to acquire things and as an investment that may bring power. The actress Rima contacts Mithu to retrieve the sex tape but Mithu, realising the commercial value of the tape in his possession, starts blackmailing Rima.

Before acquiring the tape Mithu was jobless, but later obtains a job in a MLM (Multi-level Marketing) company. Upon Rima's request, he returns the mobile phone he found to Rima but keeps a copy of the sex tape. Possession of this tape changes Mithu; he sees himself as empowered and able to move up in the consumer society to which he aspires. He uses the film to make Rima a client of his company, which brings him credit in the eyes of his employers. However, Mithu decides to take his putative control of Rima beyond using her for financial advantage; he decides to enter a world of psychosexual role-playing. First, Mithu takes Rima to his ex-girlfriend's house to make her jealous of his new girlfriend; his association with a glamorous celebrity thereby signifying his social rise. He also visits Rima's film set, which was shooting at Cox's Bazar, much to her annoyance. The role-playing concludes with an extreme act (in the Bangladeshi context), in which he compels Rima to play the role of his wife for one hour and invites her into his bed in an attempt to possess Rima as though she were like any other commodity. Rima responds to the blackmailing by Mithu, complying with his requests but refuses to go to bed with him at the end deciding that Mithu will not ruin her life. Rima's boyfriend also tries to get the copy of the sex tape from Mithu, but these efforts failed. Rima then changes her approach to the problem and arranges for gangsters to kidnap Mithu. The sudden arrival of the police at the scene of the kidnapping allows Mithu to escape, but his office then comes under scrutiny from the government and is shut down for illegal activities. Mithu's clients, alarmed by this turn of events, started visiting Mithu's house to demand the return of their investments.

From the moment the authorities are involved, Mithu's life is filled with troubles and to survive he becomes a fugitive. Rima cannot find Mithu, and she begins to fear that the release of the sex tape online will destroy her career, which drives her into depression. But Mithu's life becomes even more miserable. He has no job and no prospects, the creditors are relentless in the pursuit of their money, and he comes to fear death, which leads to a mental breakdown. His only solution is to rush home and ask his parents for their protection saying that he would be a good boy like before and would start going to school. In the last scene, he is shown in school uniform, staring at

Figure 6.2 Mithu (Noor Imran) enters Rima's (Sheena Chouhan) house and blackmails her.

nothing. His sister is sceptical about Mithu's mental degeneration and asks whether his mental status was true or false. Mithu remains silent and continues to stare at nothing.

Recit

The skill of Farooki in making this film lies in the fact that he deals with a contentious issue, sex among the young alienated members of a changing society, but never depicts anything sexual explicitly. He negotiates the grey area of sexual activity astutely, on the one hand conforming to local norms by not showing explicit images but on the other hand challenging local conventions with frankness found in few local films. The sex tape remains the central motif of the storyline. Thus, the audience is engaged with a libidinal item but without ever seeing anything explicit. The director's approach to the topic is essentially psychoanalytic, showing how an object, the sex tape, can bring change to the lives of people, either directly or incidentally, by playing off the subject's fears about sex in a repressed culture. This leads Farooki to adopt a rather gloomy view of life and apart from a few comic lines of dialogue between Mithu and his ex-girlfriend's husband, the director does not leave any comfort space for the audience. None of the depicted human relationships is in good shape; cunning, ugliness and tension occupy the storyline. Love and innocence have all taken place in the past – Mithu loses his humanity, Rima's fame is fragile and dependent on a video tape, Rima's boyfriend loses his credibility (he was responsible for losing the phone in the first place), Mithu lost his love to another guy before the movie begins. In short, Farooki takes a bleak view of humanity, suggesting that in a globalised city like contemporary Dhaka, humanity is a victim of a predatory consumer culture; it is objects and not people that are important.

Psychoanalysis

In terms of money, fame and class, Rima has status in the city, but the presence of the tape puts her in an awkward situation; in the thrall of someone inferior and insignificant in terms of class. Mithu lives outside of the city and needs to cross the river to reach his house. These two people, from different classes and backgrounds encounter one another in a context created by modern technology, which is the most obvious sign of Dhaka having entered the globalised economy. However, the main focus of the director is not the class of the protagonists; rather his interest lies in the psychology of the characters, especially of Mithu. As a result, the film can be divided into two distinct halves. In the first half of the film, the narrative trajectory tends towards docudrama, presenting the facts and commenting on contemporary life through the images and status of the main characters. In the second half, he investigates the psychological world of Mithu. This is portrayed surrealistically through dreams, such as the beach scene in which we see Mithu's imagined intimacy with Rima. Many masks are placed on the beach, as if these are representing the time and people around. Some ants attack Mithu's face while he is lying on the beach. Mithu rushes to the water to save his face. The ant is a symbol here as it is also a nickname of Rima's boyfriend Ayon, given because Ayon is a greedy ant that wants to taste Rima's sweet body. This greed was evident within Mithu as well, but it becomes the source of his ruin. The ants attack Mithu in more than one dream, which turn into nightmares.

The fugitive Mithu sleeps in a relative's clothing shop where he appropriates a mannequin from the shop as a surrogate for Rima and sleeps with it, his arms wrapped around the model. This fetishistic act symbolises his sexual desire for Rima. In another sequence, Mithu is to meet Rima for the first time, and he imagines the first encounter in three different ways. These imagined encounters, or dreams, allow the director to show us Mithu's state of mind, which is in turmoil. Rima's imagination is also given substance. Her depression, or mental disorder, is the ultimate consequence of her actions, exacerbated by her interactions with Mithu. Mithu appears to face two options, leading to an open-ended closing – he has either gone mad or to avoid the problems he has created through his desire for success and Rimi (they are virtually the same), he has taken to pretending madness.

Contemporary Bangladesh

Despite political turmoil, structural constraints and global volatility, the Bangladeshi economy maintains macroeconomic stability and is moving forward. *The Diplomat* reports on November 2, 2019:

> Since 2009, Bangladesh's economy has grown 188%. This year (2019), Bangladesh is on track to post record high annual GDP growth of 8.1%, up from 7.9% in 2018. By comparison, other South Asian countries, including India, Pakistan, and Sri Lanka, suffered significant dips in GDP growth in recent years. Yet Bangladesh has continued to thrive. HSBC Bank recently predicted that Bangladesh would be the 26th-largest economy in the world by 2030.
>
> (Ziauddin, 2019)

Bangladesh remains in the top three countries for manufacturing ready-made garments (RMG) for the global market and the money flow generated from the remittance of the Bangladeshi labour force in the global market has created a robust national reserve. Historically, the country has a strong base in agricultural production and is now self-sufficient in food production. Mithu wants to engage himself in this economic euphoria but until the mobile phone came in his possession he was destined to remain forever on the fringe. Mithu's desire for class transformation leads him to take a job in a MLM company, which is essentially a pyramid scheme that promises untold riches for very little effort. However, under the pressure of globalised consumer culture, people want to earn money any in way possible, even if it is not legal or ethical. Thus, the combination of the commentary on technology the mobile phone), human desire and economic cupidity presents a penetrating analysis of contemporary Bangladesh. In passing, it should be noted that in 2013 pyramid selling was outlawed in Bangladesh.

Bangladesh has one of the highest rates of mobile telephone usage in the region. Within a very short period, mobile phones penetrated every level of society. In many respects, the phone is a boon because of its flexibility for people like rickshaw drivers and housemaids as well as international business people, but it has also acquired the reputation for sensational misuse. The celebrity sex tape has become a phenomenon, with intimate video clips of celebrities being released online. In many cases, the boyfriend often does it after break-up of a relationship. Thus, Bangladesh has entered the world of revenge porn. In many respects, the incident narrated in *Ant Story* is similar to an actual case in which a sex tape of the actress and model Sadia Jahan Prova became available on the internet, released by her ex-boyfriend Rajib and the subject of much talk in Bangladesh in 2010.

The film also portrays the contemporary landscapes of Dhaka city. Rather than show the exotic and antique, it focuses visually on the newly made flyovers, the Buriganga river, buses and cars in the street presenting a composite picture of the city. In this way, the film suggests that Mithu's search for masculinity and the contemporary city feed from one another.

Narration

In this film, Farooki adopts some novel and interesting narrative strategies. The sequence in which Mithu coerces Rimi into pretending to be his wife is a case in point. Rima is situated in a darkened room, and the light coming from outside of the frame falls onto her face, emphasising her hatred and helplessness. Meanwhile, Mithu enters the room with a mechanical doll, suggesting it is their imagined daughter. The doll is put on a table, Mithu calls Rima to come to bed – in the background a part of the bed is seen and in the foreground the doll continues nodding its head. These scenes signify what is going to happen is not right and cannot be accepted.

The relationship with the shop owner in whose shop the fugitive Mithu passes his nights is not clear in the film. In the first encounter, the owner scolds Mithu, but neither his words nor the reason for them is clear. In other scenes, the characters are taken to an open place at the outskirts of the city, but again the reason for this action is not clear. In addition, the film is curiously paced. The first part of the film is largely occupied by the video clip issue, and at one stage, the audience might feel that the plot was limited. These might be some limitations of the film, but in many ways, it was a well-made film. The selection of the actors, cinematography, background music, use of sound – everything is done and performed in a consistent manner. The director's minimalist style can be noticed easily. The first two films made by Mostofa Sarwar Farooki (*Bachelor* and *Made in Bangladesh*) are dialogue-driven but in *Ant Story*, we find the minor characters talk less and sometimes do not talk at all. Farooki allows the images to tell the story, suggesting a mature approach to the craft of filmmaking. We see Mithu's sister several times, but she only talks in the last scene. Mithu's father was seen in many scenes, but he never talks suggesting to us, at least, something about the emasculation of males and the older values of society that have come under assault in contemporary Bangladesh. This is something Farooki captures with skill and insight in *Ant Story*

C *Under Construction*: A Document of Time and Space under Construction

Under Construction is a film about women made by women. It is also a critique of contemporary Bangladeshi society in two ways. First, the story skillfully weaves together an examination of gender relations in Bangladesh, which is followed with a powerful critique of the exploitation of labour and the underlying political structures governing it. The trope linking these two disparate social phenomena is that of building construction. The film looks at and deconstructs how gender is constructed in a conservative, patriarchal society against a backdrop of urban blight caused by the over-construction of dwellings in Dhaka. The latter is of particular importance as the construction industry and the multistory buildings signify the deep and lasting changes modernity has on shaping contemporary Dhaka. The single-story bungalow is disappearing and the social life it supported is now a thing of the past, especially in respect to the role of women. Thus, *Under Construction* has enormous relevance for our understanding of the changing worldview consumer capitalism has brought to Bangladesh. This is made abundantly clear by the way the film deconstructs a classical Bengali play, Tagore's *The Red Oleander*. Roya, the female protagonists seeks to 'modernise' the play, which antagonises some friends who revere Tagore, while a visitor (someone without deep cultural roots in Bengali culture) is attracted to the idea. Thus, *Under Construction* is a multi-layered production that is good to look at and biting in its criticism of contemporary affairs.

Histoire

The main character of the film, Roya, is an actress and theatre activist. The film begins with a performance of *Rakto Korobi* (The Red Oleander) by Rabindranath Tagore. It is quickly established that Roya is giving her final performance as the main character, Nandini. Roya has become disillusioned with the play and the manner in which it is presented but, more importantly, she is aware that she is gradually ageing, and a new girl has been cast for the character. Roya is interested in modernising the play, making it more contemporary and challenging. Other characters revolve around Roya. There are two females who relate to Roya; her mother and her housemaid Moyna, which sets up a nice contrast between the past and the present in narrative terms. The males who complement Roya are Russell, the producer and theatre owner who is the custodian of the traditional culture, and Imtiaz, a European-based Bangladeshi. Roya's husband is quite rich but marginal to the unfolding narrative; he has the wealth that enables Roya to pursue her career in theatre and consider taking the play to Europe.

Roya is highly conscious of the fact that she is ageing. Returning home from the theatre, at a traffic signal, a flower-seller child in the street called her 'aunty', which upsets her. After entering her home, Roya asks the housemaid Moyna whether she looks like an 'aunty' or not. In the bathroom, in front of the mirror, she looks at her body and tries to imagine how she will look in the future, as she ages. Roya's concerns about ageing, her husband's desire for a child, and the fact that she has played the role of Nandini for twelve years place her in a deep quandary; whether to pursue her art or let biology takes its course. Her mother and Russell also advise her to leave the theatre and have a baby.

A minor female character in the film underscores this theme. She is a woman who exudes modern attitudes but has given up her PhD studies because 'being a mother is the most precious thing' and she suggests Roya also become a mother as well before it is too late. However, the friend remains interested in how she looks, wants to bring back the body that she feels she lost for her motherhood. She wants to enjoy her life in every way. She wants to continue 'breast feeding' and 'power pumping' at the same time. This episode convinces Roya to remain childless and pursue her art.

Theatre owner Russell introduces Roya to Imtiaz, who is interested in her ideas about 'modernising' Tagore, which he sees as appealing to the European market, something Russell is deeply opposed to because he sees it as disrespectful of Tagore and all that he stands for. Roya wants to deconstruct Nandini's beautiful, loving and sacrificing character by changing her from a servant of the king to a garment worker and transforming *Jakshapuri* (the 'factory' in the play) into an RMG factory in Bangladesh. She thinks this would make the play contemporary and relevant. Russell is a traditionalist and strongly opposed to any tampering with Tagore's play. On the other hand, Imtiaz admires Roya's concept and offers her the opportunity to perform it in an international setting, which Roya sees as the crowning achievement of her career. Moreover, as her relationship with her husband Sameer cools, she finds herself sexually attracted to Imtiaz. Thus Rubaiyat Hossain, the director, very neatly sets up the central dilemma confronting Bangladesh's cultural elites; whether to continue to revere Tagore as canonical and therefore above change or adapt to changing conditions, like the advent of a westernised global consumer culture.

The relationship between the traditional, conservative, worldview and the modernist version is also explored in Roya's relationships with the other major female characters. Her mother is a conservative woman locked into a traditional view of the role of women in society. Her husband left her long ago, but she believes one day he will return and behaves accordingly, she mixes with *hijab*-clad women and expresses reservations about Roya's attire. She is also unhappy that her daughter is a theatre actress and reminds Roya in one exchange that actresses are considered as prostitutes by some segments of society. Clearly, the mother and daughter have an uneasy relationship. However, the mother cherishes her independence and refuses to change her lifestyle.

By contrast, the housemaid Moyna is young and represents the changing society. Roya is dependent upon Moyna to maintain her lifestyle. Moyna has a relationship with Sabuj Mia, the liftman at the building, and eventually becomes pregnant much to Roya's dismay, for two reasons; first, Moyna's pregnancy reveals Roya's lack of traditional femininity in refusing to have a baby. Second, it throws the house into disarray as Roya is incapable of performing normal domestic duties. Sabuj takes Moyna away from Roya and they start their new life in a *bostee* (slum).

Interestingly, Moyna starts working in an RMG factory. After initially attacking Sabuj, Roya reconciles herself to the loss of Moyna and visits her in the slum with ornaments made of gold and silver. She asks Moyna to come back, realising that she was more than a servant and was in fact her only friend. But Moyna decides to stay with her husband. The relationship between the two women allows Hossain to comment subtly on the fact that middle-class Bengali women can only sustain their cosseted lifestyles through the labour and support of the working-class maids. Moreover, Moyna's decision throws into question the orthodox view that the RMG factories are there to exploit working-class girls. Moyna chooses the factory over being a servant because it gives her identity and agency, and probably more money as well.

At the conclusion of the film, Roya realises she is at a crossroads and she makes several significant decisions in order to sustain her creative journey. She decides against having a baby. She also gives up the decision of going to London and taking her sick mother there for medical treatment, which her brother desires. Thus, her husband deems her 'selfish'. However, Roya's decision to be selfish for her theatre career is a masculine perception. Her decisions are not clearly stated in the film but signified obliquely. At the end of the film, Roya is found rehearsing the dialogue from *The Red Oleander*, the scene in which Nandini promises to support Raja with her last strength although this may cause her death, which will haunt the Raja. Nandini/Roya, indeed all women, may have no weapons, but her death will ensure that she wins. This is a confusing, open-ended conclusion; the audience must decide whether Roya has succeeded or been defeated.

Figure 6.3 Roya (Shahana Goswami) in a dream sequence with garments workers.

Recit

Under Construction was made by women who fill most of the important roles in composing the film; direction, production, cinematography art direction, production design and so on. The main protagonists are three women from different eras and differing classes. But this is not a typical feminist film, Roya is not a radical woman. Rather, she is an opportunist taking advantage of circumstances as they occur. She is dependent on her husband for her material well-being and comfortable lifestyle but there is no warmth in the relationship. Roya's affection and love towards Moyna are also ambiguous. It is partly motivated by self-interest but there is also an element of affection and genuine feeling. After Moyna and Sabuj left the house, Roya visited Moyna's house twice, giving Moyna wedding gifts but also in an unsuccessful attempt to lure Moyna back into her employment. Moyna had decided that the job as a housemaid did not provide any dignity to a woman or more importantly, an identity. In marrying Sabuj Mia, finding a job at a RMG factoty and having a baby provided Moyna with an identity. Indeed she acquires an agency that permits her to make decisions and no longer be dependent on Roya.

On the other hand, Roya's conservative mother lives a religious life; like a conventional wife, she waits for her husband to return after a long absence with a belief that he will come back one day. However, she is self-dependent and has the mental strength and capacity to live her life by her own. She has the management capability and entrepreneurship to earn money for herself and other hijabi women by sewing clothes. Both Roya and Roya's mother have identity and agency that Roya seems to lack as she oscillates between her husband, Russell and Imtiaz, always seeking their approval for her actions. It is Roya's sincere love of the theatre, and her aspirations to creative freedom to re-interpret a classic text, that provide the capacity for her to make a decision about life. The creative journey she chooses gives her character shape.

By comparing the RMG factory with *Jakshapuri*, Hossain establishes a clever interplay between the past and the present. In both institutions, labourers are repressed and victimised. Both in the *Jakshapuri* and in the RMG factories we see the exploitation of labour, where the workers are seemingly the extension of machines. Here we may recall Fritz Lang's film *Metropolis* (1927) for the similarity of the subject matter. By exploiting the workers' labour, Bangladesh earns foreign currency, but the security of the labourers is the least concern of the owners and authorities. The Rana Plaza accident in 2013 illustrates this and makes Roya's adaptation of the original storyline contemporary and disturbing, as it is in death that the workers are remembered, not through their work.

Addressing recent events in Bangladesh is a pivotal aspect of the film. It is surprising that this aspect is near absent in the art and independent cinema of Bangladesh. Bangladeshi independent cinema has not yet completed its journey. The culture and the authorities seem to demand that the films focus on the 1971 War of Liberation, but it is the RMG that is synonymous with Bangladeshi identity to the outside world. *Under Construction* has put contemporary issues dealing with gender and class at the centre of the plot. In *Runway* (2010), Tareque Masud also addressed recent Bangladesh society and included RMG in his narrative, but as a sideline to the major concern of fundamentalism. Rubaiyat Hossain's *Under Construction* not only deals with RMGs but also tries to tell a story of Dhaka, a city under construction. The lives of the citizen's mirror the material reality of a life in which the streets, the buildings, the Art Academy (Shilpakala Academy) and theatre as cultural forms together portray the identity of a city and a country, under construction.

Narration

The film does not reach to any overwhelming or even satisfying climax; everything remains unfinished and under construction. In that way, the film has a poststructuralist feel; rather than neatly packaging events, the director leaves much to the imagination of the viewer. To establish the theme, some non-diegetic elements have been inserted into the narrative – female workers are working on the construction sites, newly built buildings are being constructed, tiles have been cut and sometimes the whole building is shown as under construction. This non-diegetic insertion describes the situation in the storyline and at the same time symbolises the city in which the story is taking place. It is a way of implying that Dhaka City or Bangladesh as a nation is growing but is not completely grown – it is under construction.

The director uses metaphors in other scenes. Once Roya dreams of her husband in bed as a python, suggesting perhaps the power of the patriarchy to crush the aspirations of women; Roya, it is suggested, slept with Imtiaz and after that the pet goldfish and tortoise are found playfully and freely swimming in the bathtub. In one scene, Roya puts her hand inside the aquarium and after stirring the water the movement seems to scare the fish. In another dream sequence, Moyna is working in the RMG factory where her hand has been trapped in a sewing machine and she turns to Roya for help; this was unconvincing in its execution compared to the rests of the film. However, Shahana Goswami as Roya, Mita Chowdhury as the mother and Rikita Nandini as Moyna all perform well in their respective roles. The Indian actor Rahul Bose as Imtiaz and Shahdat Hossain as the husband do not have much to do as their roles are limited dramatically, providing little scope to explore the characters in any depth. In the role of the custodian of classical culture, the puritan Russell, played by Towfiqul Islam Imon was a much more rounded character. Martina Radwan's camera had an informal style; it does not want to seduce spectators with beautiful images. *Under Construction* is not a compact story, rather it is a film of the statement which means that the camera plays the role of interpreter, raising questions that the audience are asked to answer – if they can.

Shayan Chowdhury Arnob's background score and Sujan Mahmud's sound design have the capacity to attract the attentive audience and able to enhance the impact of the film on spectators. By contrast, the editing by Sujan Mahmud is not always as convincing. For example, after Imtiaz gave his approval to Roya, there was a debate between Roya and Russell on the deconstruction of *The Red Oleander*. We then cut away to a street scene where Roya observes a monkey dancing in the street. We then cut to a scene =e in which Roya and Sameer have a cup of noodles for dinner. Sameer is disgruntled and asks: 'how long do I have to eat food like this?', which is a reflection on Roya's domestic skills and the absence of Moyna. The monkey dance scene is placed between the debate and the dinner – and it is not clear why this is the case. There is no internal logic to the sequence. Again, this may symbolise the idea that we are all performing monkeys trapped in a cage, but it is possible to be sceptical here and question whether it was used in the right place in the narrative or not.

The film has additionally touched on many contemporary issues – the accident of Rana Plaza, the rally of fundamentalists and the demand of the death sentence of atheists and so on; but the biggest political event of the age, the Shahbagh movement was not addressed. By giving the film a contemporary edge *Under Construction* adds a new dimension to independent film in this country and Hossain is to be congratulated for this fact.

D *My Bicycle*: Changing Indigenous Life on the Advent of Modernity

My Bicycle (*Mor Thengari*) is the first feature film made in the Chakma language, used by a large indigenous group, the Chakma people. According to the Bangladesh census 2011, there live nearly 5,00,000 Chakma people in CHT, the south-eastern part of Bangladesh. This population is nearly 60% of the total indigenous people who live in CHT and 0.33% of the total population of Bangladesh (See Choudhury, 2017: 15).

This is also a debut feature by Aung Rakhine, a member of another indigenous group, the Rakhine. The film tells a story of a Chakma family living in a hill of the CHT. The tribal culture and lifestyle of the Chakma people are depicted in the film. It also delineates how modernity and its changing agents are making the simple Chakma lives complex.

The film did not get the censor certificate for depicting a 'sensitive' issue which we have discussed later in this chapter. However, the film has been screened in several international festivals including the Tallin Black Night Film Festival 2015, Estonia, Goteborg Film Festival 2016, Sweden, Zanzibar International Film Festival 2016, Tanzania. The film bagged the best screenplay award in the Ufa Silver Akbuzat Ethnic Cinema

Festival 2016, Russia and Honorable Mention at the Cine Kurumin – Int. Indigenous Film Festival 2016, Brazil.

Histoire

Kamol, a Chakma man, comes back home from town after six months. While he was absent, his wife Devi and his little son Debu struggled yet managed to survive. Kamol lost his factory job and before that he was also unpaid for several months. However, he came back with a new bicycle which was identified as a new technology in the remote hilly Chakma village. Kamol thought of using the bicycle for earning money. He started carrying people and goods from the village to the nearby Bazar in exchange for small fares. This new earning source brought happiness in his family. He sent his son to the school. He repaired his dilapidated house. Meanwhile, there was an accident during a trip and a passenger was injured. In a village court, it was decided he could carry only goods and not people anymore. Everything was going fine until some muggers demanded money as they saw that he had become 'rich'. He refused to do so. On a bad morning, he found his bicycle damaged and left under the hill. Shattered Kamol travels to town to repair the bicycle. While he was crossing the Kaptai Lake, another boat approached from the opposite direction towards the village with a new bicycle along with a television set and a motorbike.

Recit

The film *My Bicycle* describes the ethnic lifestyle and culture that include agro-based professions, tribal justice system and human relations. However, the film also portrays how modernity affects the tribal life. The political

Figure 6.4 Kamal (Kamal Mani Chakma) with his bicycle.

aspect of their lives, military deployment by the government in the CHT area is also depicted, but via metaphors.

A Historiography of Indigenous People

CHT is the habitat of most of the small indigenous and ethnic groups of Bangladesh. According to Jamil L. Iqbal (2009), despite their close ethno-cultural affinities with other peoples of Sino-Tibetan origin in the Indian state Tripura and Mijoram, and the lack of ethnic or religious identity with Bengalis, the eleven diverse ethnic groups – Chakma, Marma, Tripura, Bawm, Chak, Khami, Kheyang, Lushai, Mrung, Pankho and Tanchangya found themselves instead in (East) Pakistan and after 1971 in Bangladesh.

British rulers identified this part of the country as an 'exclusive area' in terms of the different characteristics of its land, agricultural pattern and the unique religious, cultural and ethnic identity of its inhabitants. They ensured its exclusivity by implementing 'Chittagong Hill Tracts Regulation of 1900'. However, in the Pakistan era, the new country incorporated the region into its modernisation projects, most notably the construction of the Kaptai hydroelectric dam, which submerged about 40% of cultivable lands of the Rangamati district and displaced about 100,000 people (Choudhury, 2017: 17). The Chandraghona Paper Mill evicted people from Marma villages at Bandarban. After the liberation in 1971, the CHT people demanded recognition and protection of their earlier exclusiveness. However, this was rejected by the Bengali rulers as they decided that Bengali nationalism was the basis of national identity. CHT people formed a political party named Parbatya Chattagram Jansamhati Samiti (PCJSS) and its militant wing *Shanti Bahini* became infamous for its guerrilla operations. Post-1975 military governments responded to it with force and wanted to change the demography with a state-sponsored resettlement programme in the 1980s. The prolonged conflict between *Shani Bahini* and the Bangladesh Army received national and international attention and concern. In 1997, there was a peace accord initiated by the Bangladesh government that addressed many of the core issues in the conflict. However, the CHT issue was never completely resolved. CHT people are still suffering from earlier problems. A newer problem is that the settler Bengalis have gradually been occupying the land and the civil and military administration are biased towards the settlers. In 1947, the Bengali people constituted only two percent of the CHT, and now Bengali settlers constitute a major part of the CHT population (Choudhury, 2017: 17, 148).

Amena Mohsin (2000) observes that the Bangladesh state was predicated on the idea of Bengali nationalism which is reflected in its constitution. Article 9 of the constitution defined Bengali nationalism to be based on Bengali culture and language. Through Article 3 Part 1 of the constitution Bengali was adopted as the state language and Article 6 Part 1 declared that the citizens of Bangladesh were to be known as Bengalis (Mohsin, 2000: 79). And through this existence of 45 ethnic communities with their own language and culture was ignored. The Hill people of CHT rejected this hegemonic imposition. Manobendra Narayan Larma, their representative in the national parliament refused to endorse the constitution and walked out in protest of the above in 1972 and later he founded PCJSS in the same year in demand of an autonomous status of the CHT people. Mohsin states, it is interesting to note here that Bengali nationalism with its emphasis on Bengali language and culture was constructed by the Bengali politicians to counter the hegemony of Pakistani nationalism. The same was now being used to impose the hegemony of the Bengalis over the non-Bengali population of the state (Mohsin, 2000: 79). Even after 1997 peace accord, the hegemonic influence and systematic repression of the state run by the dominant Bengali people had never stopped, Hana Shams Ahmed (2017) argues, violence against the CHT has not ceased, and instead, the presence of the military has become normalised. On the other hand, the state promotes the Hills as a tourist site where tourists may enjoy the landscape and the 'exotic' inhabitants.

The film *My Bicycle* does not tell the whole historiography of CHT, but its opening scenes provide some historical references, especially how the Kaptai dam had flooded the Chakma agricultural land and turned it into an artificial lake. At the beginning in the film, the camera focuses on the water of the huge lake through which Kamol approaches his home on a tiny boat with the new bicycle. The boatman is also a villager, known to him and Kamol tells him by pointing his finger:

'Grandpa and grandma's house used to be on that side'.

'On that side, there used to be a cemetery'.

'I remember a King's palace was on that side, there was a jungle there'.

The boatman agreed. These statements suggest that the post-dam flood occurred during Kamol's childhood. His ancestor's house, the cemetery, the jungle and even the Chakma King's palace was destroyed by the flood that had been created by the hydroelectric project. Kamol is not aggrieved, like some of the Chakma people, who became militant later. Kamol is an ordinary man trying to have a regular life, with a desire to prosper. Nor are other characters of the film shown having strong political views. Rather, the film's focus was on the simplistic or traditional life of Chakma people gradually being affected by modern technological agents. However, the director rightly puts some references of historical incidents upon which the community presently stands.

Depiction of an Ethnic Identity and Culture

The film shows the identity and culture of Chakma people who live a tribal way of life, different from the modern and urban lifestyle. Women are the bearers of the originality of the culture. Devi wears *Pinon*, a very distinctive Chakma clothing made of ethnic handloom. However, Kamol wears modern trousers and a jacket as he went to town for his job. Devi does *Jumma* cultivation, a particular type of agricultural method used in CHT. The film also depicted a sequence of a village court, headed by the *Karbari*, also a traditional form of administration found in CHT. Just before starting the business with the bicycle, we see Kamol family arranging a special prayer session led by a monk. In that prayer, all members of the family – husband, wife and child – participated. As a minor detail, we also see that people are smoking with a special kind of *hukkah* made from bamboo. The film rightly shows wide use of homemade liqueur by Chakma people. The Karbari shows his concern in the film as Chakma youths are getting spoilt by excessive drinking of liqueur and gambling. In a remote society, simple-minded people with Mongoloid features, living in tiny huts on top of hills surrounded by jungle and a wide lake – that's the picture of a typical Chakma community, and the film substantially portrays that.

Advent of Modernity and a Changing Society

As an indigenous community, Chakma is a tribal society. However, unlike other small indigenous communities, it is going through some changes. The arrival of modern change agents such as technology, education and transportation are in play in the society. For earning money Kamol went to the town and found a factory job. Due to retrenchment in the factory, he came back home with a bicycle for himself and a football for his son. The bicycle has wheels and it can speed up the slow lifestyle of his remote community. Kamol started earning money from the bicycle and eventually his family felt economic progress. He sent his son to school. He initiated repair of his dilapidated house. But his progress was envied by the others, especially by the drunken youths who tried to extort money from him. Upon his refusal, they destroyed his bicycle. This incident shows that modernity makes your life complex and that you need extra attention to resolve the complexities. At the end of the film, we see another bicycle and television are entering into the village. Who does not know that television is the best vehicle of modernity as well as consumer culture?

Military and the Censorship Fiasco

There is no elaborate description of military insurgence at CHT in the film. Just after the Kamol's bicycle was destroyed, to increase their misery, some members of Bangladesh military suddenly crossed the yard. Devi and Debu became scared and hid inside the home and Kamol exchanged wishes to them humbly. The military members did not respond; instead, they broke Debu's toys with their boots while leaving. The breaking of toys was showed in a close shot, giving added emphasis to the symbolism.

BFCB asked the producer to cut that scene. The producer-director of the film Aung Rakhine resubmitted the film. Now the BFCB issued another letter advising for a few more cuts that calculates total duration of nearly 25 minutes of film. The new advises included the historical and contextual discussion between Kamol and the boatman at the beginning of the film. This time the producer denied cutting the scenes and the film remained stapled until today since 2016. The producer Aung Rakhine told the whole story of censor process over telephone to the authors on June 2, 2020. However, the film was screened at different international film festivals. There were also some non-theatrical alternative screenings within the country. But after the censor fiasco, no more screening could take place anymore.

Narration

The narrative of the film is simple, which resembles the simplicity of Chakma lifestyles. The camera is slow or sometimes static. Sometimes it could not focus properly in transition shots from the foreground to background or vice versa. However, the camera was very sincere in portraying the beauty of the lake and the hills. To create the background scores, western instruments like a piano and violin have been used. Traditional hill tunes or fusion of Chakma and western tunes might have been better choices. We see the best scene at the end of the film – while Kamol was going to town to repair his bicycle, a large auto-run boat passed by his tiny boat and created large waves. Kamol's boat was dancing helplessly on the top of the waves – this is a symbolic shot suggesting how helpless Kamol is after the destruction of his bicycle. The arrival of three new technologies including a bicycle, a motorbike and a television was excessive as a new bicycle entering the village could be enough to create the contrast and conflict in the storyline. However, the inclusion of television as a new changing agent might have a different dimension – it is the best vehicle of modernity as well as bearer consumer culture.

References

Ahmed, H. S. (2017). Tourism and state violence in the Chittagong Hill Tracts of Bangladesh (2017). Electronic Thesis and Dissertation Repository. 4840. https://ir.lib.uwo.ca/etd/4840, Accessed on 9 July 2021.

Choudhury, Z. U. A. (2017). *Mapping in the Chittagong Hill Tracts (CHT), 1997–2013*. Dhaka: Adarsha Books.

Iqbal, J. M. (2009). The Fate of the Chittagong Hill Tracts Tribe of Bangladesh at https://www.marxist.com/fate-chittagong-hill-tracts-tribes-bangladesh.htm, Accessed on 1 June 2020.

Mohsin, A. (2000). Identity, Politics and Hegemony: The Chittagong Hill Tracts, Bangladesh. *Identity, Culture and Politics*, 1(1), 78–88.

Rashid, A. (2001). *Taliban: The Story of Afghan Warlords*. London: Pan.

7 Representing Identity through Cinema

Most of the independent films in Bangladesh, as those are 'third world texts', as we recall Frederick Jameson's (1986) words again, are 'necessarily 'national allegories'. These filmic allegories often address the Liberation War as the subject or uphold political ideologies derived from the experience of the birth of the nation. The directors, especially the senior directors like Tanvir Mokammel, Morshedul Islam and Tareque Masud, have their own justifications for making most of their films with the Liberation War as a subject. Before extracting the findings from the textual analysis of ten selected films, it is important to look at the overall position of identity issues in independent films.

In the interview taken for this book, Tanvir Mokammel (2007) interprets why they are eager to deal with identity issues:

> The filmmakers, being rooted to the soil and committed to the people, obviously try to uphold these age-old beliefs, traditions and struggles of our nation. Naturally their endeavours go against the state patronised official communal identity, a garb that our ruling classes are so eager to put on our people.

Tareque Masud (2007) told us why the subject of the early independent films was the Liberation War, 1971:

> You must look at the then situation in the country. The egalitarian ideologies of 1971 were almost buried in late 1970s and early 1980s which let the country ruled by dictatorship, anti-democratic forces and anti-liberation forces. All these elements, which can be put in bundle of the term non-egalitarian, were active forces. We were from that generation who has seen the war in the childhood and post-war incidents in the young age. We had seen the rise of a heroic generation and fall of the generation. We were going through post-71 frustrations. We upheld the spirit of 1971 but at the same time we were very much frustrated. We as youths, went through the turmoil period from 1975 to 1982, which was basically ruled by military. So, our filmmaking was reaction to military, reaction to lack of

DOI: 10.4324/9781003271093-8

Representing Identity through Cinema 161

democracy, reaction to Islamisation, and reaction to communal politics. We were inclined to secular, pro-democratic and pro-1971 struggles. It was an overall standpoint, though individual differences were there.

Echoing Tareque Masud, Morshedul Islam (2006) explained to us, why he chose the subject of his first film *Towards* that upholds the spirit of Liberation War in the context of the early 1980s in Bangladesh:

> I chose our Liberation War as the subject of the film and I tried to substantiate the Liberation War at the perspective of that time. General H M Ershad just took the power; we saw earlier that there was a conspiracy in the state to down the spirit of Liberation War. The collaborators of the Liberation War reorganised themselves and our freedom fighters had to see this occurrence helplessly, but they could not do anything. I tried to portray this situation in my film. The film was ended with a hope that our next generation may bring back the magnitude of our Liberation War.

In the foundational and transitional phase, the Liberation War was a regular subject matter. Seven out of Tanvir Mokammel's 20 films, five out of Morshedul Islam's 14 films, four out of Tareque Masud's 11 films and one out of Abu Sayeed's 10 films have been made on the Liberation War of Bangladesh. Although Abu Sayeed has made only one film on the Liberation War (*Dhusar Jatra* 1992, a short feature) he (Sayeed, 2006) thinks more films on the issue should be made. The reason for his low number is due to his belief that the stores of the Liberation War demands bigger canvas and great funding, which he never gets. Other than these films on the Liberation War, some films have been made which transcended 1971[1] and portray the greater identity of the population. However, it does not matter how many films are made on identity issues here the important issue is the director's view towards identity of the nation.

While narrating the national history of the country on the screen, some secular-modernist film directors have clearly taken the position on behalf of Bengaliness and against Muslimness. Their portrayal suggests, they consider the two are conflicting identities that should remain in conflict. This is mostly true for the films made by Tanvir Mokammel and Morshedul Islam (Raju, 2008: 134). Although some of Tareque Masud's earlier films contributed to the nationalist narratives, he also had some complex and nuanced views which were evident in *The Clay Bird*.[2] Abu Sayeed's film does not build a Bengali nationalist ballad in excess, and although Sayeed wants to make more nationalist films, he has a sense of viewing things from a complex perspective, which is evident in his 'non-1971' films. Rubaiyat Hossain *Meherjaan* went further to challenge the grand narratives of the Liberation War, although in a haphazard way, and created much chaos among the Dhaka-based intelligentsia and audiences in 2011.

162   *Representing Identity through Cinema*

If some filmmakers have a clear position about Bengaliness and Muslimness, the two major identity approaches of Bengali Muslim identity, examining the third approach, popular religion, in the independent films are also needed. This identity approach is not explored even in the general identity discourse in Bangladesh. Therefore, our study aims to address this issue. All three approaches can be found in some foundational and transitional films. *A Tree Without Roots* and *Television* predominantly deals with Muslimness, *Dollhouse* with Bengaliness, *Meherjaan* with both Bengaliness and Muslimness, *Kittonkhola* with popular religion, and *The Clay Bird* comprises all three approaches. In Chapters 4–6, we showed how these approaches have been addressed by the directors as a part of the whole cinematic representation. Textual analysis of the selected films reveals an ambivalence in the construction of identity– mostly anti-Islamic and pro-Bengaliness and sometimes clear endorsement for popular religion or a sensible representation of Muslimness. In the contemporary films, the Bangladesh society is portrayed as under transition, largely due to two external factors – neoliberal globalisation and globalisation of Jihadist Islam. In addition, the economic growth based on an export-oriented RMG sector and the remittances sent by immigrant workers have given a new identity to Bangladesh – with one of the highest rates of GDP growth in the world, a robust national reserve and rapid urban growth. The exploitation of cheap labour is the key to this growth, which is creating a financial disparity in the society. The selected films show, this transformation in identity is not only visible in contemporary Bangladesh but has been occurring for ages (as portrayed in *Kittonknola*) due to poverty and other socio-cultural factors. However, slow internal transformation cannot be compared with the contemporary situation, which is rapid and has a global context. In one film (*My Bicycle*), we saw that not only the majority Bengali Muslim society, but also the indigenous or *Adibasi* groups are going through a transformation due to modern technologies. For them, the additional factor is the aggression of the state which is formed by the majority Bengali people.

Bengaliness and Muslimness as Conflicting Identities

While describing national identity on the screen, some secular-modernist independent film directors have clearly taken the position on behalf of Bengaliness and against Muslimness. While adapting novels and writing scripts, they are increasing elements of Bengaliness in their filmic texts and curtailing humanist components. By preferring Bengaliness and undermining Muslimness they are portraying these two identity approaches as opponents from the Islamist characters. In Chapter 1, we quoted Kath Woodward (2000) who said that identity is not fixed and unchanging, but the result of a series of conflicts and different identifications. Some independent film directors seemingly try to say in their films that the national identity of Bangladesh is not fluid, it should remain unchanged, and it would be solely based on Bengaliness.

One will find the enthusiastic representation of Bengaliness in the film *Dollhouse* by Morshedul Islam. He has made several films related to the Liberation War of Bangladesh, including his first film, *Towards* (Agami 1984), and the recent film *A Day of Anil Bagchi* (Anil Bagchir Akdin 2015) in which a monolithic nationalist narrative is found that includes persecution by the Pakistani Army, brutality of Islamist collaborators (*Rajakar*s) and bravery of *Mukti Bahini*. The storyline of *Dollhouse* was a bit different as the focus of the film was not on the bravery of the *Mukti Bahini* or brutality of the Islamist collaborators rather on a rape victim woman which signifies the persecution by the Pakistani Army. One important change from the book was made in the very end of the film – Yakub, one of the main protagonists of the text, is transformed from a naïve, passive observer to an active participant. Making Yakub willing to join *Mukti Bahini* is the construction of a nationalist narrative of resistance by the director which did not appear in the novel. In our interview, Morshedul Islam (2006) says, 'I had thought after happening everything there should be a change within Yakub'. Aloofness is a common portrayal of the main characters in the novels by Mahmudul Haque. However, in the film of *Dollhouse* Yakub turned from a distant observer into a potential guerrilla at the end, in accord with the director's desire and the wish fulfilment of potential audiences.

In the film *A Tree Without Roots*, Tanvir Mokammel is delineating the role of Muslimness in the peasant society of Bengal. It is described as a totally fatalistic society; in the name of Islam, one can manufacture fear among people, annihilate ordinary lives and victimise women. In *Tree Without Roots* and Mokammel's other films a kind of Muslimness is seen that is primitive, anti-modern, annihilating, monstrous and against nation and people. He clearly supports Bengaliness, although this was not evident in *A Tree Without Roots*, but available in other films. In Tanvir Mokammel's earlier film, *The River Named Madhumati* (Nadir Nam Madhumati 1995), an Islamist, middle-aged character appears in a monstrous role – he collaborates with the occupying Pakistani Army and kills freedom fighters. He also snatches a Hindu's property, tries to rape his wife but the wife requested him to marry her first and he made her the second wife. The collaborator has a nationalist guerrilla son who kills his father. In *Rabeya* (2008) by Tanvir Mokammel, there is also an aged *Rajakar* character who orders villagers not to bury the dead body of a freedom fighter who was killed by the Pakistani Army. This brutal character appears as a demon when we discover that the freedom fighter is his nephew. The film progresses with the conflict between the *Rajakar* and the freedom fighter's sister Rabeya, who wants to bury her brother. In both of Mokammel's films, the character of the bad Islamist guy was performed by Ali Zaker (this also includes Islam's film *Towards* 1984), which contributes in creating an archetype of an Islamist who was bad in all aspects.

If Mokammel's Islam is monolithic and scholastic in *A Tree Without Roots*, Tareqe Masud has portrayed a nuanced view of Islam in *The Clay Bird*. Kazi is the follower of scholastic Islam, but he is not a 'monster' – he is not a *Rajakar* collaborating with the Pakistani Army. He was perhaps like a lot of Bengali Muslims who joined the Pakistan movement in the 1930s and 1940s the break-up of Pakistan broke his heart. However, his house was smashed by the Pakistani Army, which doubled his pain. If Kazi is the representative of scholastic Islam, *Baro Hujur* prefers political Islam, and Ibrahim Hujur is the representative of Sufi Islam. However, there was no *Rajakar* character in *The Clay Bird*.

In the independent films related to the Liberation War, generally a *Rajakar* character would be found who collaborates with the Pakistani Army and has Islamic mannerisms and features. He would be a middle-aged man with beard and wearing white *pyjama-panjabi-tupi*. It is true that the *Rajakar*s were the members of Islamic parties, but they were not necessarily middle-aged, a lot of them were clean shaved and dressed in shirt and pants like in the west. Because of their westernised worldviews – either capitalist or socialist – the film directors could not differentiate scholastic Islam from political Islam. Even popular Islam is synonymous with other forms of Islam to them. The whole of religious identity is bundled together stereotypically. Instead of looking at diverse religious orientations and approaches, the community is judged in black and white. While describing the national history of the country, the religious people were identified as demons. It is done from the ultra-secular point of view of the filmmakers. The problem lies with the secular, nationalist and historiographical discourse of the nation. The basic notion of the birth of the nation in 1971 was a secular worldview towards Bengaliness, which is repeatedly seen in the art and literature. This is especially applicable to the foundational independent films.

However, the construction of archetypes for the religious community in cinema has reversed in contemporary times, as observed by Tareque Masud (2007). In some films, such as *Joyjatra* (Journey for Victory 2004) by Tauquir Ahmed and *Shyamol Chhaya* (Dark Shadow 2004) by Humayun Ahmed, the whole archetype had been reversed. Both films were made in the same year and the subjects of the films were similar. Set in the backdrop of the Liberation War, both films, people who tried to escape from the attack of the Pakistani Army are gathered in a boat moving towards a free zone occupied by freedom fighters. But how does this reversed portrayal of religious people take place? It is not by the maker or writer; it is the audience of a new time that dictates the terms and subconsciously influences the maker or writer. The backlash of 9/11 and the emergence of Islamic sentiment have created this environment. Now Bengali Muslim is primarily identified by the Europeans or Americans as 'Muslim', so an affinity has been created with the 'bearded *other*', the Islamists. So, he cannot portray himself villain as he is endorsing his Muslim identity now. In the earlier texts, *Rajakar* and *Moulavi* were synonymous. In *Joyjatra*, the first protest against the Pakistan Army came from the *Imam* of the village mosque and the *Moulavi* in *Shyamol Chhaya* was the first man who joined the Liberation War. The first martyr was a *Moulavi* in *Joyjatra*. In *Shyamol Chhaya*, Muslims did not want to take people from the Hindu community in the boat, but they got shelter because of the involvement of the *Moulavi*, the bearded Islamist. While the boat was moving, the Hindus were worshipping, Muslims asked them to stop, as the Pakistani Army would attack them if the worshipping was seen. But the *Moulavi* resisted them by saying that all religious communities had the right to their rituals, which was unnatural to be carried on in 1971 as the Hindu minorities were the primary targets of Pakistani Army. This reversed construction is dictated by the peoples' feelings in the post 9/11 and post-Afghan-Iraq war time. Even the director who portrayed religious people one-way earlier now portrays them differently. Religious people are now in the role of heroes of the Liberation War in contemporary art films in Bangladesh.

In *The Clay Bird*, Bengaliness is represented through Milon, the young Marxist and his friends. Milon participated in a demonstration at the town and was concerned about the election results for the AL and later he was engaged in a guerrilla fight during the war. But there was no jingoism within the character; instead, he was criticised by a village bard, a representative of popular religion, for seeing the concept of freedom in a narrower way. In *A Tree Without Roots*, there was no portrayal of Bengaliness, as it was a story set in the backdrop of late 1940s Bengal peasantry but it was an anti-Muslimness text. In *Kittonkhola*, the message about identity is subtle as the film represents the cultural elements and traditions of Bengaliness. *Jatra*, folk music, myth and *Purana* – all formed the cultural features of Bengaliness. Thus, *Kittonkhola* describes crises within this context.

The transitional film *Meherjaan* provides a different interpretation of the conflict between Bengaliness and Muslimness. There is the *Mukti Bahini* in the village and there are *Rajakar*s. In addition, there are leftists with their mission of revolution. The Pakistani Army also enters the village. All groups are seeking permission from the grandfather to act. His role was to keep everybody calm. Grandfather's guiding principle is to prevent bloodshed. He witnessed the excesses of Partition and wishes to avoid them at all costs. However, he was not in favour of the *Rajakar*s (he refuses to sign on as the head of the 'Peace Committee', the committee that consisted of the pro-Pakistani Bengalis of the locality) or the Pakistani Army. He gives shelter to revolutionary leftists and he feeds the members of the *Mukti Bahini* but he does not allow them to cause bloodshed. The central theme of the film is 'loving the other'. The director wanted to break the conceptions used to justify war, killing and violence. The director's position is to face the masculine conflict with feminine emotions and sensibilities. But the furor created in Bangladesh after the release of the film was indicative of the reality that loving the other is not easy and perhaps impossible. Hatred and jingoism are the norms of members of the nation state who believe that hating 'others' gives them the fuel for loving 'us'.

Like the foundational film *A Tree Without Roots*, the transitional film *Television* deals with only Muslimness. But unlike *A Tree Without Roots*, it does not portray a monolithic or fundamental religious identity, which was thought to be very rigid, anti-progress and annihilating. Like Majid, Amin Patwary is also rigid and follows scripture too, but Amin is not a fraud as he believes Islamic governance shows people an acceptable path of living. He was flexible in his governance; for example, he allowed Kumar Babu's television in the village. Majid was able to resist an initiative to establish a school in the village, but Amin could not resist the advent of modern technologies in the village. He was ready to perform his hajj at distance via television. Majid was portrayed as detestable, but Amin was depicted as solicitous. Majid was an Islamist character who was like a demon, but Amin was a human being with a limitation. The character Majid is depicted as an agent of Muslimness fighting with Bengaliness, but Amin is not. Mostofa Sawar Farooki (2016) says in the interview conducted for this book, 'although *Television* raised some highly challenging questions, they (the audience) got some catharsis'. Majid might be disliked or hated by the audience, but the character Amin is built with care and instead of hatred the audience will feel attached to him.

Bengaliness as the Preferred Identity Approach

Some independent filmmakers contribute directly or indirectly in maintaining and even enhancing the conflicts between Bengaliness and Muslimness that depict Bengaliness as the preferred identity approach of the nation. As a cultural institution, cinema has impacted the audience to some extent as it deals with the two conflicting identities frequently. Its repeated representation of these two identities always conflicting with each other had ensured this contribution. Raju (2007) says:

> The pro-Islamist and anti-Islamist forces, i.e. Islam and the Liberation War, found in the films by Tanvir Mokammel and Morshedul Islam are depicted as black and white division. But the things are not that simple. Islam and the Liberation War were not always opponents. You cannot analyse religion in that simple way. In reality, Islam is related to human life in such a manner that it is not only a religion.

However, another film scholar, Sajedul Awwal (2007), has different views:

> After assassination of Sheikh Mujibur Rahman, the leader of the Liberation War, in 1975, an artificial crisis of national identity was imported. The four fundamental principles of the Liberation War – nationalism, secularism, democracy and socialism – were altered towards pro-religious stands by subsequent governments. We have not worked anything in any front that we could be back to the earlier position. As

cultural activists, filmmakers had the responsibility to bring back the secular characteristics of the nation.

He prefers making more narratives from the Bengaliness point of view to curb the prevalence of Islamisation through state patronisation, although he admits that religion is a great institution and has a social role to play. He refers to Max Weber when he says that religion organises society systematically and mitigates the psychological crisis of being human. But when religion wants to grab other intuitions, then the problem arises. He mentions that films like *A Tree Without Roots* play the role of de-theolisation.

These two different points of view are found among the film directors as well. Agreeing that the independent films contribution in widening gaps between the two identities, Tanvir Mokammel (2007) says:

> Ethnically we were, and are, Bengali. There is no argument about that. But for the religious identity, our people can be Muslim, Hindu or Christian. The problem emerged, as during and even after Pakistan, this religious or communal identity of ours was overemphasised ... The independent filmmakers, being rooted to the soil and committed to the people, obviously try to uphold age-old beliefs, traditions and struggles of our nation. Naturally their endeavours go against the state patronised official communal identity, a garb that our ruling class is so eager to put on our people.

The notion of 'state patronised official communal identity' can easily explain why a filmmaker stands against that patronisation, and thus set Muslimness as against of Bengaliness. However, the same director (Mokammel 2007), in the interview talks about Islam, he says the following:

> Being of its Arabic origin and delinked with the fertility rituals of a peasant society, [Islam] as a religion in Bengal, has some problem with a populace whose traditions and culture are rooted in the soil and shaped by the productive means of our agriculture and its cycle of rice producing calendar.

He thinks Islam is a religion that came to Bengal from the outside and yet to be linked to the local culture and lifestyle. For people like him, the members of the nation unite through a 'moral conscience', as Earnest Renan (1990) suggests, and in the Bangladesh context, this moral conscience should be developed through Bengaliness, not through Muslimness. Some directors resort to uniting the nation with Bengaliness, but they are contributing to dividing the nation by rejecting Muslimness. Although Islam came to Bengal nine hundred years ago from the outside, Sufis and early sultans of Bengal tried their best to indigenised themselves and established themselves as 'locals'. This localised Islam got a new identity as the 'Islam of Bengal' and there is minimum scope to treat it as 'foreign'. This anti-religion/Islam and secular/western worldviews of some filmmakers portray the Muslimness approach of identity as anti-modern, non-progressive and worth abandoning. In their films, they demonise the Islamic people and thus bundle the pro-Muslimness community as opponent of national progress. In the 'imagined community' (Anderson, 2006) of some filmmakers, there is no place for the followers of Islam – be it scholastic, political, or popular. Having a different and nuanced notion, the filmmaker Tareque Masud (2007) says:

> Independent films of Bangladesh are widening the gap of the conflicting secular and Islamist identity. Filmmakers are part of the polarization. They are reaffirming the secular and middle-class discourse. He is catering his class position, re-establishing nationalist narratives and dominant ideology. He is not questioning his catered audience. He just re-perpetuates the dominant ideology.

This 'catered audience' are urban, middle-class people who are thought of as the followers of Bengaliness and who are dominant in creating discourses of identity. Due to the 'othering' of the pro-Muslimness these films appear as a foreign narrative to the followers of Muslimness. The linear and stereotypical treatment of Islam in the films has created a gap between the secular-modern director and the audience who are the followers of Muslimness. Perpetual and continuous treatment of that kind had been increasing the gap. We would like to recall the idea of Arjun Appadurai (2001: 257) who says, 'one man's imagined community is another man's political prison'. Although he was referring to the majority's nationalist treatment of the minority within a nation, the relentlessly antagonistic treatment to Islamists contributes to widening gaps.

Among the selected films, *A Tree Without Roots* by Tanvir Mokammel is considered anti-Islamic and *Dollhouse* by Morshedul Islam appears to be pro-Bengaliness and *The Clay Bird* by Tareque Masud tried to capture all types of Islamic thoughts (scholastic, popular and political). But the nuanced visualisation of religion, ethnicity and identity in *The Clay Bird* are generally absent in the foundational independent films. Other than *The Clay Bird*, the transitional film *Television* deals with Muslimness with sensibility and a nuanced point of view.

In the contemporary films, the portrayal of identity issues has changed in comparison to earlier works, contemporary filmmakers are more subjective; they are no longer obsessed with the historiography of the Liberation War, and they are looking at a globalised and post-9/11 Bangladesh with different lenses. We discussed earlier that recently these portrayals had been reversed in films like *Joyjatra* and *Shyamol Chhaya* after the backlash of 9/11. This is again to cater to audience thinking.

The transitional film *The Clay Bird* represents a breakthrough in the dominant discourse of the Liberation War and thus helped people look at Bengaliness and Muslimness with fresh eyes and from a different point of view. *Meherjaan* also challenged the dominant discourse, but as it was not a neat argumentative narrative, and sometimes ignored some historical facts, it could create chaos among the audience instead of guiding them to a discursive notion. However, like *The Clay Bird* and *Television* looked at the Islamist people closely, leaving hatred towards them behind. The contemporary films are no longer interested in portraying the clichéd narratives of the Liberation War, rather they are focusing more on contemporary crises of globalised Bangladesh. The extreme form of Muslimness, Jihadist Islam, is portrayed in the film *Runway*, by Tareque Masud expressing his desire to bring back the 'derailed' young men to 'normal' life. The issue of Jihadist Islam is not limited within the local identity politics between Bengaliness and Muslimness; rather it is very much connected with the globalisation of Jihadist Islam.

Bengaliness was the preferred identity over Muslimness for some of the earlier independent filmmakers. Their relentless attempts, selected here or not, could be found in the foundational films. Amena Mohsin says:

> The construction of one identity denotes the separation of the group/community from the other. In the context of the modern state based as it is on the nationalist discourse that is inextricably biased towards the dominant/majority community it results in the hegemony of the dominant identity over the weaker ones.
>
> (Mohsin, 2000: 78)

Foundational filmmakers tried to separate their catered audience to separate from the idea of Muslimness considering Bengaliness as the dominant identity. And for sure, they would treat the same to the 45 ethnic minorities living in CHT and plain land. Mohsin's statement evolved in the context of the dominance of Bengaliness over CHT people which is not convincingly portrayed in any film. But in *My Bicycle*, it was stated how the development projects (i.e. the Kanrnafuli Dam in the 1960s) for serving the majority Bengali people became the reason of teardrops of CHT people.

In short, we believe that foundational films were interested in upholding the greatness of Bengaliness and demeaning Muslimness as backward, anti-modern and portraying it as an evil omen for society. But in transitional films there was a change in the dominant discourse of identity politics – Bengaliness was still important to the directors, but they studied Islamist characters closely by leaving prejudice behind. In contemporary films, age-old identity politics is not the area of interest for the directors; rather, they are attentive to the contemporary issues of globalised Bangladesh. Contemporary film like *My Bicycle* also tended to set a discourse of the hegemony of Bengaliness over CHT people.

Popular Religion in the Selected Films and the Greater Identity Questions

Chatterjee (1993) suggests an 'imagined community' has a sovereign 'spiritual domain' that contributes in developing a 'national culture' in the colonial context that did not allow the colonialists to intervene. It is in this sovereign spiritual domain that nationalism is said to have begun via the development of native language and the writing of prose and novels, establishment of institutions like secondary schools, reforming the family and community and on. We also spot on popular religions are a part of the spiritual domain, which did not allow Bengaliness or Muslimness to intervene and either way influenced them. Sufism and Baul songs and poems helped Muslims (who are Bengalis at the same time) to internalise liberalism and Bengalis (who are Muslims at the same time) to create humanist literature and culture since the Middle Ages.

We have already said the film *The Clay Bird* dealt with three aspects of the national identity of Bangladesh: Bengaliness, Muslimness and popular religion. But the film made a deliberate attempt to explore the presence of syncretic identity – the popular religious practices in traditional Bangladesh. This exploration was the first attempt of its kind on the screen.

Kazi, who believes in Muslim brotherhood, was criticised by Milon and Ibrahim *Hujur* respectively and Milon (who is a Marxist) is criticised by the boatman Karim, who believes in syncretic popular religion. Milon tagged Karim as 'fundamentalist' but Karim's response to that was 'true faiths open your eyes'. Milon was unable to respond.

One can easily differentiate Kazi from the *Baro Hujur* of madrasa who believes in Jihad to uphold Islam. His political Islam was also criticised by Ibrahim *Hujur*, who believed in popular Islam. *Baro Hujur* tries to inspire his students towards Jihad, but Ibrahim thinks that the role of the teacher is not to pull students into extremism. He reminds Halim Mia, the other instructor, that Islam in Bengal did not begin by means of the sword; rather, the creative and poetic invitation to Islam by Sufi saints converted people to Islam.

Some *bayati*s sing and debate in *The Clay Bird*. Sometimes they deliver mystic, philosophical thoughts and engage in *bahas*, on which one is the true way of Islamic life – *Shariah* (scholastic) or *Marfat* (popular)? The former is rigid, and the latter is liberal. The *Marfat* wins at the end of the *bahas* and again the director (Masud, 2004) expresses his preference to the popular religion and culture.

> The title *The Clay Bird* symbolises the main theme of the film as a mystic metaphor. As Sufism teaches us, the human being is made of clay and the soul is always associated with a free bird. The soul is caged in the body of clay and the body is limited, transitory, fragile, and weak; the soul has an immense desire to be free. This brings in the question of

freedom versus different kinds of human limitations – social, political, and religious. The characters and the nation are pursuing an identity that is supposed to be free. In this way, the title of the film through mystic metaphor carries the philosophy of Sufism, which again endorses popular religion.

However, other independent films do not deal with popular religions extensively as *The Clay Bird* did. In *A Tree Without Roots*, a popular religious act was attacked by Majid. Majid stops a Baul song programme in the evening declaring singing to be un-Islamic. In *Kittonkhola,* there are mystic songs sung by mystic characters like *bayati* and *Palakar*; *jatra* performances from Mangalakavya are represented in such a way in the film that shows its inclination to popular religion. Just before Banasreebala's suicide, a rhyme from *Manasamangala* was recited in the voice-over who prefers to perform the character of Manasa Devi instead of virgin Behula. Manasa is a non-Aryan deity who receives the worship from the non-Aryans of East Bengal. The traditional popular religious elements provide entertainment, thoughts, philosophy and mental food for ordinary people of Bengal. This is all displayed in the Kittonkhola fair in the film.

In *Meherjaan*, Meher's friends Arup and Rahi were two village bards and they gave shelter to wounded Pakistani soldier. Arup and Rahi were soul mates to each other and indicate their homosexual relations, however, it was evident in the film that they were followers of popular religion. Rahi sings, 'Tell me now where is my divine love?' and Arup explains to the soldier that, this is man's love to the god. The soldier Waism asks, 'What about the love between men? It binds the hearts and bewilders'. Rahi replies, 'Love is absolute, and love is the religion'. Love and peace are the ultimate messages of popular religions.

Bengaliness and Muslimness are two dominant identities and debates evolve around these two; popular religions are far away from the debate, rather they deal human society from a philosophical perspective that is elevated to greater identities of human beings which are liberal, humanist and peace oriented and the film like *The Clay Bird* rightly portray that.

Bangladesh Society in Transition and Deterritorialisation

Bangladesh's identity is currently going through a transition, and this transition is captured, as expected, in the contemporary films. This transition is shaped by the 'deterritorialisation' (Appadurai, 2001) of predominantly two external factors – neoliberal globalisation and the globalisation of Jihadist Islam. Pre-globalised Bangladesh and post-globalised Bangladesh are different in nature. The globalised reality is characterised by the establishment of a strong consumer culture and prevalence of telecommunication technologies and the mushroom growth of supermarkets with international foods in both centre and periphery. The urban skylines are covered with high rises and flyovers. Peoples' moral values are no longer solely determined by traditional Bengali cultural norms; rather consumer culture is the factor that is shaping the minds of Bangladeshi people. However, this economic progress has resulted in rapid urban growth, increase of an ultra-rich group that evolves due to a corrupt politico-commercial nexus among elites and of course through labour exploitation. The benefit of the growth is limited to the privileged class and social and economic disparity remains intact. Yet the consumer culture is highly prevalent among all strata of the society. This culture is also affecting the practicing and scholastic Muslim community, who generally believe in the Islamic ideologies of simple living.

Other than neoliberal economic and cultural globalisation, the globalisation of Islam, jihadist Islam to be more specific, influences contemporary Bangladesh. Several jihadist attacks took have taken place since 2000 but the attack on Holey Artisan Bakery at Gulshan on July 1st, 2016 shook the country and earned headlines in the international press. These attacks were not isolated incidents. The backlash of 9/11 and subsequent attacks on middle eastern countries contributed to the rise of Islamisation throughout the world and that affected Bangladesh as well. Extremist activities inside Bangladesh got moral support from a large portion of the population. This was especially true for the, targeted killing of atheist bloggers, writers or publishers, and LGBT rights activists and the government spokespersons also blamed the victims. This means there was a shift in the psyche of a large segment of the public, if not all. Sufi Bengal can now be described as political Islamist Bangladesh. The increase of *Hijab* in women's attire and the popularity of the sermons of Islamist speakers in the social media are some of the indicators of the shift.

However, it would be misleading to say the transition is only a contemporary phenomenon. different societies and nations have always gone through transition and Bangladesh is no exception. Peasant Bengal society has had a different political identity during different phases of history. The affluent Bengal in the Sultani period (from the 13th century to the 18th century) lost its financial solvency in British colonial period (from 1757 to 1947) and turned into one of the poorest areas in the world in the 20th century (in the Pakistan era from 1947 to 1970 and in the Bangladesh era, from 1971 to 1980). Poverty and other socio-cultural realities compelled the people of Bangladesh to experience transitions. Bangladesh society has been going through transitions since its ancient period, although it is happening more rapidly in contemporary times. Such transition is clearly described in the film *Kittonkhola*.

Kittonkhola is basically a tale of the transformation of ordinary people, whose existence is constantly threatened by the miseries of life. This transformation has been taking place for ages and in many cases, the transformations are alterations of identity and sometimes of the profession. The struggle of life compels people to think even to change his or her ethnicity and religion. While singing a song in the village fair, Sonai wished to go to *Shantipur* (the land of peace). Idu grabbed his property, he could not stay in his present living place at Toitam village. The Bedey boy Rustam wants to leave his 'ill-fated' gypsy life and wants to go to *Dukhaipur* although he knew it was a land of sorrow. Yet he wanted to leave his gypsy life and to settle permanently in a land. He was ready to alter his ethnic identity by any means. Chhaya Ranjan, a member of a *jatra* troupe who are predominantly Hindus, due to the miseries in his life, he sometimes thinks of changing his religion or of migrating to Kolkata, India, the dwellers of which are predominantly Hindus. Basir, who grinds oilseed by profession wished to torch the oil-grinding machine and leave the home forever in search of a better place to live. Moreover, the central theme of the continuous transformation process has been enhanced by a *Panchali* song in the film, which is also a theme song of the film which was used thrice in the film – 'Oh my mad horse, You ride men from place to place...'.

Among the contemporary films, *Runway* predominantly focuses on Jihadist Islam which is a recent concern in Bangladesh society. What is the true way of Islam – like Ruhul, many of the practicing Muslims in Bangladesh are searching the answer of this question. The ultimate question has haunted the Bengal Muslims – primarily what they are, Bengali or Muslim? The rise of global Jihadist Islam after 9/11 is a result of several complex but interrelated factors – global Muslim fraternity, a fight against imperialism, opposing the aggression of 'harmful' western culture, and attacks on Muslim countries by the western military which is perceived by the Muslims as a Judeo-Christian conspiracy. The rise of Jamayatul Mujahidin (JMB) and Harkatul Jihad in Bangladesh in the 2005–06 periods was connected to this globalisation of Jihadist terrorism. They wanted to capture power through Jihad, implement Islamic *Sharia* law, and ultimately form a government. The film *Runway* was made in 2010 and the film selected the rise of *Jongibad* in Bangladesh as a subject matter.

In *The Clay Bird*, the head teacher in the madrasa believed in Jihad and tried to inspire disciples to join, if necessary, in the context of the Liberation War in the late 1960s. In *Runway*, the leader of a Jihadist group in 2005, Urdu Bhai (performed by Md. Moslem Uddin, the same actor who played the Jihadist character in *The Clay Bird*), in *Runway* was an extremist Mujahid, having experienced the war in Afghanistan and Kashmir. He had tech savvy Arif and madrasa dropout Ruhul with him. Arif joined him from a political stand – after the fall of communism, when the imperialist aggression by the USA-led western powers has been perceived synonymous to abusing Muslims, the resistant Palestine militants or Taliban fighters have become the inspiration to the person like Arif. However, *Jongibad* provides poor Ruhul an ideology as well as some money. The Jihadist jingoism drives them insane to implement Shariah in a coercive manner. We cannot expect Arif coming back to normal life, but Ruhul might be brought back; at least the director's desire was to bring him back. Ruhul understood the path he took was not right, especially

174 *Representing Identity through Cinema*

after Arif's death in a Jihadist mission. But the director's proactive message to bring them back did not create impact in Bangladesh. The film *Runway* was released in 2010 and more lethal Jihaidst attacks took place after that.

In post-*Runway* (2010) time, in the infamous Holey Artisan Attack, we see the planners of the attack were Bangladeshi born Jihadists living in Canada or Japan and the attackers were not a poor young man like Ruhul, rather they were from urban and rich backgrounds and were studying in private universities at home and abroad. These tech savvy and smart young men (Arif, as indicated in *Runway*) were connected through new media technologies and inspired by or directly connected with global Jihadist organisations like IS or the Al Qaeda Network. Whereas once Jihadist Islam only existed theoretically in Bangladesh, it is now practiced here and that is the transition that is giving the nation a new identity. Within a restricted environment of freedom of expression, filmmakers like Tareque Masud tried to record all these transformations. Mostofa Sarwar Farooki has recently made *Saturday Afternoon* (Shonibar Bikel, 2019) which is based on the Holey Artisan Attack, but the BFCB banned the film[3] although it participated in international festivals. The deterritorialisation of Jihadist Islam from the Middle East to Bangladesh has only minimally been depicted by filmmakers in Bangladesh. It is considered to be a 'sensitive' issue in the society; the ban on *Saturday Afternoon* proves that. When the film was in the pre-production phase, in the interview conducted for the book, Farooki (2016) says:

> I got a wire asking is it necessary to poke into the wound again? They think being silent is the best way to heal the wound. I am trying to get their point ... I am trying to cope with them, and I want to be loved by them, so I don't want to shoot this film right now, though my Indian partner wants to make the film. The difficult part is they are not saying to me anything directly, whatever I am hearing, through other channels that it would be dangerous to make a film about the Holey Bakery massacre.

Besides Jihadist Islam, neoliberal consumer culture in a globalised Bangladesh providing a new identity. In *Ant Story*, we see under the pressure of neoliberal consumer culture, people want to earn money any way possible, even if it is not legal or moral. Mithu's desire for class transformation leads him to take a job in a multi-level marketing (MLM) company, which is essentially a pyramid-style scheme that promises untold riches for very little effort. In passing, it should be noted that in 2013 such schemes were outlawed in Bangladesh. Bangladesh was having one of the highest GDP growth in the world in the 2010s and Mithu wanted to engage himself in the financial euphoria until actress Rima's mobile phone into his possession. In contemporary Bangladesh, occasional leak of the celebrity's sex tape was evident and thus, Bangladesh entered the world of revenge porn. Mithu was depicted coming across to a sex tape of Rima, a celebrity. However, the film created discomfort even among a portion of the cult followers of Farooki. The director himself could sense that:

> People loved *Television* like nothing else before, but they did not love *Ant Story*. They were challenged by *Ant Story*. It gave them discomfort, an utter discomfort. The subject, the content, the hollowness in the tunnel of the story, the melancholy and the unresolved riddles – they are not used to this kind of storytelling. They went to the theatres, but they got challenged. They thought oh, no, this is not the film I want to watch.... You enter the tunnel and you are left there. The director is not helping you to come out from the tunnel.
>
> (Farooki, 2016)

The urban character of Dhaka City was completely absent in foundational films or transitional films. It is the contemporary films that portray the city, which was established 400 years ago, even before Kolkata, India. The city was depicted in Rubaiyat Hossain's *Under Construction* as a major character and as a background of the plot in Tareque Masud's *Runway* and Mostofa Sarwar Farooki's *Ant Story*. In *Under Construction*, under the rapid growth of the city, the director narrates the human relation – Roya's uneasy or ambivalent relation with her husband, mother, maid Moyna and the international theatre curator Imtiaz; her creative journey on the stage as an actor and the director, the labour exploitation in the RMG industry and the physical city itself; everything is unsettled and incomplete, all are under construction. In a way, Hossain is saying that Bangladesh as a nation going through a transition (in her depiction, it is under construction). To establish the theme, some non-diegetic elements have been inserted into the narrative – female workers are working on the construction sites, newly built buildings are being constructed, tiles have been cut and sometimes the whole building is shown as under construction. Thus, *Under Construction* has enormous relevance for our understanding of the changing worldview, consumer capitalism has brought to Bangladesh.

The film *Television* by Mostofa Sarwar Farooki portrays the conflict between tradition and modernity and narrates how a conservative rural Bangladesh is going through a transition after the arrival of modern communication technologies. Amin Patwary, the village leader wants to preserve the traditional values that are manifested through religion and tries to ban television in the village. He allows men to use mobile phones without cameras but tried to restrict women from their use.

In Chapter 5, we discussed Raymond William's (2003) optimistic notion to call television a tool for 'long revolution' and that it can be contested in terms of its 'counter revolutionary' effect Amin Patwary could only see television through a religious lens. According to Islam, drawing or appreciation of the image of living animal is *haram*, and he watches television is the greatest source that continuously produces the bulk of moving images. In his view, this is the invention of Jews and Christians to contaminate the minds of Muslims. However, his brother Razzab Patwary talks on television regularly on religious issues and sermons the nation in Dhaka-based broadcast channels, but Amin thinks Razzab is 'spoilt' and his path is not truly Islamic. Amin is such a religious person, who only follows scriptures which was introduced 1400 years ago and who is not agreed to accept any interpretation given in the modern context. But he had to allow almost everything he contested. He had to give permission to use all modern technologies and he himself had to use 'necessary evils' to travel and perform Hajj. Mostofa Sarwar Farooki considered that there was 'pathological interest' (Farooki, 2016) in the vulnerable characters; he found Islamist characters like Amin Patwary to be too 'vulnerable' to the endless supply of visual images – from television, internet, mobile phone and other information and communication technologies.

Communication technologies have ultimately brought a change in the minds of Muslims as well – they not only use them now; they use these technologies to disseminate the message of Islam to others. Muslim preachers appear on talk shows on television, give speeches on YouTube and open pages on Facebook. Even the Jihadists keep contacts with the members of their network through social media or encrypted Apps on hand phones.

The transformation is also going on in the tribal lives of indigenous people in Bangladesh. *My Bicycle* documented the transformation in ethnic Chakma life, especially due the advent of modern changing agent such as wheel. Kamol came back home from town with a bicycle and with its wheels he brought changes in his life. Kamol started earning money with it and eventually there was a financial progress in Kamol's family. He sent his son to school. He initiated to repair his dilapidated house. But his progress was envied by others, especially by the drunk youths who tried to extort money from him. Upon his refusal, they destroyed his bicycle. This incident also proves that modernity makes your life complex and you need extra attention to resolve the challenges. At the end of the film, we see another bicycle and television are entering into the village. The ending of the film suggests more changes are coming in the tribal Chakma life and we know television is the best vehicle of modernity as well as the bearer of consumer culture.

In this way, the expansion of consumer culture and jihadist Islam across borders has been portrayed in a very few films. In addition, few films mention what Appaduari (2001) calls the deterritorialisation of people from one world to the other, although Bangladesh's migrant workers would be a good example of that. *Runway* has a small reference to migrant workers and there is only one film (*Unnamed* 2016) made by Tauquir Ahmed that completely focuses on the plight of migrant workers. In that film, we see an unidentified dead body of a migrant worker arrived in a village, through which it was revealed how labour is exploited by employers in the Middle East and the corruption of the whole labour exporting market.

Women in the Identity Politics: Victim, Labourer and Rebel

Gender aspects might not be a major focus of discussion in identity politics in Bangladesh, however, we cannot refrain from discussing the issue. In the Liberation War women were raped and assaulted; in the peace time women are the victim of religious bigotry and they are labourers at home and outside for little or no pay. However, within the patriarchal society, women often become rebellious. In contemporary times, women are more empowered than before, as they are coming out of their homes for jobs or do something meaningful in the society, but still they are being victimised, their labour is exploited and as expected,. Rebellion is evident, as expected, in the contemporary society. they are becoming rebellious. Among all the selected films there are major female characters and we will find women are in all roles – victim, labourer or rebel. In the foundational films, the victim part is predominant, although the role of labourer and rebel are also seen.

Banasreebala in *Kittonkhola* and Rehana in *Dollhouse* are two among some victim characters. Ill-fated Banasreebala wanted to play the character of Manasa, the local deity who was also a born destitute yet later became powerful. The social condition did not allow Bansareebala, the sex worker turned actress, to have a decent life, and instead, the rich man Idu Contractor wanted to fulfil his lust perceiving a *jatra* actress like Banasree very available for sex. Subal had consent on this and Banasreebala could not bear her wretched life anymore and committed suicide.

In any war, women are the inevitable victim – assailants target their bodies, which may bring to the psychic disorder of women. Rehana in *Dollhouse* was raped and tortured by the invader army and she symbolises Bangladesh in 1971 which was shattered by invaders. She was taken away and was raped in the army camp and these traumatic experiences haunted Rehana with an ultimate result of the psychic disorder.

Even if she is not a powerless woman like Banasreebala in *Kittonkhola* or a wartime rape victim like Rehana in *Dollhouse*, a modern empowered woman in contemporary can be victimised under patriarchal conditions. Rima in *Ant Story* is a famous actress, yet the leak of her intimate video made her vulnerable to Mithu.

In several films, women characters are found in the role of the labourer. The prime victims of the aggressive and authoritative nature of Muslimness portrayed in the film *A Tree Without Roots* were women. The expression of basic and natural feelings became forbidden to Rahima and Jamila. They were not allowed to talk and laugh loudly, go outside the house and stand in an open place after a bath. Rahima used to massage Majid's legs regularly, which symbolises slavery. Rahima was found always working within the domestic sphere – processing crops, feeding cattle or serving Majid. Rahima is always accompanied by 'mother of Hasuni', the housemaid. Peasants grow and harvest paddy in the field, but the paddy is processed and preserved by silent labourers at home – Rahima and mother of Hasuni. Those peasants can be easily recognised as workers, but the contribution of the housewives in agriculture has never been recognised, let alone being paid.

In *Runway*, both Ruhul's mother and sister are characterised as labourers. Although Ruhul earned no money and did not take care of the house, he tried to rule the family with the *Shariah* norms he learned from the Jihadist group.

Other than victim and labourer, some women characters in the selected films are seen strong in sustaining their culture. This was true for Devi in *My Bicycle* and Dalimon in *Kittonkhala*. Some of the women actively resisted against patriarchal repression. Although Jamila, the second wife of Majid was rarely seen at work she becomes the nemesis of hypocrite and fraudulent Majid. Jamila was a rebel and she was not interested to obey Islamic rules imposed by Majid. Jamila's rebellion ultimately made Majid vulnerable and helpless. The mighty Majid had to seek help from the silent and obedient wife Rahima. Jamila continued her rebellion till the end of the film. When she was found senseless in the *majar* where she was tied by Majid as a punishment, Jamila was found lying on flooded water and keeping her leg on the part of the grave of the *pir*, which was symbolically, an ultimate rejection to the false grave of a saint.

The character of Ayesha in *The Clay Bird* represents the woman who is the victim of patriarchy and scholastic Islam. When modern Kazi became religious, Ayesha became his prime victim. She had to go inside *Purdah*; she lost her right to sing, draw picture, and to go outside. Later she had to lose her friend and brother in-law Milon, because he was deeply involved in nationalist movement. As the narrative progresses, emancipated Ayesha stopped talking to him and when the Pakistani Army attacked, she left Kazi and moves forward by taking the son Anu with her. Ayesha was primarily a victim, but she revolted at the end.

In *Meherjaan*, Neela, the cousin of Meher was a rape victim of war, though mentally shattered, she was not ashamed about what happened to her. For the first time in the cinema of Bangladesh, a rape victim talked about what she experienced and joined the war as a fighter. If we look beyond the text, the protest against the film that compelled the producer to pull it from theatres, was a 'hyper-masculinist response' (Chowdhury, 2015: 760) as the psyche of the normative masculinity found 'the enemy' (Wasim) is winning 'our girl' (Meher) and because of that 'our boy' (Sami) is refused and eventually slapped by our 'derailed girl' (Meher). The dominant masculine narrative accepted the rape of hundreds of thousands of women, by mentioning them in one line in the historiography, but was not ready to accept one girl's love to a Pakistani soldier.

Rubaiyat Hossain's film *Under Construction* portrayed women in a different way, as we have analysed in Chapter 6. *Under Construction* is made by women who fill most of the important roles in composing the film, direction, production, cinematography art direction, production design and so on. The main protagonist is three women from different age groups and differing classes. Ambivalence in their characters is especially important. Roya is not a radical woman. She is aware of her career and does not want to take baby, but she does not hesitate to depend on her husband for her material well-being and comfortable lifestyle. Roya's affection and love towards Moyna are also ambivalent – she needs Moyna to accomplish the household jobs so that she can do her theatre activism freely. Moyna got pregnant by the liftman Sabuj Mia, left Roya, started living independently in a slum with Sabuj Mia and got a job in a RMG factory. In this way, she acquires agency that permits her to make decisions independently which was not possible for her living in Roya's house as a maid.

On the other hand, Roya's conservative mother lives a religious life, like a conventional wife she has been waiting for her husband to return for years yet she is self-dependent and she has the mental strength and capacity to live her life by her own. She has her own management capability and entrepreneurship to earn money for herself and for other *hijabi* women by sewing clothes. Again, the character has an identity and agency that Roya seems to lack as she oscillates between her husband, Russell and Imtiaz, always seeking their approval for her actions. It is Roya's sincerity to theatre, her aspirations to creative freedom to re-interpret a classic text, that provides the capacity for her to take decisions about life. The creative journey she chooses gives her character a shape.

How does identity politics determine the fate of women in Bangladesh? According to the films we are discussing, the utmost victimisation of women in Bangladesh was in wartime. Rehana was a direct victim of war and she could not overcome the trauma of the experience. Neela was also a rape victim and was traumatised. But she could translate it to anger and revolt and joined the *Mukti Bahini* to fight at the front. This war erupted due to the fight between two conflicting identity approaches – Bengaliness and Muslimness. Between the fight and difference in identity politics between East and West Pakistan, women's bodies were one of the primary targets for victimisation.

In peace time, women are victimised by the followers of Mulimness, especially by scholastic Muslims at home. Majid tried to victimise both Rahima and Jamila, but he was unsuccessful in the case of Jamila. Ayesha was a sufferer for Kazi's religious bigotry, but she managed to come out from Kazi's hold. In *Television*, Kohinoor was punished by the religious and administrative leader Amin Patwary, but she could show her disobedience on the spot. In popular religions, women are important – they are described as the 'nature' (see Dasgupta, 1976). But the hegemonic Bengali state-system through the military deployment in the CHT has left the lives of women like Devi and her family in distress and humiliation. The transition to neoliberal consumerism due to the flexibility of digital technology and overall moral degradation also victimises women, as seen in the character of Rima.

Class as a Component in Identity Politics

Some films portray class differences and class exploitation that have connections with identity politics. In *Kittonkhola*, Idu Contractor is one of the most powerful men in the human settlement in both sides of river Kittonkhola. Other than his business, he is also a landlord, who wants to snatch away more lands from simple and poor people like Sonai by any way. He organises the village fair for profit and he wants *jatra* actress Banasreebala for one night. He has a good connection with Shafiq Chairman, the head of the local government, and that enhances his power. The film shows the politico-commercial nexus exploits the poor people in the peasant society of Bengal. In the film *Kittonkhola*, Idu represents the rich peasant category as Chowdhury (2004) suggests and Sonai as the poor peasant who will soon be landless as of Idu's application of power.

The film *Runway* depicts the issues of labour exploitation and labour discontent in the RMG sector. In the labour market of Middle East, the Bangladeshi labourers are exploited by the Muslim 'brothers'. The mighty NGOs pressurise the poor credit holders to return the instalments – the mother returns the credit from the daughter's salary, not from the milk of the cow, which was bought by the credit. The issue of fraudulence of telecom companies towards users is also mentioned in the film. People like Ruhul live in non-privileged and oppressed class. It is suggested in the film that Ruhul's social experiences of being discriminated might be one of the reasons to be interested in the terror network. Ruhul's sister, Fatema's salary in her factory was suspended for two months. She says, if there is oppression, there would be protest.

By comparing the RMG factory with *Jakshapuri* (a space that was suggested by Tagore in *The Red Oleander*) Hossain in the film *Under Construction* establishes a stunning comparison between the two ages. In both institutions, labourers are repressed and victimised as subjects leading a diminished life. Both in the *Jakshapuri* and in the RMG factories, the presence of the exploitation of labour, where the workers are seemingly the extension of machines that reminds us Fritz Lang's classic film *Metropolis* (1927). By exploiting the workers' labour, Bangladesh earns a bulk of foreign currency, but the security of the labourers is the least concern of the owners. The Rana Plaza collapse in 2013 or Tazreen Fashion Factory fire in 2012 illustrates this and makes Roya's adaptation authentic. Roya deconstructed *The Red Oleander* into a modern time play where the character

Nandini, an ideal beautiful Bengali woman was changed into an exploited RMG worker.

Mithu, in the film *Ant Story,* wanted to transform his class which leads him to take a job in an illegal and immoral MLM company and to blackmail the actress Rima. In the contemporary globalised Bangladesh, there is a desire among people to become rich hastily. The neoliberal ideologies have established a deep impact in the society and there is a sharp rise of consumer culture. There are opportunities of class transformation, but the opportunities are limited. Mithu's company was banned by the government and he was haunted by the creditors.

The issue of class has a prominent position in contemporary films that are set in recent Bangladesh, which is in a transitional period. However, class exploitation has been taking place for a long time in society as the foundational film *Kittonkhola* has depicted.

'Oriental's Orientalism': Re-reading the Case for Independent Films in Bangladesh

Zakir Hossain Raju (2015) first applies the term 'oriental's orientalism' to global independent and art films produced in Bangladesh. He borrowed the idea from Chinese American scholar Rey Chow (1995) who herself derived the idea from eminent scholar Edward Said's (1979) theoretical notion of Orientalism in analysing the films made by Fifth-Generation Chinese filmmakers. After discussing *The Wheel* (1993) by Morshedul Islam and *The Clay Bird* (2002) by Tareque Masud, Raju (2015) says:

> Being caught up in meeting the demands of a westernised, national middle class as well as the western view on a Third World country like Bangladesh, and like *The Wheel*'s bullock-cart, Masud bring together all these aspects as a new ethnography for Bangladesh and its people.
> (Raju, 2015: 198)

Bangladeshi independent cinema started appearing in global markets through *The Wheel* (Chaka 1993) by Morshedul Islam. The film received three awards in the 1993 Mannheim film festival and another three at the Dunkirk Film Festival, 1994 in France. *The Wheel* also enjoyed theatrical release in metropolitan centres like Paris and Tokyo. After an interval, independent cinema started appearing regularly in the Western festival circuits in the new millennium. *Shankhonad* (2004) by Abu Sayeed was commercially released in Europe and *The Clay Bird* by Tareque Masud was released on both sides of Atlantic. Films like Masud's *The Clay Bird* and *Homeland* (Ontorjata 2006), Mokammel's *A Tree Without Roots* or Sayeed's *The Flute* (Banshi 2007) and *Transformation* (Rupantor 2008) received western funding. The DVD of *The Clay Bird* was released both in France and the USA.

182   Representing Identity through Cinema

Currently, exploring foreign funds is becoming the norm for the leading independent filmmakers. In fact, all upcoming projects of Mostofa Sarwar Farooki, Kamar Ahmad Simon, Rubaiyat Hossain and a few others will be partially or fully funded by foreign agencies, will be screened in international festivals and will (perhaps) be commercially released in foreign countries. In this way, contemporary independent cinema is becoming part of global cinema. We have discussed this in Chapter 3.

Considering these global aspects of independent films, Raju's analysis becomes important. Another film scholar, Sajedul Awwal (2007) also echoes Raju's accounts in this regard:

> When it is a foreign funded film, then the ideology comes along with the fund. And there is an unwritten dictation what would be the message, what would be the storyline. The film may be rich technically, but one can easily identify the presence of the ideology, which came with the fund.

However, before looking for the elements of 'oriental's orientalism' in the selected independent films, we must look back at the original discussion of the concept. We want to include the analysis of Sheldon Hsiao-peng Lu (1997) along with that of Rey Chow. Both have analysed the Fifth-Generation Chinese films, especially the films of Zhang Yimou, to explore the ethnography, identity, nationhood of China.

By analysing Yimou's 'appreciated-by-the-west' films like *Ju Dou* (1990) and *Raise the Red Lantern* (1991) Rey Chow says that directors such as Zhang are producing a new kind of orientalism. This orientalism is constructed through subalternizing and exoticizing China to the West. They lend themselves to the western appropriation. Chow says Zhang is producing

> exhibitionist self-display. ... what we may call the Oriental's orientalism. ... It turns the remnants of orientalism into elements of a new ethnography. ... In its self-subalternizing visual gestures, the Orient's orientalism is first and foremost a demonstration.
>
> (Chow, 1995: 171)

Chow refers to Thomas Elsaesser's (1989) work on New German Cinema and indicates the Chinese directors' strategy of treating artifacts and cultural objects as commodities, in order to make them enter and create markets in a modern, global, capitalist economy. Chow adds that this is the sign of cross-cultural, commodity fetishism precisely because ethnic practices are presented in a theatrical way as arcane and archaic.

Sheldon Hsiao-peng Lu's observation is partially resonant to Rey Chow's and he has some different views as well. Lu partially agrees with native Chinese critics regarding Zhang Yimou's films (which include Chinese American, Rey Chow) as they say:

Zhang's international popularity is dubious. He has been taken as an exemplary instance of the willful surrender to Third World cinema to the Orientalist gaze, as a classic case of the subjugation of Third World culture to western hegemony.

(Lu, 1997: 107)

Lu agrees that Zhang Yimou's films made in the 1990s are not strictly 'Chinese' or 'Mainland' films. The target audience of his films is not Mainland China but the international community. He has offered the western viewer a 'museum' of precious Chinese objects, costumes and artifacts. His films are periodically banned in his home country, but they have been regularly screened in movie theatres around the world. Zhang's film career is synonymous with the globalisation of Chinese cinema. Zhang is not so warmly welcomed in his home country. And Zhang's capital is not Mainland's, rather it is transnational.

In favour of the presence of Orientalist elements in 'Oriental' films, Lu appreciates Zhang's films by saying:

Under the condition of global capitalism, Zhang has been able to pursue and sustain a critical project that has become impossible in his home country. Transnational capital is therefore at once a constrictive and a liberating force for Chinese cinema.... These films offer alternative histories, stories, and images of nations and peoples that are unseen and unavailable in ordinary Hollywood films.

(Lu, 1997: 107)

Lu has other pragmatic reasons for approving transnational films by Zhang and others. He summarises, under the dual pressure of censorship and the rapid shrinking of the domestic market, entering the international market seems to be the inevitable solution.... Joint film production is the rule, not the exception today (Lu, 1997: 131). He indicates that what is termed 'orientalism' or the exit to the global cultural market, is also a strategy of survival and renewal for Chinese filmmakers (Lu, 1997: 132).

Orientalist elements and this issue of Oriental orientalism can be analysed by comparing the independent films of Bangladesh with those of China. In both cases, in Chow's language, directors are working to exoticise their culture for the global audience or to westernise the selected audience at home. According to Lu's words, the directors are offering a 'museum' of precious Bangladeshi objects, costumes and artifacts to the global audience. Such efforts to make native objects and culture seem exotic are found in the film *The Clay Bird*.

In *The Clay Bird*, folkloric cultural elements from the traditional Bengal have been widely used though these were not essential components of the narrative. Several rural festivals and folk concerts are seen in the film such as the boat race, village fair, ballad of Qurbani in a *puthipath* programme, *bahas*in Baul songs, Eid festivals and so on. The boat race was not merely a race; it was added with a lot of 'cultural shows' taken from the Hindu mythology at the bank as a part of the race. In every cultural event, protagonists were present as audience. These events do not contribute to the storyline and represent a 'cultural package' of traditional Bengal. The director (Masud, 2004) says, I wanted to convey my own image of my country as a moderate Muslim Bangladesh to bring out its social, cultural and political diversity.

Self-exoticisation also can be found when comparing films to the novels on which they were based One must recognise the colour and magnificence of rural Bengal as captured in *A Tree Without Roots* by the eminent cinematographer Anwar Hossain. This beauty was not described by the novelist but can be considered as an additional narrative in the film. Although the main theme of the novel *Dollhouse* has nothing to do with nature in the war-shaken country, in the film, the beauty of Bengal is presented strongly which can be counted again as an additional narrative in the film. In *Kittonkhola*, not only the cultural elements like local theatre and village fair are part of the storyline, deliberate attempt of describing the beauty of Bengal can be clearly identified.

In *Television*, the beauty of the countryside of Bangladesh was exoticised by focusing on the wide river and lavish greenery. In *Meherjaan*, the green field, foggy morning, sandy riverside, bushes and jungles etc. were repeatedly used just to frame some beautiful shots with little connection to the narrative. For *My Bicycle*, the whole plot and the physical environment was an exotic commodity – the tribal norms and practices, the lake, the mountains, the jungles – all were components of self-orientalism. Ahmed (2017) mentioned Bangladesh state promotes the Hills as a tourist site where tourists may enjoy the landscape and the 'exotic' inhabitants. The director of *My Bicycle* was also entrapped in that exoticism.

But other than exoticising, the approach of seeing Islam in *A Tree Without Roots* is Orientalist – Muslim society is depicted as very conservative; it appears to annihilate life and victimise women. The Islam presented in the film is monolithic and no other version of Islam is present. This is very clear in the portrayal of Majid as a demon instead of a man with limitations. We have discussed in Chapter 2 that the *majar*s are the centres of Sufis, a place of non-scholastic Islamic practices. In the novel *Lalsalu*, the *majar* has been portrayed as a place of monolithic and scholastic Islam. The enormous popularity of the novel misrepresented *majar* culture to the people of Bangladesh. Now it has been misrepresented to the global audience by the film *A Tree Without Roots*.

Now agreeing with the case of Oriental's orientalism in independent films, we would like to take this issue further from Raju, as Lu partially agrees with Chow considering the existing cine-situation in China. Like China, by borrowing Lu's observation, we would like to say that under the dual pressure of censorship and the rapidly shrinking domestic market, entering the international market seems to be inevitable for independent film.

We would like to briefly discuss the current cine situation in Bangladesh and thus indicate the likelihood orientalism increasing in order to obtain the foreign funds and global distribution necessary for the survival strategies of independent films. Independent films have always received unfavourable treatment from the BFCB. Transnational funds or the success at international festivals can be helpful for compelling the BFCB to be 'favourable'. *The Clay Bird* primarily was banned in Bangladesh. Its success in Cannes was helpful in lifting the ban. Regarding the shrinking local market, Morshedul Islam (2006) says:

> The kind of film we make cannot make profit from local market. I got $30000 from *Dipu Number Two* from the cinema halls in 1996. At the present situation, we can get maximum $7000 from local market. Audiences have been split in sections. Some watch a film on the television[4] some in theatres and some watch and preserve DVDs. The culture of watching films has been changed totally.

There is almost no out-of-studio professional producer in Bangladesh to produce independent films. Only Machhranga Productions produced some independent films occasionally, but they lacked professionalism. They do not have country-wide distribution system. The other source for films is TV channels, especially Impress Telefilm, which emerged as an alternative studio to BFDC. Yet it is very difficult to stay independent under their corporate influence. Lack of professionalism is also seen with Impress. Thus, in order to combat the shrinking local market, absence of producers, and censorship pressure, foreign funds and global release become the automatic choices for filmmakers. Everybody must be reminded that foreign funds and global release required high quality in the storyline and film techniques. In exchange for Orientalist representation, the country becomes famous and Bangladesh gets a position in global cinematic discourse. The challenge is how an independent filmmaker can protect him/herself from exploitation and create his/her space in global cinema at the same time. Filmmaker's awareness to the issue is much needed here.

Independent Cinema as a Cultural Institution: It's Influence in Constructing Identity

An institutional analysis of independent cinema is needed to judge its influence in constructing identity. The institutional analysis enables us to relate the text of films to broader social, political and historical aspect of the country.

Film director Abu Sayeed (2006) thinks that:

> Independent cinema as a cultural institution of Bangladesh is not very influential. It is not widely distributed and not accessed by mass

audience. But independent cinema has some influence on the advanced urban audience.

But research scholar Zakir Hossain Raju (2007) thinks in other ways:

> The independent cinema can be found apparently as a less influential cultural institution. Because these films are not accessed by mass people and the target audience of these films in home or abroad is very limited. But these films create national-modernity discourses which are very important. As nation-state is predominantly a modernist concept, these films imagine and want to see Bangladesh as a post-colonial modern state. Independent films are creating the discourses of cultural-modernity of the nation which includes ethnic and traditional roots of Bengal society or upholding Bengali cultural forms.

Christian Metz (Metz 1977 cited in Casetti, 1999) recognised the cultural institution as a threefold *machine*: the industrial one, which works toward the output of the product that is as effective as possible; the mental one, which seeks to perpetuate the spectators' capacity to enjoy film; and the one that finds expression in critical, historical, or theoretical arguments, which attempt to valorise each work. Independent cinema is not that effective as an 'industry'. By emphasising its the 'mental' role, it may not be very successful in perpetuating the spectators' capacity to enjoy the film; but it plays an important role in offering 'critical, historical, or theoretical arguments'. It produces or sustains discourses regarding identity.

As Raju (2007) says, independent films are creating the discourses of cultural-modernity of the nation. However, this cultural-modernity can be in opposition to Muslimness. According to Tanvir Mokammel (2007):

> All the independent filmmakers were product of the Liberation War and were steeped with the spirit of secularism and Bengali nationalism. They had nothing to do with Muslimness, rather more radical ones among them were opposed to the very idea of a Muslim identity. If the alternative film-makers of Bangladesh have done anything at all regarding construction of a cultural identity, then they have been sabotaging the assiduously peddled idea by the Bangladeshi ruling class to give the people of Bangladesh a religious or communal identity, an idea which was already defeated at the cost of millions of lives in 1971.

But filmmakers' pro-Bengaliness and anti-Muslimness stands, which Tanvir Mokammel wants to uphold, have been criticised by another director, Tareque Masud (2006). He says, most of the independent films are trying to build the uniform national narrative and identity as very few independent cinemas raise questions against the uniformity of national narrative and identity. He agrees like other cultural institutions, independent cinema plays a role in nation building, representing identity, creating cultural taste and forming ideological values of public. But according to him, this role was supposed to be played by the mainstream cinema industry. In a strange way, independent cinema in Bangladesh has taken on the responsibility of playing the role of a predominant cultural institution. The failure of mainstream cinema, for its poor quality in relation to content and form, has driven independent cinema to play this role and endorse diversities of sub-cultures or alternative approaches in religion, race and gender.

The pro-Bengaliness and anti-Muslimness positions of independent filmmakers had been discussed, debated and criticised in this study. We have also highlighted the tendency of these filmmakers to construct identity repeatedly and with much eagerness as part of their cinematic mission. Thus, as a predominant cinematic institution, independent cinemas build and perpetuate culturalist-modernist and nationalist discourses.

On the eve of the victory day or other national days, these films are screened in television channels. Sometimes, these films are re-released on national days. Parents buy the DVDs of these films to help their children consider identity questions. Abu Sayeed (2006) says, these films have been telling the history of the nation on celluloid or through digital bytes which is positively perceived by younger generation of Bangladesh. It becomes very important when the true history of Bangladesh as a nation sometimes being distorted by politicians and rulers.

Notes

1 *In the Bank of Chitra* (Chitra Nadir Pare 1999) by Tanvir Mokammel deals with identity questions. It is a story of a Hindu minority family whose members do not want to leave their homeland and migrate to India in the post-partition period in (East) Pakistan. In *Homeland* (Ontorjatra 2006), by Tareque and Catherine Masud, an expatriate Bangladeshi mother and her son in London come back to Bangladesh after hearing the news of the death of the boy's father, who was separated from herlong ago. The film is, for the son especially, a search for his own identity.
2 Tareque Masud's documentary *The Song of Freedom* (*Muktir Gaan* 1995) tells the story of musical troupe that sings for the refugee and freedom fighters to inspire them during the Liberation War, 1971. But his next documentary *Tales of Freedom* (*Muktir Katha* 1996) is based on the audience's reaction to *The Song of Freedom*. There he shifts his earlier position and welcomes the nuanced views in representing nationalist narratives where sub-altern people raise questions against the absence of their contribution in the nationalist narrative made in *The Song of Freedom*. Tareque and Catherine's short feature *The Barbershop* (Naroshundor 2009) creates someway a counter nationalist narrative. In the dominant narrative discourse the non-Bengali and Urdu-speaking Bihari people were against of the Liberation War and they were closed to Pakistani Army and killed freedom fighters. But in this film, we see Bihari people are saving a freedom fighter from the *Rajakars* and military.
3 See 'Shonibar Bikel, a Film Based on Gulshan Café Attack, Banned' at https://www.thedailystar.net/city/news/shonibar-bikel-film-based-gulshan-cafe-attack-banned-1689409, Accessed 09 December 2019.
4 Some films of independent makers are produced by television channels, which are premiered at the channel first and released in theatres later.

References

Ahmed, H. S. (2017). Tourism and state violence in the Chittagong Hill Tracts of Bangladesh (2017). Electronic Thesis and Dissertation Repository. 4840. https://ir.lib.uwo.ca/etd/4840, Accessed 9 July 2021.

Awwal, S. (2007). Interview conducted for the study on 02 February 2007.

Anderson, B. (2006). *Imagined Community: Reflections on the Origin and Spread of Nationalism*. London: Verso.

Appadurai, A. (2001). Disjuncture and Difference in the Global Cultural Economy. In S. Seidman and J. C. Alexander (eds.), *The New Social Theory Reader: Contemporary Debates* (pp. 253–265). London: Routledge.

Casetti, F. (1999). *Theories of Cinema: 1945-1995*. Austin: University of Texas Press.

Chatterjee, P. (1993). *The Nation and Its Fragments: Colonial and Postcolonial Histories*. New Jersey: Princeton University Press.

Chowdhury, E. H. (2015). When Love and Violence Meet: Women's Agency and Transformative Politics in Rubaiyat Hossain's Meherjaan. *Hypatia*, *30*(4), 760–777.

Chowdhury, B. M. (2004). Changing Class and Social Structure in Bangladesh: 1793–1980. In A. F. S. Ahmed and B. M. Chowdhury (eds.), *Bangladesh – National Culture and Heritage: An Introductory Reader* (pp. 253–266). Dhaka: Independent University, Bangladesh.

Chow, R. (1995). *Primitive Passions: Visuality, Sexuality, Ethnography and Contemporary Chinese Cinema*. New York: Columbia University Press.

Dasgupta, S. (1976). *Obscure Religious Cults*. Calcutta: Firma KLM Private Limited.

Deen, S. A. (2006). On Kittonkhola' (Kittonkhola Prosonge). In S. Zakaria (ed.), *Complete Works of Selim Al Deen-2* (Selim Al Deen Rachonasamogro-2) (pp. 350–356). Dhaka: Maola Brothers.

Farooki, M. S. (2016). Interview conducted for the study on 09 December 2016.

Islam, M. (2006). Interview conducted for the study on 10 December 2006.

Jameson, F. (1986). Third World Literature in the Era of Multinational Capitalism. *Social Text*, 15 (pp. 65–88). Autumn.

Lu, S. H.-p. (1997). *Transnational Chinese Cinemas: Identity, Nationhood, Gender*. Honolulu: University of Hawaii Press.

Masud, T. (2004). The Clay Bird: Asia Source Interview with Tareque Masud at http://www.asiasource.org/news/special_reports/masud.cfm, accessed 04 March 2008.

Masud, T. (2006). Interview conducted for the study on 13 December 2006.

Masud, T. (2007). Interview conducted for the study on 11 February 2007.

Mohsin, A. (2000). Identity, Politics and Hegemony: The Chittagong Hill Tracts, Bangladesh. *Identity, Culture and Politics*, *1*(1), 78–88.

Mokammel, T. (2007). Interview conducted for the study on 26 April 2007.

Raju, Z. H. (2007). Interview conducted for the study on 05 May 2007.

Raju, Z. H. (2008). Madrasa and Muslim Identity on Screen: Nation, Islam and Bangladeshi Art Cinema on Global Stage. In J. Malik (ed.), *Madrasas in South Asia: Teaching Terror?* (pp. 125–141). London: Routledge.

Raju, Z. H. (2015). *Bangladesh Cinema and National Identity: In Search of Modern?*. London: Routledge.

Renan, E. (1990). What is a Nation?. In H. K. Bhabha (ed.), *Nation and Narration* (pp. 9–22). London: Routledge.
Said, E. (1979). *Orientalism*. New York: Vintage.
Sayeed, A. (2006). Interview conducted for the study on 15 November 2006.
Williams, R. (2003[1974]). *Television: Technology and Cultural Form*. London: Routledge,
Woodward, K. (2000). *Questioning Identity: Gender, Class and Nation*. London: Routledge.

Conclusion

Who am I first, Bengali or Muslim? – This unresolved identity question has been haunting the people of Bangladesh for a long time. Muslims of undivided Bengal generated the 'Pakistan Movement' in the early 1920s and accepted the 'Partition of India' in 1947 that took place in the communal line-ups. Later, the large portion of the same group in (East) Pakistan fought for an independent Bangladesh in 1971, which was based on secular ideologies and Bengali culture. For that, Rafiuddin Ahmed says, a Bengali Muslim may have seen himself primarily as 'Muslim' in the past, as a 'Bengali' yesterday, and a 'Bengali Muslim' today, depending on objective conditions (Ahmed, 2001: 4). Ahmed extends the idea further – this dual pull is often reflected in people's continued hesitation to define the cultural boundaries of their identity in specific terms (Ahmed, 2001: 4). This journey of looking for 'real' identity went on in post-independent Bangladesh during turbulent political changes. Moreover, in the contemporary globalised and post-9/11 era, the question of national identity has emerged with great intensity and complexity.

Independent filmmakers in Bangladesh regularly engage themselves in identity discourses and attempt to resolve the identity questions. This book tried to examine how Bengali Muslim identity, the national identity of majority people of Bangladesh, is represented in independent films. Theoretical applications of national identity by Earnest Gellner (1983), Benedict Anderson (2006), Arjun Appadurai (2001), Homi K Bhabha (1990) and Stuart Hall (1999) and the notion of representation by Stuart Hall (1997) were instructive in guiding this inquiry. For textual analysis of selected films, film narratology derived from the theory of 'narrative discourse' by Gerard Genette (1980) has been applied. Bangladeshi scholars who theorise the national identity of the country such as Chowdhury (2020), Hossain (2016), Mohsin (2000) and Hussain (2010) were also consulted to comprehend the local views in the analysis.

Some of the independent filmmakers of Bangladesh tried to depict Bengaliness (the ethno-linguistic identity approach) as the preferred identity of Bengali Muslims and portray Muslimness (the religious identity and popular religion) as the 'other' identity. The 'further other' identities are not

DOI: 10.4324/9781003271093-9

portrayed at all. Within the domination of Bengali language, the Chakma-language film *My Bicycle* based on the lives of ethnic Chakma people was made by a director who comes from another small ethnic group Rakhine. Mohsin (2000) rightly spotted on the dominant identity's aspiration to hegemonise the weaker identity. In the mainstream cultural discourses, the tension between Bengaliness and Muslimness could be seen, though some independent filmmakers prefer Bengaliness, but as the weaker identity, the small ethnic communities are destined to be hegemonised by both.

On a different aspect, to sustain the ethnic and cultural elements of Bengaliness on the screen, influential cultural institutions do not hesitate to orientalise themselves toward the interests of the global audience. However, national identity is going through a transition, as Chowdhury (2020) rightly marked the ever-changing nature of Bangladesh's national identity – people are deterritorialised, Jihadist Islam combines with Muslim identity, and technologies are pushing boundaries of Bengali cultural domains by adding consumer culture to neoliberal and globalised Bangladesh. The use of information technology by Islamists and Jihadists is also a new phenomenon, someway Hussain (2010) called it 'Islamic modernity'.

The constructionist view of the theory of representation by Stuart Hall (1997) was used to look at the film texts critically, as in constructive approach, meaning is constructed, not by things, but by using representational systems such as concepts and signs. We have found that the directors' politico-cultural backgrounds and their class positions have shaped their concept of national identity, which has driven them to construct identity in a particular way and with certain codes and signs in their films. Different aspects of the theory of identity elucidated by different scholars have enabled us to understand the nature of identity representation in the film texts. We were able to start the analysis of identity representation in the films with a few pre-studied ideas of nation, such as it is a contingent, artificial, ideological invention; an imagined community; a system of representation; a production of image; and/or homogenised by the dominant class. In all these descriptions, one person's imagined community is a political prison to another. We have found that some of the independent filmmakers are very eager to homogenise the nation with a particular approach to the national identity of Bangladesh through their cinematic system of representation, even though their approach was imagined and ideologically invented within a certain context of history.

In the foundational and transitional phases, the Liberation War was a regular subject. Some secular-modernist film directors have clearly taken the position on behalf of Bengaliness and against Muslimness, considering the two identities should remain in conflict. This is mostly true for the films made by Tanvir Mokammel and Morshedul Islam, two *auteurs* from the independent film tradition of Bangladesh. When considering Bengaliness as the preferred 'imagined community' (according to Anderson's [2001] terminology) the independent films widen the existing gap between the conflicting identities. Bengaliness as 'one man's imagined community' appeared as 'political prison' to the followers of Muslimness (in Appadurai's [2001] term). Gellner (1983) mentions nation as an artificial and contingent construction, Hall (1999) terms it a 'system of representation' and Bhabha (1990) calls it 'production of image'. The intention of Yakub to join *Mukti Bahini* in *Dollhouse* is a constructionist effort from the director as in the novel Yakub was inactive and apprehensive till the end. By portraying Majid as shrewd and heartless in the film version of *A Tree Without Roots* (which was not the case in the novel) the director has created another construction. The mannerism and dress codes of Majid and the majar as the symbol of Islam construct Muslimness as a primitive, fraudulent, rude and inhuman approach to identity. When Rubaiyat Hossain's *Meherjaan* challenged the grand narratives of the Liberation War it created much chaos among the Dhaka-based intelligentsia in 2011.

If some filmmakers have a clear position about Bengaliness and Muslimness, there needs to be the examination of the function of the third approach, popular religion, in independent films. This identity approach is not explored even in the general identity discourse in Bangladesh. Now if we look at the foundational and transitional films, these three approaches can be found to varying extents. *A Tree Without Roots* and *Television* predominantly deal with Muslimness, *Dollhouse* with Bengaliness, *Meherjaan* with both Bengaliness and Muslimness *Kittonkhola* with popular religion and, *The Clay Bird* comprises all three approaches. Chapters 4 and 5 showed the ambivalence in the construction of identity in these films – mostly anti-Islamic and pro-Bengaliness and sometimes clear endorsement for popular religion or sensible representation of Muslimness. In the contemporary films, we have seen that the Bangladesh society is under transition, largely due to two external factors – neoliberal globalisation and globalisation of Jihadist Islam. Also, economic growth based on export-oriented RMG sector and remittances sent by immigrant workers is giving a new identity to Bangladesh as a place with one of the highest GDP growth in the world, a robust national reserve, and rapid urban growth. The exploitation of the cheap labour is key to this growth, which is creating a financial disparity in society. The selected films show this identity of transformation is not only visible in contemporary Bangladesh; the society has been under the transformation (as portrayed in *Kittonknola*) for ages due to poverty and other socio-cultural reasons. However, the slow internal transformation cannot be compared with contemporary rapid transformation, which can be discussed by connecting it with the global context. The film *My Bicycle* shows that like the majority Bengali Muslim society, indigenous or *Adibasi* groups are also going through a transformation due to modern technologies. For them, the additional factor is the aggression of the state, which is formed by the Bengali majority of people.

To some directors, popular religion is a preferred identity approach. In the film *The Clay Bird* by Tareque Masud, the plurality of religious thought and nuanced views of national identity have been portrayed. To express his statements, the director of *The Clay Bird* loosens the narrative and adds popular religious elements in the film as fragmented clips that have little connection to the storyline. In *Kittonkhola* by Abu Sayeed, some popular religious forms of expression and components like *jatra*, *Manasamangal*, *Kavigan* and *Panchali* songs have been used as essential parts of the film.

We find here that independent cinema is an influential cultural institution, an ideal 'system of representation', which portrays national identity to perpetuate the idea of nationness. Like other cultural institutions, independent cinema plays a role in nation building, representing identity, creating cultural taste and forming ideological values of public. The failure of mainstream cinema, because of its poor quality with respect to content and form, has driven independent cinema to play this role. In central or even in peripheral areas, groups of people celebrate by screening these films. These films have been telling the history and culture of the nation in celluloid or digital formats that are positively perceived by the younger generation of Bangladesh. The most important point here is that these films contribute to the identity discussions existing in the country, either by perpetuating the existing discourse or by creating new discourses.

We also found, to uphold the ethnic and cultural elements of Bengaliness on the screen, independent film directors do not hesitate to orientalise themselves to the global audience. The depiction of cultural and religious roots of Bengal in *The Clay Bird* and *Kittonkhola*, the additional narrative of capturing scenic beauty or rural Bengal in *Dollhouse* and *A Tree Without Roots* are presented as exotic attractions to the global audience. But the study sees this self-orientalising process as an inevitable survival strategy in a shrinking industry that is under the rigid censorship practices. By comparing the situation with independent filmmaking in China, the study tends to show that, directors have to target a global market or global fund in order to keep their relative independence. The type of films they make cannot survive from the local market. To get foreign funds and to satisfy global audiences sometimes they have to surrender wilfully to the western gaze.

While representing the national identity, the filmic texts organically portrayed gender politics in the narrative. Although some of the women characters in the selected films were primarily the victims of patriarchy and religion, they revolted at the end. Strong and complex characters like Rehana and Banasreebala can be considered as interesting characters for investigation. *Dollhouse* is basically the story of Rehana, who was raped by the occupant army. Rehana symbolises Bangladesh, which has been shattered by invaders.

In *Kittonkhola*, the issue of feminine dichotomy has been raised by the character Banasreebala. Banasree knows that although she plays the role of Behula, an ideal housewife, her life is unlike that of Behula. Rather, she is more like Manasa, who is born destitute and who is hungry for the worship of anyone, even an audience who throws filthy comments while she dances for them. Behula may represent or expected to be represented as the ideal Bengal womanhood, but the same society produces a destitute like Banasree.

The prime victims of the aggressive and authoritative nature attributed to *Muslimness* as portrayed in the film *A Tree Without Roots* are generally women. Besides being the victim of religion and patriarchy, women of *A Tree Without Roots* are labourers and rebellious. If Rahima and 'mother of Hasuni' fall into the labourer category, Jamila is the rebellious one. Jamila's rebellion makes Majid vulnerable and elevates Rahima to a strong position at the end.

In *The Clay Bird*, the victim of Kazi's zealotry was his daughter Asma, who died due to his maltreatment. The wife Ayesha was primarily submissive to Kazi, but in the latter part of the film, she was firm. After the attack of the invader army, Ayesha leaves the village and Kazi.

Class exploitation is represented in some of the selected films. Labour exploitation in the RMG factories is overtly as well as covertly portrayed in *Under Construction*. The same issue has been dealt with in *Runway*. In *Runway*, it is also suggested that Jihadist Islam has a class dimension; unemployed and poor madrasa students like Ruhul are easy targets for this movement. It is also evident in films like *Kittonkhola* that the poor peasants have been exploited by the feudal class since the earlier period of Bengal society.

The issue of censorship is an increasing concern for the filmmakers. The present AL government led by Sheikh Hasina has become authoritarian since taking power in 2009. A sense of fear is driving the people of Bangladesh. Arrests, abductions and killings are very prevalent. Surveillance and censorship are regular weapons of the government. At the end of January 2018, the German organisation Bertelsmann Stiftung reports that Bangladesh is among five countries that lack a minimum standard of democracy. Also, Bangladesh ranked 151st in the annual World Press Freedom Index 2020 report published by Reporters Without Borders. In this restrictive environment, a filmmaker cannot choose a script that would be translated into an expensive media without having concern to pass through BFCB. The selected film *My Bicycle* did not get the censor certificate. We have discussed the contemporary situation of freedom of expression in Chapter 3. So self-censorship is prevalent among the filmmakers. Mostofa Sarwar Farooki's film *Saturday Afternoon* (2019) which dealt with the infamous Holey Artisan Bakery terrorist attack in 2016, struggled to receive a certificate. In a totalitarian sociopolitical environment, directors are not able to make films independently that contribute to the further examination of national identity.

Even under these circumstances, some films are being produced every year in Bangladesh. Films made by Mostofa Sarwar Farooki, Rubaiyat Hossain, Kamar Ahamd Simon, Abdullah Mohammad Saad and others are addressing contemporary issues of jihadist Islam, labour exploitation in RMG factories and deterritorialisation of people in the globalised Bangladesh. The films also narrate the ongoing conflicts between tradition, modernity and new technologies and state that the change from traditional to modern and even post-modern is inevitable.

One encouraging observation is contemporary directors are more interested in addressing changing Bangladesh society whilst the foundational filmmakers were interested in addressing the conflict between Bengaliness and Muslimness. Therefore, the idea of upholding Bengaliness can be continued, but the existence of Muslimness should not be denied or ignored and attention should also be given to popular religion. Popular religion is a syncretic identity that can resolve identity debates and conflicts and it has the characteristics by which the whole 'imagined community' can be brought together under one umbrella. The followers of Bengaliness can find progressive elements and followers of Muslimness can see religiosity within it. But above all, it provides the message of freedom for both spiritual and worldly belief systems. Popular religion is usually attacked by adherents to Muslimness and ignored by adherents to Bengaliness. Now, it is the time to bring back popular religion as the mainstream identity, as it was in the ancient and medieval Bengal. Cinema can play an important role as a system of representation by mainstreaming this approach of identity which contributes to the formation of the identity discourse and ensures the co-existence of diverse ideologies of identity. Hossain (2016) also proposes a democratic system of politics, which accommodates aspects of secularism, language, Muslim identity for forming and consolidating the country's multi-racial, multi-religious national identity over the long run and its survival as a sovereign state. Independent filmmakers have a role to play here.

References

Ahmed, R. (2001). Introduction – The Emergence of the Bengal Muslims. In R. Ahmed (ed.), *Understanding the Bengal Muslims: Interpretative Essays* (pp. 1–25). Oxford: Oxford University Press.
Anderson, B. (2006). *Imagined Community: Reflections on the Origin and Spread of Nationalism*. London: Verso.
Appadurai, A. (2001). Disjuncture and Difference in the Global Cultural Economy. In S. Seidman and J. C. Alexander (eds.), *The New Social Theory Reader: Contemporary Debates* (pp. 253–265). London: Routledge.
Bhabha, H. K. (1990). Introduction: Narrating the Nation. In H. K. Bhabha (ed.), *Nation and Narration* (pp. 1–7). London: Routledge.
Chowdhury, A. (2020). *Sheikh Mujibur Rahman and Bangladesh: the Quest for a State (1937–1971)*. Dhaka: Shrabon.
Gellner, E. (1983). *Nations and Nationalism*. London: Blackwell Publishing.
Genette, G. (1980). *Narrative Discourse*. Oxford: Basil Blackwell.
Hall, S. (1997). The Work of Representation. In S. Hall (ed.), *Representation: Cultural Representations and Signifying Practice* (pp. 1–4). London: Sage Publications.

Hall, S. (1999). Culture, Community, Nation. In D. Boswell and J. Evans (eds.), *Representing the Nation: A Reader* (pp. 33–44). London: Routledge and The Open University.

Hossain, A. A. (2016). Islamism, Secularism and Post-Islamism: The Muslim World and the Case of Bangladesh. *Asian Journal of Political Science*, *24*(2), 214–236.

Hussain, N. A. (2010). Religion and Modernity: Gender and Identity Politics in Bangladesh. *Women's Studies International Forum*, *33*(2010), 325–333.

Mohsin, A. (2000). Identity, Politics and Hegemony: The Chittagong Hill Tracts, Bangladesh. *Identity, Culture and Politics*, *1*(1), 78–88.

Index

9/11 (2001) 5, 52, 72, 76, 127–8, 139, 164–5, 168, 172–3, 190
16 mm format 2, 57, 59, 61–4, 83–4, 88, 94
35 mm format 59, 62–4, 69, 70, 84, 88, 94
1947 (Partition of India) 8, 10, 35, 36, 39, 42, 43, 49, 50, 57, 62, 90, 129, 156, 172, 190
1952 (Language Movement) 4, 37, 39, 43, 119
1971 (Liberation War of Bangladesh) 1, 3–4, 8, 14–5, 19, 30, 36, 37–9, 43, 48–50, 56, 58–9, 60, 78, 103–5, 107, 112, 114–5, 120, 125–9, 137, 153, 156, 160–1, 164–5, 172, 177, 186–7, 190

Adam Surat 16, 59, 61, 78
Agami 16, 58, 59, 61, 87, 106, 163
Ahmed, Humayun 128, 164
Ahmed, Rafiuddin 40, 41, 190
AL government 53, 64, 194
alternative cinema 24, 28–9, 86, 110
alternative film 25, 57, 186
Anderson, Benedict 5–9, 10–1, 27, 168
Anil Bagchir Akdin 106, 163
Anisuzzaman 39, 43, 54
Ant Story 4, 74, 137, 143, 147–8, 174–5, 177, 181
anti-Islam 37, 83, 99, 100, 139, 162, 166, 192
Appadurai, Arjun 5–6, 10, 18, 27, 50, 54, 168, 171, 188
Arab 33, 40, 41
art cinema 22–4, 29, 56–8, 72, 76, 188
artisanal 23, 56
Aryan 32, 90, 92, 171
Asia 5, 14, 17–8, 29
Asia Pacific Screen Award 73–4, 129, 143

Australia 50, 73
Awwal, Sajedul 27, 98, 101, 110, 166, 182, 188
Aynabaji 72, 75

Bacchu, Nasiruddin Yousuf 75, 80, 85, 87–8
Bangladesh Awami League 11, 37, 47
Bangladesh Nationalist Party (BNP) 11, 48, 49, 50, 83
Bangladesh Shilpakala Academy 58, 153
Bangladeshi Muslims 11, 45
Bangladeshiness 19, 48–9
baul cult 4
baulism 30, 41, 45–6
BCTI 81
Bengali (ethnicity) 1, 30, 33, 36, 45, 51, 53, 55, 81, 149, 156, 190
Bengali language 1, 4, 22, 31, 34, 37–9, 46–7, 157, 191
Bengaliness 4–5, 9, 11, 31, 34–5, 38–9, 40, 43, 47, 50, 59, 115, 161–9, 170–1, 179, 186–7, 190–3, 195
BFA 81
BFCB 81–3, 113, 159, 174, 185, 194
BFDC 2, 15, 16, 25, 28, 59, 65, 72, 81, 84, 185
BFIA 57–8
Bhabha, Homi K. 5–6, 10–1, 27, 29, 189, 190, 192, 195
bhadralok 36, 41
bhakti 30
Bhutto, Julfiqar Ali 38
Bihar 32, 36, 42
Bollywood 20, 125
Bordwell, David 26–7
British colonial 40, 172
British imperialism 35
British policy 41

Index

Buddhism 31, 32, 44–5
Buddhist 4, 31–3, 45–6, 98, 118

cable TV 2
Calcutta 20, 36, 57, 82
Canada 50, 76, 95, 174
Cannes (International Film Festival) 73–5, 112, 185
captive audience 2, 61
Casetti, Francesco 13, 186
CD/DVD 2
celluloid 68, 81–2, 88, 108, 187, 193
censor board 82–3, 113
censorship 24, 57, 76, 80–5, 126, 156, 183–5, 193–4
Chaka 62, 73–4, 88, 108, 181
Chalachchitram Film Society 58
Channel I 66–7
Chatterjee, Partha 5, 9, 170
Children's Film Society 58
Chinese Cinema 17–8, 183
Chitra Nadir Pare 62, 64, 187
Chittagong 33, 79, 95, 126
Chittagong Hill Tracts (CHT) 1, 10, 31, 48, 138, 154, 156–9, 180
Chow, Rey 17
Chowdhury, Afsan 11, 190, 191
Christian 31, 48, 141, 167, 173, 186
cinema hall 2, 6, 63, 67, 185
cinephile 2
class 5, 7, 21, 41, 51, 134–5, 142, 146–7, 153, 168, 172, 174, 180–1, 191, 194
The Clay Bird 4, 20, 23, 25, 47, 64, 69, 71, 73–6, 85, 112, 122, 128, 140, 161–2, 164–5, 169, 170–1, 173, 178, 183, 185, 192–4
Communal Award 36, 41–3
Congress (The Indian) 9, 36, 41–2
constructive approach 13, 191
Culler, Jonathan 13, 26
cultural institution 5, 166, 185–7, 193

Dasgupta, Shashibhushan 43–5, 180
Day After ... 74
Deen, Selim Al 62, 88–9, 90, 93
Delhi 16, 33–4, 95
Deterritorialisation 50, 171, 174, 176, 195
Dhaka 2, 20, 25, 34, 37–9, 40, 42, 52, 54, 57–8, 60, 62, 66, 69, 72–3, 75–6, 79, 80, 88, 95, 103, 106, 109, 114, 116, 123, 133, 143, 146, 148–9, 153, 161, 175–6, 192
diaspora 50
digital filmmaking 68, 70
Digital Security Act (DSA) 85
Dill-Riaz, Shaheen 77, 79
documentary 25, 58, 62, 70, 73–4, 77–8
Dolhouse 4, 69, 87, 102–9, 125, 162–3, 168, 177, 184, 192–3
DVD 16, 65, 70, 113, 181

East Bengal 14, 35–9, 42, 91, 110, 118, 171
East Pakistan 20, 37, 43, 57, 119, 156, 187, 190
electronic media 65–7
Europe 17, 59, 66, 149, 181

fana 45–6
Farooki, Mostofa Sarwar 3–4, 27, 66, 72–6, 85, 112, 129, 131, 137, 143, 145–6, 148, 166, 174–6, 182, 194
Ferdousi, Shabnam 77, 79
FFSB 58
fiction film 26, 80
film narratology 5, 7, 25, 88, 190
film society 16, 56–8, 61–4, 138
film society movement 56–8, 61
FIPRESCI 73, 112
France 63, 71, 73–5, 113, 181
free market economy 10, 51

GDP 54, 157, 162, 174, 192
Gellner, Ernest 5, 8–9, 10–1, 190, 192
gender 1, 5, 7, 17, 21, 75, 83, 148, 153, 177, 187, 193
Genette, Gerard 5, 26–7, 190
Ghatak, Ritwik 20, 57, 87
global cinema 73–4, 77, 182, 185
government grant 73–4, 77, 182, 185

Hall, Stuart 5, 10–1, 13, 190–2
Hasina, Sheikh 49, 50, 52–4, 84, 194
Hayat, Anupam 20
Hefajat-e-Islami 50, 53
Helal, Saiful Wadud 77
hijab 12, 150, 172
Hinduism 1, 30–1, 33, 38, 42, 44–6, 98
histoire 26–7, 88, 95, 103, 113, 122, 129, 138, 144, 149, 155
Hollywood 2, 15, 56, 68, 76, 183

Index

Hong Kong 17–8
Hooliya 6, 16
Hossain, Rubayiat 3–4, 72, 75, 112, 122, 125, 137, 150, 153, 161, 175, 179, 182, 192, 194
HUJI 52

IDFA 73–4
imagined community 8–9, 10, 168, 170, 190–2, 195
Impress Telefilm 66–9, 70, 88, 185
Indian sub-continent 2–4, 119
Inner Strength 16, 59, 61, 78
Islam, Kazi Nazrul 1, 44
Islam, Morshedul 3–4, 16, 23, 27, 57, 59, 60–4, 66, 69, 70–4, 82–3, 87–8, 106, 108, 125, 161, 163, 166, 168, 181, 185, 191
Islamic culture 11, 98
Islamic State (IS) 52, 119

Jamaat-e-Islami 49, 52, 83, 142
Japan 17–8, 63, 74, 95, 142
jatra 88–9, 90–2, 94, 109, 139, 141, 161, 165, 171, 173, 177, 180, 193
jihadist Islam 1, 5, 30, 51–3, 137, 140, 142, 162, 169, 171, 173–4, 176, 191–2, 194
Jinnah, Muhammad Ali 37, 39
JMB 52–3, 141, 173
Joyjatra 128, 164

Kabir, Alamgir 20, 57, 105
Kabir, Yasmine 77–8
Kashmir 14, 37, 139, 141, 173
Khan, Fauzia 77, 79
Khan, Habib 64, 85
Khoo, Gaik Cheng 21, 22
Kittonkhola 4, 87–9, 91–3, 162, 165, 171–2, 177, 180–1, 184, 192–4
Kolkata 1, 20, 34, 36, 39, 40–1, 43, 76, 85, 90, 103, 173, 175

Lahore 39, 82
Levy, Emanuel 15, 17
LGBT 52, 172
Locarno Film Festival 73–4
London 51, 95, 103, 151, 187
Lu, Hsiao-Peng 17, 182

madrasa 25, 53, 113–4, 116, 118–9, 120, 139, 141, 170, 173, 184
mainstream cinema 3, 20

Malaysian film 21–2, 50, 56, 65, 187, 193
marfat 47, 116, 170
Masud, Catherine 62, 64, 68–9, 70, 78, 85, 112, 188
Masud, Tareque 3–4, 16, 20, 23, 27, 57, 59, 61–2, 64, 67, 68–9, 70–4, 77–8, 83, 85, 112, 117–9, 120–2, 137–8, 140, 153, 160–1, 164, 168–9, 174–5, 181, 186–7, 192
Matir Moina 4, 69, 71, 74
Meherjaan 4, 112, 124, 128, 161–2, 165, 169, 171, 178, 184, 192
MK2 71, 113
MLM 144, 147, 174, 181
moderate Muslim 118, 184
Mokammel, Tanvir 3–4, 16, 23–5, 27, 57, 59, 61–2, 64, 67–9, 70, 77–8, 82, 87, 95, 100–1, 160–1, 163, 166, 168, 186–7, 191
Mor Thengari 4, 154
Moviyana Film Society 58
mufassil 1, 137
Mughal 34
Mujib 38, 47, 48
mukti bahini 87, 103, 106, 125, 127, 163, 165, 179, 192
Muktir Gaan 62, 77, 187
multiplexes 2, 84
multi-racial 12, 195
multi-religious 12, 195
Murad, Manjare Haseen 24–5, 58, 77–8, 80
Murshid, Golam 31, 33, 38, 41, 43, 45
Muslim League 36, 39, 42–3
Muslim rule 33, 44
My Bicycle 4, 10, 22, 138, 154–5, 157, 162, 169, 176, 178, 184, 191, 194
myth 18, 26, 96, 122, 165

narration 11, 13, 25–7, 93, 100–1, 108, 118, 128, 134, 143, 148, 153, 159
narrative discourse 5, 7, 26–7, 88, 187, 190
narratives 3, 10, 18, 23, 31, 72, 124, 161, 167–9, 187, 192
national cinema 3, 14–6, 56
nawab 34–5
neo-liberalism 50
NGO 69, 77, 133, 138

Oggatonama 75–6
The Ominous House 58, 160
Open Doors Programme 73–4

The Orange Ship 75
orientalism 17–8, 23, 76, 181–4, 185
OTT 3, 75–6

Pakistan Movement 4, 36, 127, 164, 190
Pala Empire 32–3
partition 8, 14, 35–7, 39, 41–3, 48–9, 50, 62, 122, 165, 187, 190
Pather Panchali 20, 118
Piprabidya 4, 72
political Islam 45, 52, 53, 142, 164, 170
popular Islam 43, 115, 120, 164, 170
Porobasi Mon Amar 77–8
post-9/11 5, 168, 190
product placement 66
pro-Islam 24, 83, 115, 166
prophet 53, 116
puthipath 116–8, 183

Quran 43, 141
qurbani 116–8, 183

Rabeya 69, 163
Rahman, Sheikh Mujibur 37, 127, 116
Rahman, Ziaur 49, 60
Raihan, Zahir 58–9
Rainbow Film Society 58
rajakar 83, 87, 106, 163–5, 187
Raju, Zakir Hossain 2, 20, 22–4, 27, 56–8, 76, 112, 161, 166, 181, 184, 186
Rakhine, Aung 3–4, 154, 159, 191
Rasul, Polash 77, 79
Ray, Satyajit 20, 57, 108, 118, 120–1
recit 26–7, 89, 96, 104, 115, 124, 131, 139, 145, 152, 155
Rehana Maryam Noor 73–5
Renan, Earnest 7, 167
Riaz, Ali 127
RMG 75, 137–8, 140, 147, 150–3, 162, 175, 179, 180–1, 192, 194
Robin, Noman 75, 77, 80

Saad, Abdullah Mohammad 72, 74, 194
Saturday Afternoon 85, 174, 194
Saussure, Ferdinand De 13
Sayeed, Abu 3–4, 23, 27, 59, 61, 64–5, 67–9, 71–3, 83, 93–4, 161, 181, 185, 187, 193
scholastic Islam 43, 116, 119, 120, 164, 168, 170, 172, 178–9, 184
SFF 58

Shah, Lalon 46, 68
Shariah 47, 116, 118, 139, 141, 170, 173, 178
Shilpakala Academy 58, 153
short film 16, 23, 58–9, 64–5
Shunte Ki Pao! 73–4, 77
Simon, Kamar Ahmad 73–4, 77, 79, 182, 194
Singapore 74–5, 103, 143, 50, 73
social media 1, 52, 131, 172, 176
Song of Freedom 62–4, 77–8, 85, 187
South Asia 51, 54, 72
Stop Genocide 58
studio system 15, 59, 60–1, 63
sufism 4, 9, 44–6, 117–8, 121, 170–1
Surya Dighal Bari 58
syncretic identity 44, 170, 195

Tagore, Rabindranath 1, 30, 43–4, 88, 109, 110, 149, 150, 180
Taiwan 17, 74
Tantric Buddhism 44–5
Television (film) 4, 72–5, 112, 129, 134, 162, 166, 169, 175, 179, 184, 192
Tododrov, Tzvetan 25–6

UK 50, 71, 73, 95, 103
Umar, Badaruddin 49
Un Certain Regard 73, 75
Under Construction 4, 72–5, 122, 137, 148–9, 152–4, 175, 179, 180, 194
Unnamed 66, 75, 176
USA 15, 17, 50, 59, 71, 76, 103, 113

vaishnavism 4, 44–6, 118
van Schendel, Willem 30, 48–9

web series 3, 76
West Bengal 2, 39, 42, 46, 48, 76, 118, 141
West Pakistan 4, 37–8, 179
Westernised 22, 24, 141, 150, 164, 181
The Wheel 23, 62–4, 71, 74, 88, 108, 181
Williams, Raymond 132, 175
Woodward, Kath 7, 8, 11, 162
World Cinema 75, 125, 183

Yimou, Zhang 17, 182

zamindar 36, 41

Printed in the United States
by Baker & Taylor Publisher Services